RANK

Picturing the social order 1516–2009

"We have found ourselves living in an elaborate and barely understood system of castes."[1]
Jonathan Raban, 'Soft City', 1974

"All societies are unequal... but they describe their own inequalities differently."[2]
George Watson, 1998

"A humanist... does not admit of rank."[3]
EH Gombrich, 1998

1. Jonathan Raban 'Soft City', 1974, (London: Harvill Press) p128
2. Quoted by David Cannadine in 'Class in Britain', 1998 (New Haven: Yale UP) p20
3. In interview in 'Henri-Cartier Bresson at 90', BBC TV, first broadcast 1998

CONTENTS

'THE WAY WE RANK OURSELVES NOW'

This timely exhibition is a powerful reminder that although rank, status, class and hierarchy are as much with us now as ever, we have lost the language and the imagery to describe it. It has become the great unmentionable in an era where the right to vote and the imagined opportunity for anyone to make it to the top masquerades as equality.

In recent years there has been an unacknowledged political conspiracy across all the parties to pretend the mighty inherited social differences of previous ages are dead and gone. The 'modernisation' of politics makes MPs at ease with worrying publicly over differences of race, gender, disability, region or religion while the politics of class has vanished from the mainstream agenda. All these various social differences are assiduously catalogued and analysed, avoiding the inconvenient truth that they are only less important sub-sections of the one great inequality.

But outlawing the vocabulary of class has not made it disappear. Banishing the cloth cap, the bowler and the top hat has only disguised class and rank a little better – to the advantage of the bowler and top hat classes and the frustration and confusion of those at the bottom bereft of a modern politics or language to describe their condition.

Pecking orders exist among all social animals from bees to monkeys to humanity. This biological fact has in recent years been used as an excuse for social Darwinism – an idea that red-in-tooth-and-claw instincts are natural, irrepressible and good, leading to the survival of the fittest and the success of the human species. Indeed, humans will always rank themselves – but the question is the degree of privilege we should tolerate. It is almost impossible to imagine a human society without rankings. Utopias here represented have a heart-sink sense of a life not only unachievable, but awful and certainly no fun. Like religious images of heaven, the sameness and goodness of everyone equal in all things, doing the right thing all the time for the greater good of all is simply not human. In a post-Soviet age, we look on such visions now with double the scepticism, revulsion and amusement. But the death of Utopian thinking has left the field to the social Darwinists. If the extreme ideal of equality is no longer credible, more, then the danger is that winner- takes-all turbo-capitalism can pretend to be the only alternative.

How should we think about the way we rank ourselves now? Money, rank and class are so intimately linked, that how wealth is shared stands as a very good proxy for hierarchy of every other kind. There used to be a sense that social progress and growing equality in rank and fortune were an inevitable part of the march of modernity – but that came to an abrupt halt. All through the twentieth century up to the mid 1970s Britain was becoming progressively more equal in income and wealth – but that went into abrupt reverse in the early 1980s, after which it has never regained momentum. In the distribution of wealth, we have now returned to the same level as 1937, when Evelyn Waugh was writing. In the UK the top tenth take 54% of disposable wealth and nearly a third of all earnings, while the bottom tenth earn just 2.6% of GDP.

It makes any general measure of the growth in GDP per capita pretty meaningless: it all depends where you are on the social scale whether you enjoy any of our shared economic growth at all. A remarkable recent surge upwards of wealth to the top means that whilst 20 years ago the CEO of a top FTSE company earned 17 times as much as the average worker in that firm that has now risen to 75.5 times as much. The gap between the bottom and top in all organisations has stretched the very fabric of society.

How easy is it for anyone to rise up the social order these days? A middle class child is 15 times more likely to stay middle class than a working class child is likely to make it into the middle classes: it's not impossible, but it's not very likely. Social mobility only happens in a society which is far more equal than either Britain or America. Among western nations the Nordic countries are the most socially mobile because they are also the most equal in terms of incomes, education and life-style. The ladder is easier to climb when it is shortest.

The American Dream – the myth that anyone can make it if they have the talent and determination – has become a part of British thinking too, in a post trade union age. Where thirty years ago there was a class identity, a sense of class interest in organised labour, now there is virtually no public voice representing the bottom third of society. Celebrity culture instead spreads the false hope that fame and fortune means anyone can make it through football or pop star success. Contemplating individuals who made it against the odds takes the place of political awareness. The need to organise in order to get a fairer share of the nation's spoils is replaced by an individual yearning for personal success, unattainable except in the pages of celebrity magazines.

Birth still predicts destiny to an alarming degree and yet those born with few opportunities are encouraged now to see it as their personal failing that has left them with a lesser slice of life's best opportunities. Rank rules still from generation to generation, but it is cleverer about disguising its grip on power and money these days.

Throughout history the turbulent sense of social injustice bubbling beneath the surface has found its expression, as this remarkable exhibition shows. The question for us is now is what has happened to our understanding of class? Why do today's politics make class the great unmentionable?

Polly Toynbee is a columnist for the Guardian, whose recent publications include 'Unjust Rewards' (Granta) and 'Hard Work' (Bloomsbury).

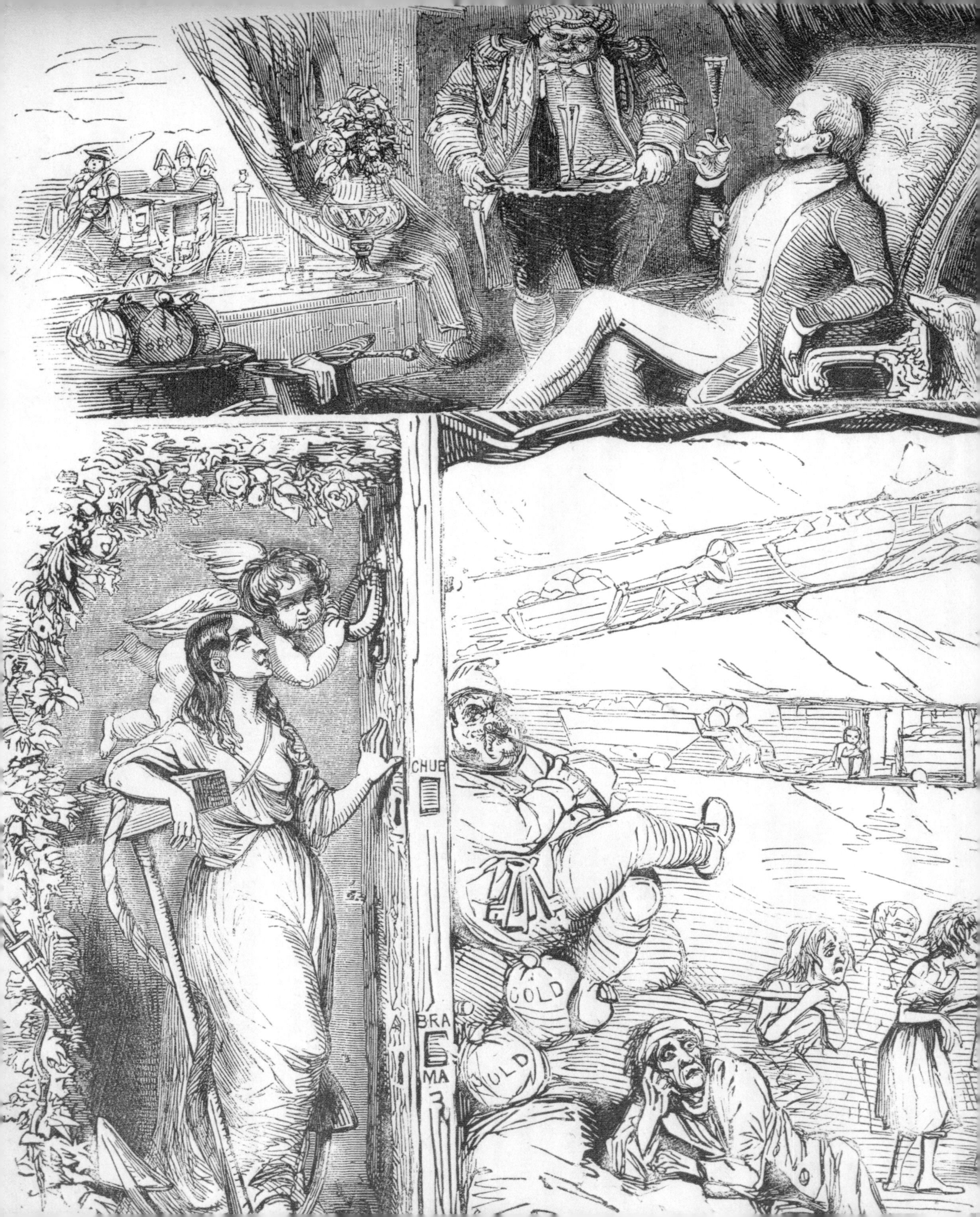
CHUB
BRA
MA
GOLD

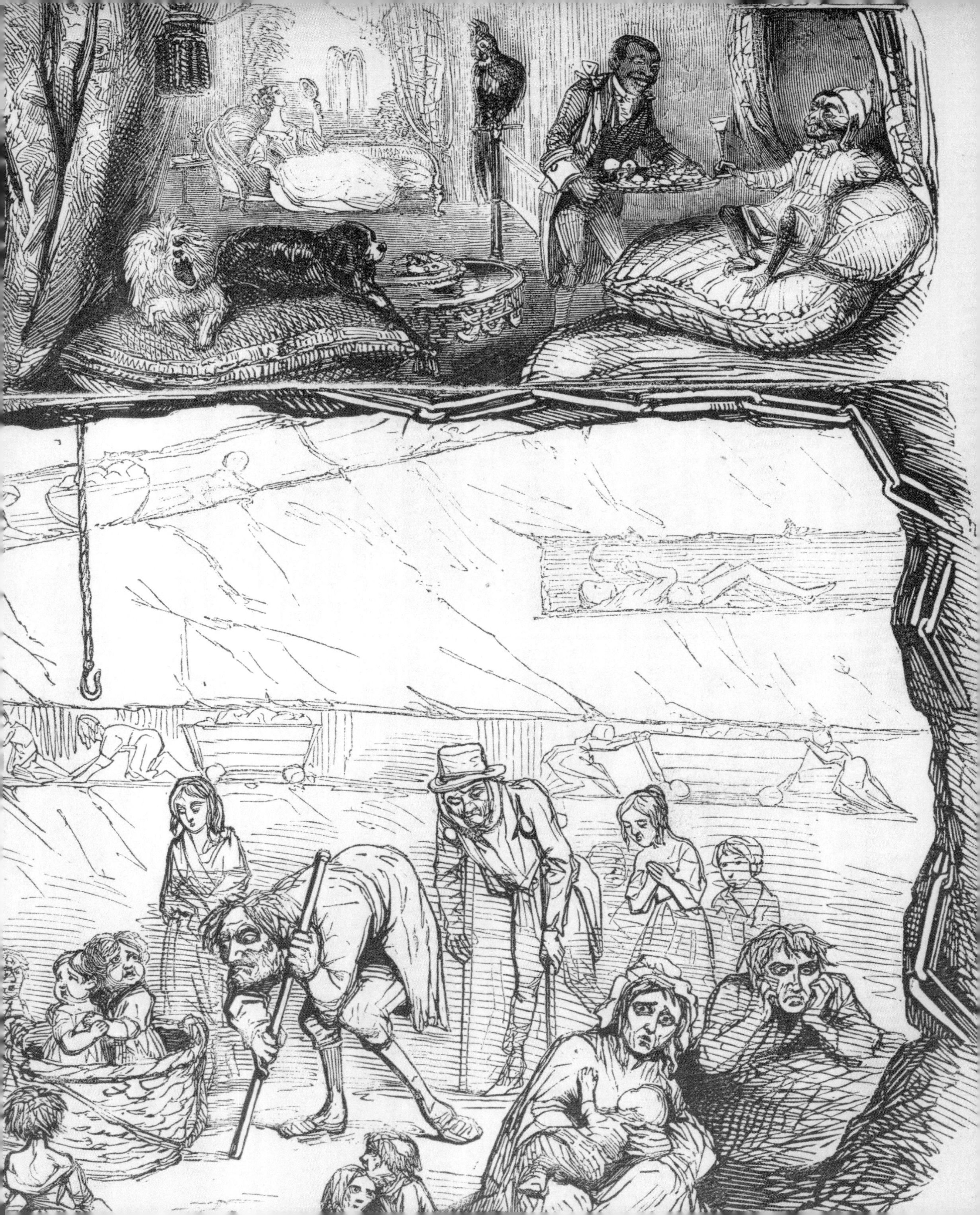

'PICTURING THE SOCIAL ORDER'

"When Englishmen set out to describe their society, they began by making distinctions, by classifying and ranking... This mental habit... is of the first significance. It bears witness to the fact that the most fundamental structural characteristic of English society was its high degree of stratification, its distinctive and all-pervasive system of social inequality... [of] hierarchical distinctions of status, rank and power. Order, degree, rank and hierarchy seemed self-evident, even natural... a scheme of ranks or degrees, of hierarchically arranged social categories were intended to simplify the complexity of reality and clearly distinguish the principal social groups."[1]
Professor Keith Wrightson, 'English Society 1580-1680'

'Rank' brings together diverse images from six centuries across the English speaking world. The show asks the two questions the historian David Cannadine has posed: "what are the ways in which [we] have visualised our social worlds and social identities?" and "how, across a long time span, and from a broad geographical perspective, can we recover the ways in which Britons saw and understood the manifestly unequal society in which they lived?"[2] All of the participants address the problem of how we imagine and visualise our own place in our wider society. This raises other questions: in what ways do we classify the world, and what are the criteria upon which our scheme of classification rests? To represent a 'society' is to represent an abstract idea: it is not possible to imagine or visualise 60 million people in one picture or phrase. Each of us has an imaginative model of the society we inhabit, whether articulated or not. The questions here then, are: how do we picture the world around us; how have others done so; and how might we yet understand the world more fully by visualising it anew?

The exhibition rests on the contention that we think through images, and that all of our language to describe social difference is based on visual imagery. In English as in most world languages, hierarchies are always expressed as spatial metaphors. 'Higher' is preferable to 'lower': to make a value judgment and to order or rank things is to have an imaginary vertical axis already in mind. Is it possible to see the social world other than in hierarchical terms? David Cannadine has observed that "man is also intrinsically and essentially a hierarchical animal, both by his nature, and throughout most of his history. Thus regarded, men and women are predisposed towards rank and order – towards class as hierarchy".[3]

The four sections here explore images of the nation as a political unit; of how inequalities are ordered in space; what myths and stories explain our differences; how we might picture the entirety of society; and how we imagine our place in the economy. The exhibition ranges widely – bringing images together from quite distinct historical periods and from disciplines way beyond the field of fine art. There are works by some of the greatest names in the history of British art including Hogarth, Gillray, Cruikshank and Eric Gill.

The long timescale is important: together, the works offer us a chance to see how different, or how similar our worldview is to those of our predecessors. The academic AH Halsey has suggested that there has been an "extraordinary combination of solidarity and hierarchy in British society" that stretches from the pre-industrial to the post-industrial world."[4] It is only possible to imagine how our relations to others are structured by comparisons over time or space: the images here present us with the opportunity to undertake the former.

As Gordon Fyfe argues here, there are direct connections between different social strata and the type of media used to create and distribute images. Whilst some of the works are painted, most were printed. Few patrons of the arts prior to the 20th century commissioned images attempting to picture a worldview, critical or otherwise. Few outside the social elites had access to the resources or technologies of 'high art'.

Alongside canonical works of art are images created to forward a political argument, whether by Thomas Hobbes or by the International Workers of the World. Alongside these are images which diagnose the state of the nation or of the world, based on hard facts about the levels of inequality between nations or within them. Images created specially for the show which dramatise statistics from the Office for National Statistics or the World Bank ask us to imagine our own place in the bigger scheme of things – indeed the biggest scheme of things. The juxtapositions created throw some light on the ideas that underpin our worldview. They also ask us to imagine how else we could picture the world.

The title of the exhibition is no accident. There have been dozens of terms to describe social stratification across such a long timescale: 'degrees', 'sorts', 'orders', 'estates', 'stations', and 'ranks' amongst them, with 'classes' a relatively recent addition. The only term that has been in use from 1516 to 2009 and kept the same meaning is 'rank'. This has also been one official term: mid-Victorian censuses explicitly record a subject's 'rank mid-Victorian censuses explicitly record a subject's 'rank or occupation'. Moreover, a person's 'rank' describes their entire social worth, not merely their birth, wealth, or occupation. As Keith Wrightson has argued, there are always a "multiplicity of criteria employed in the allocation of rank". It is with some irony, that the term has, since the seventeenth century, had a parallel negative meaning as in 'rank and file' or 'the rank multitude'.

'Rank' invites us to see the political imagination over a long timescale. Walter Benjamin asked about works of art, "what sort of visibility should the presentation of history possess?"

Benjamin's answer to his own question was that "What [the artwork] has to fix, perceptually, are the images deriving from the collective unconscious."[5] The similarities between 'Leviathan' and the distribution of global wealth when shown at relative human scale are not entirely accidental. Taking such a long timescale reveals some of our structures of thought.

Alistair Robinson is Programme Director of Northern Gallery for Contemporary Art, and the curator of 'Rank'.

1. Wrightson, 1982 (London: Hutchinson) pp5-8
2. Cannadine, 1998,p19
3. Ibid, pp22-23
4. AH Halsey, 'Social Change in British Society', 1986, (Oxford: Oxford UP) p 6
5. Walter Benjamin, The Arcades Project, translation 2000 (Harvard: Bellnap)

What does possession mean to you?

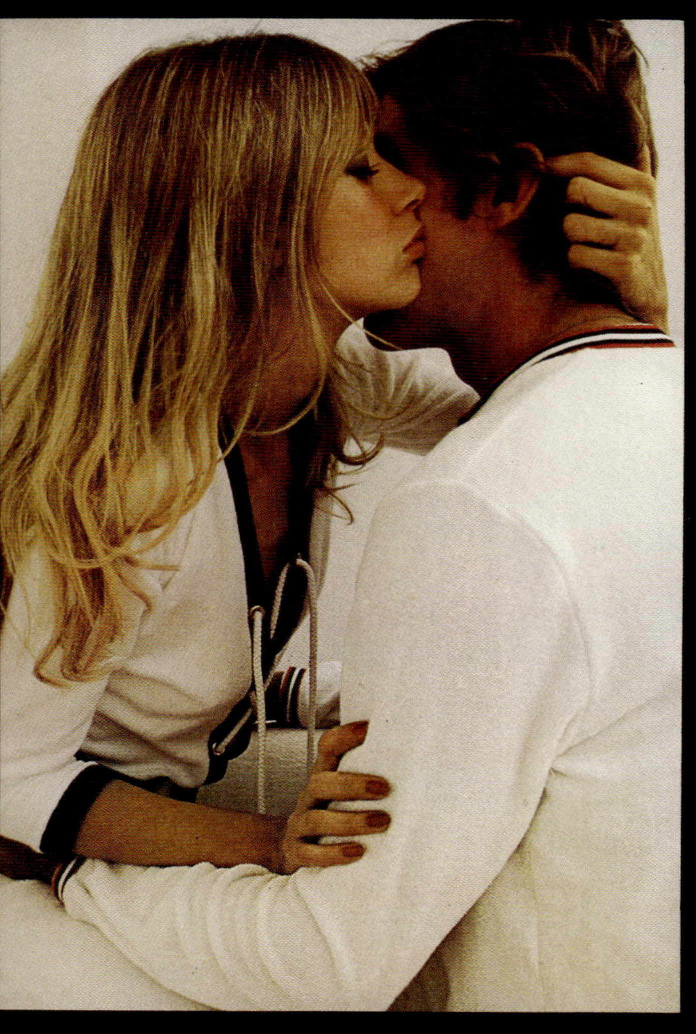

7% of our population own 84% of our wealth

The Economist, 15 January, 1966

PICTURING POLITICS:

'FROM MONARCHY TO DEMOCRACY – THE FACE OF ORDER'

"Democracy cannot be represented. It can only be 'enacted'."[1]

Peter Weibel and Bruno Latour, 'Making Things Public', 2005

How can political thought be visualised and represented? The first section of the exhibition presents images which attempt to encapsulate a political system, or are made to stand in for 'the nation', and present it as a single icon.

This section is subtitled 'the face of order' as personification has been the primary means by which artists have given physical form to their imagined community, or the abstract idea of 'society'.
The metaphor of 'the body politic', most readily visible in Thomas Hobbes' 'Leviathan' continues to inform our language: the political leaders of the English-speaking world are still known as the 'head of state'. Whilst the monarch remains the principal symbol of the nation even now, other personae have a long history.
John Bull, as a representative figure of 'the people' has been lodged in the popular imagination for three centuries. The allegorical figure of Britannia, personifying the nation-state, was revived in the late seventeenth century under Charles II, after being invented in Roman times. There are a surprising range of other visual metaphors for the constitution or society here, though. The image of 'the ship of state' features in three works; that of the constitution as a sturdy English oak tree with deep roots in several others. Hogarth's metaphor of the nation as a building that we all share and inhabit has been reworked by satirists up to the present day.

There are noticeably short periods from which most of the works here are drawn. The transitional periods when power structures have been openly challenged or even fiercely contested in Britain are well known – such as the Civil War, after the French Revolution, and during the extension of the franchise in the 1830s.
The English Civil Wars gave a voice to groups proposing alternative political arrangements as state censorship of publishing was temporarily suspended.
Cheap printing presses provided a simple way to distribute radical or novel ideas, and this period has been described as "the birth of a political nation" accordingly.[2] There are moments subsequently which picture the country's tentative steps towards 'democracy' in its modern sense, such as a record of the Chartists' march. Representing democracy as a system or process poses its own particular problems.
As Weibel and Latour argue above, is it even possible? Moreover, as modern Britain lacks a singular constitution, and combines a monarchy and a parliamentary democracy, oblique ways of picturing the body politic have seemed necessary to several of the artists here.

1. Weibel in Peter Weibel and Bruno Latour, 'Making Things Public: Atmospheres of Democracy', 2005 (Cambridge, MA MIT Press), introduction
2. JH Plumb, quoted in Ellen Meiksins Wood, 'Why It Matters', London Review of Books, 25 September 2008, p3

'DEGREES OF PEOPLE'

When sixteenth and seventeenth century Englishmen set out to describe their society, they began by making distinctions, by classifying and ranking. 'We in England', commenced William Harrison in 1577, 'divide our people commonlie into foure sorts.' A century later the curate of the Kent parish of Goodnestone-next-Wingham, in listing the local population, automatically divided the householders into five social categories. This mental habit, of which many more examples could be cited, is of the first significance. It bears witness to the fact that the most fundamental structural characteristic of English society was its high degree of stratification, its distinctive and all-pervasive system of social inequality.

The reality of inequality was displayed everywhere. Massive and very visible distinctions of wealth and living standards impressed themselves on the casual observer who travelled the countryside or walked the streets of the towns. Hierarchical distinctions of status were reflected in styles of address. Rank and power were recognized in dress, in the conventions of comportment which governed face-to-face contacts between superiors and inferiors, in the order in which seats were taken in church, in the arrangement of places at table and in the ordering of public processions. Order, degree, rank and hierarchy seemed self-evident, even natural.

That English society was highly stratified and that such stratification reflected major differentials in the social distribution of wealth, status and power, all historians would agree. Their disagreements derive from their different conceptions of the relative importance of the actual criteria upon which social stratification was based and their varying interpretations of the nature of the relationships between individuals and social groups of different rank. Was English society, as some would assert, essentially a hierarchy of status, based upon the estimation accorded to different social functions, or was it, as others would argue, a hierarchy founded upon the possession of wealth? How far did relative position in this hierarchy affect the experience and opportunities of individuals? Were relationships between people of different social position characterised by vertical ties of patronage and clientage, or by the animosities generated by horizontal class solidarities?

These questions are fundamental to our understanding of the nature of English society in this period and they are not easily answerable. It is easier for the historian to be aware of the system of social inequality than to generalize about it in more than the shallowest manner. Once familiar with the records of the period we can more readily feel its force, almost intuitively, than analyse its characteristics with real precision. Yet such an analysis must be made. In attempting it, we must take care to steer between on the one hand, an uncritical acceptance of contemporary perceptions of the social order and on the other hand, the forcing of the complex historical realities of the time into conformity with our own, perhaps anachronistic, conceptions of the nature of social inequality.

We can best approach the problem by asking first a number of simple questions. What were contemporary ideas about social inequality? What do they reveal about the criteria of evaluation upon which social distinctions were grounded? How far do these ideas confirm to what we can discover of the actual distributions of wealth, status and power in society? By answering these questions we may arrive at a description of the social order which encompasses both contemporary perceptions of its nature and discoverable historical reality.

It is a commonplace to assert that sixteenth- and seventeenth-century Englishmen were deeply preoccupied with the problems of order and degree. In their most elevated discussions of the nature of the universe they envisaged a 'great chain of being' stretching down from the deity to the very elements, in which each creature, each created thing, had its appointed place. In their accounts of the 'tree of the commonwealth' or the 'body politic', they presented society as an organism of functionally interdependent, though unequal, parts. Such accounts of society were at once an explanation of social inequality and a scheme of values. They portrayed society as it *ought* to be, providing a prescription for an ideal harmony in social relations. The scheme of social order thus propounded was the conventional bombast of sermons and homilies, of proclamations and of preambles to statutes. That it was platitudinous is not to say that it was not employed with sincerity often enough, but even its most enthusiastic protagonists knew very well that it was an ideal, an aspiration.

In trying to describe society as it *was*, or rather as it seemed to them to be (for systematic social investigation was to await a later age) contemporary writers came down to earth more firmly. They invariably put forward a scheme of ranks or degrees, of hierarchically arranged social categories which were intended to simplify the complexity of reality and clearly distinguish the principal social groups.
The nature of the actual ranking frequently varied, usually in accordance with the principal concerns of

the writer (in general sixteenth century writers were primarily interested in the polity; those of the seventeenth century gradually turned their attention to questions of national resources and manpower). Despite these variations, however, contemporary analyses of the social order usually have at least two features in common. By and large they present accounts of what is recognizably the same society, though with different degrees of detail and clarity. Again, they tend to show an overlap, even a confusion between different criteria of social rank. The broad structure of society emerges clearly enough, yet the social order was also far too complex to be anatomized in terms of any single criterion. It had burst through the constraints of traditional classifications into functional 'orders' and only with difficulty could its component parts be adequately divided.

William Harrison's scheme of society can provide an example. Of the four 'degrees of people' distinguished by Harrison, the first degree consisted of gentlemen. Though internally differentiated into the titular nobility, knights, esquires and 'last of all they that are simplie called gentlemen', this group was defined in general as 'those whome their race and blood or at least their vertues doo make noble and knowne.' Next in Harrison's scheme came the citizens and burgesses of England's cities, a group defined by their occupations and by their possession of the freedom of their cities. Third came the yeomen of the countryside, defined either as freeholders of land to the value of 40s a year, or as farmers to gentlemen, and further as possessing 'a certine prehemineence and more estimation' among the common people. Finally came a category embracing day labourers, poor husbandmen, artificers and servants, people who had 'neither voice nor authoritie in the common wealthe, but are to be ruled and not to rule other.'

A striking feature of his accounts is the multiplicity of criteria employed in the allocation of rank. Gentility, as we have seen, was broadly defined in terms of birth and blood. Yet in his account of different degrees of gentlemen Harrison showed himself very aware indeed of the importance of wealth to the establishment and maintenance of station. Knights, for example, were described as being not born, but made; for their valour in war, their service to the monarch in peace, but 'most commonlie according to their yearelie revenues or abundance of riches, wherewith to mainteine their estates' at a level appropriate to 'a knight's living' – though he quickly added that not all gentlemen of sufficient wealth were knighted. Again, gentle status could be achieved as well as inherited; by obtaining a university degree, by appointment to governmental or military office, or by any man who 'can live without manuell labour, and thereto is able and will beare the port, charge and countenance of a gentleman'.
With these qualifications Harrison passed from the ideal of gentility as an independent condition conferred by blood to its reality as a status dependent upon a compound of occupation, wealth and life-style in addition to and sometimes independent of birth.
He also gave frank recognition to the reality of social mobility, to the fact that the social order's apparent stability was a condition not of stasis, but of dynamic equilibrium.

Keith E. Wrightson is Randolph W. Townsend Jr. Professor of History, and one of the most widely respected historians practising today. His publications include 'English Society 1580-1680' (Hutchinson)

THOMAS HOBBES / ABRAHAM BOSSE

Frontispiece to 'Leviathan' 1651

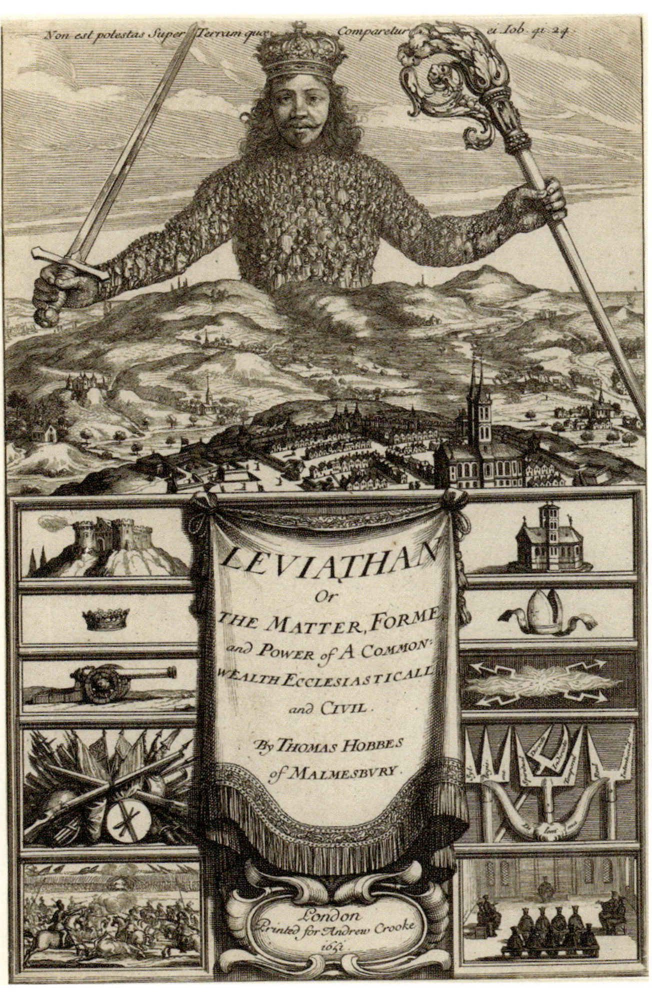

British Museum

"Kings are compared to the head of this microcosm of the body of man." [1]
King James I, speech to the houses of parliament, 21st March 1610

Thomas Hobbes commissioned Abraham Bosse to create an image under his direction to introduce his book 'Leviathan'. Written in the middle of the civil war, it argued that "In those Nations, whose Common wealths have been long-lived, and not been destroyed the Subjects never did dispute of the Soveraign Power." The print makes visible the verbal image of the time that the nation is 'the body politic', making literal the idea that the monarch is the nation 'embodied' and the 'head of state' who governs the other parts of the body. Each 'part' is necessary and is interdependent, but the monarch provides governance over all.

Hobbes's king is, like a Biblical patriarch, a father-figure towering over and protecting his subjects. James I also argued that, "In the scriptures, kings are called Gods, and so their power after a certain relation compared to the divine power. Kings are also compared to Fathers of families: for a king is truly *parens patriæ*, the political father of his people."[2] Hobbes' monarch towers over an agricultural landscape and a town. The art historian John Barrell notes that the metaphor has it that we 'command' a view: "those who can comprehend the order of society are the observers of a prospect, in which others are merely objects – some are fit to survey the extensive panorama, some are confined within one or other of the micro-prospects, which to the comprehensive observer, are part of a wider landscape".[3] Hobbes's king, towering 'above' the people, is the only figure able to see the whole picture and to act in the national interest.

1. http://history.wisc.edu/sommerville/351/Jamesdrk.htm
2. Ibid.
3. Quoted by Gordon Fyfe, 'On the invisibility of the visual' in Fyfe and Law, eds, 'Picturing Power' 1988, (London: Routledge) p2

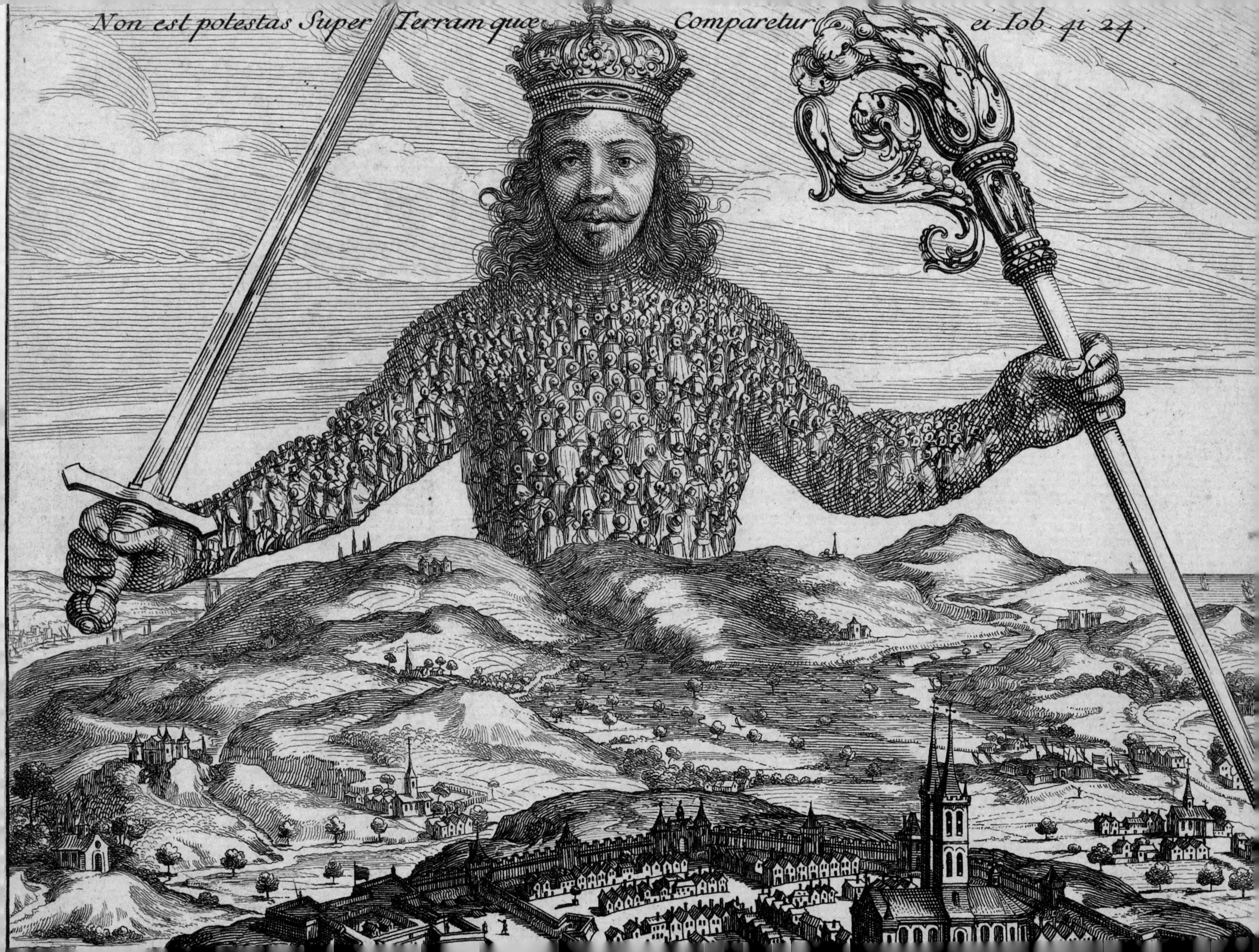
Non est potestas Super Terram quæ Comparetur ei. Iob. 41. 24.

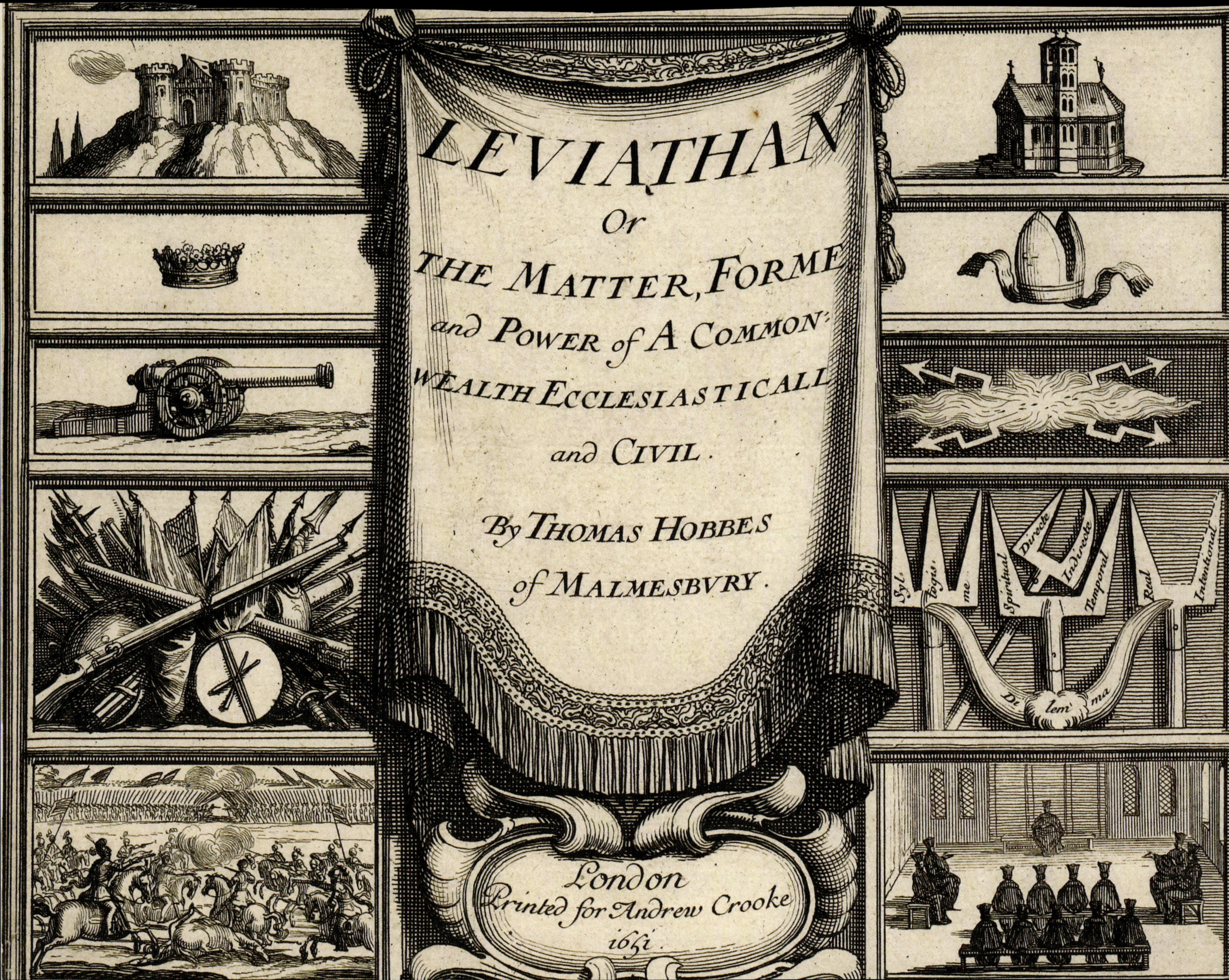
LEVIATHAN
Or
THE MATTER, FORME
and POWER of A COMMON-
WEALTH ECCLESIASTICALL
and CIVIL.
By THOMAS HOBBES
of MALMESBVRY.
London
Printed for Andrew Crooke
1651.
Syl
logis
me
Spiritual
Directe
Indirecte
Temporal
Real
Intentional
Di
lem
ma

"We have been living like kings...."[1]
Eric Hobsbawm

The novelist and artist Alasdair Gray created printed images as part of his greatest novel 'Lanark'. Here he adapts Thomas Hobbes's image for 'Leviathan', updating it to describe his own imagined country, closely based on Scotland. Gray works between image and text, and his greatest novel 'Lanark' diagnoses 'the state of the nation' on an epic scale. Gray's use of Hobbes and Bosse's composition underlines his aim to create a panoramic view of the country and its political character, by surveying both the country and the city, and the nation's sources of wealth. Here, North Sea Oil features prominently. In the middle ground, cooling towers and oil tankers flank the new Forth bridge, completed a few years earlier.
The image departs from Hobbes' model in some crucial ways. Gray is blunt about the political tools necessary to ensure order is maintained. His sword and sceptre are labelled 'force' and 'persuasion' respectively. Most of the miniscule figures inside the monarch face upwards to obey him., just as in 'Leviathan', but a few wave their arms in protest.

1. Quoted in The Guardian Saturday Review, 2007

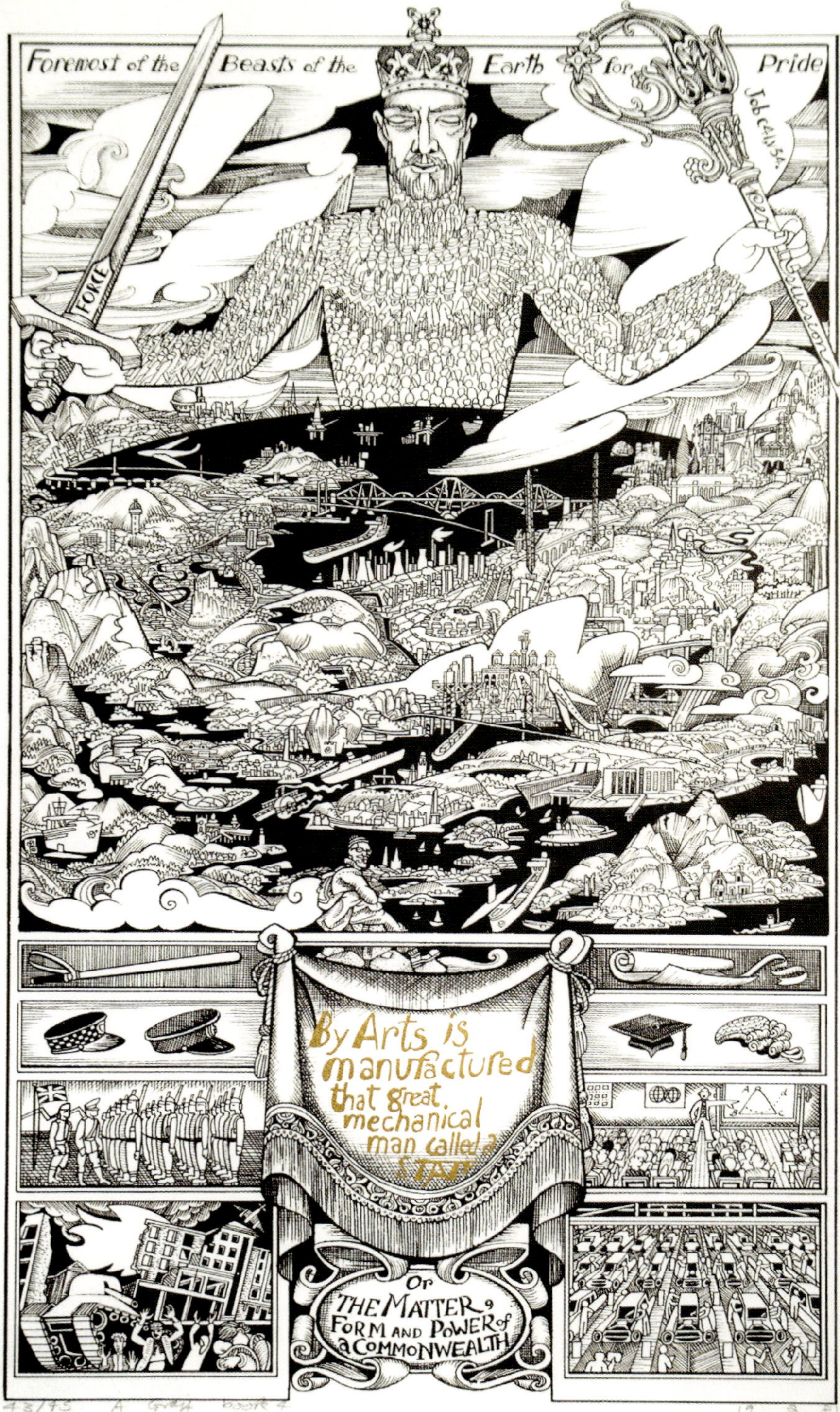

Frontispiece from 'Lanark' book four, 1982

Courtesy Sorcha Dallas Gallery, Glasgow

UNKNOWN ARTIST / CLEMENT WALKER

'The Royall Oake of Brittayne' from 'Anarchia Anglicana' 1649

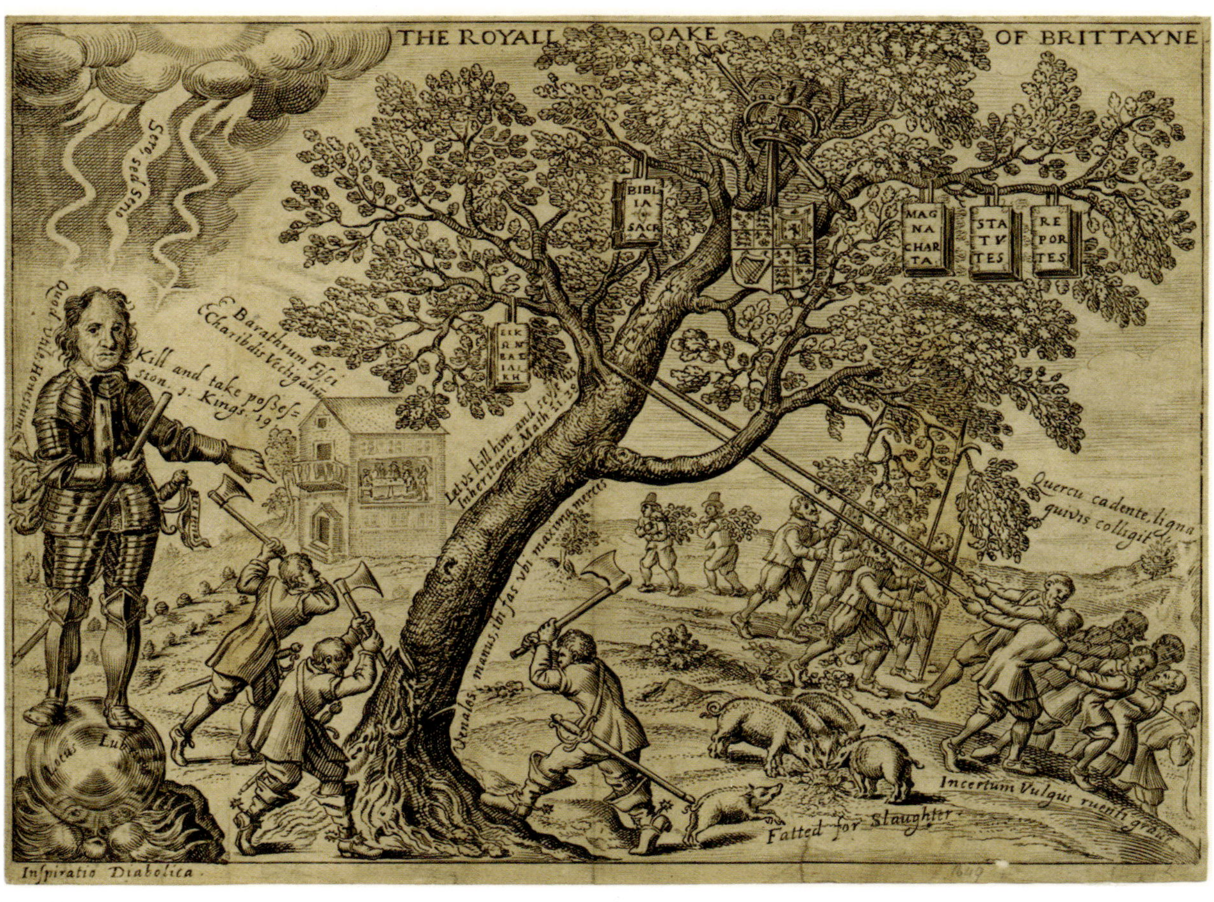

British Museum

"The Lord maketh the earth... waste, and turneth it upsidedown... And it shall be, as with the people, so with the priest, as with the servant, so with his master... The earth shall reel to and fro like a drunkard... The Lord shall punish the host of the high ones... and the kings of the earth." Isaiah xxiv, 1-2, 20-21

Publishing this print landed the MP Clement Walker in the Tower of London. Walker was one of Oliver Cromwell's loyal followers, until Cromwell supported Charles I's execution. At this point he was expelled from parliament. The Biblical quotation above was seen as a prophecy or description of the chaos and bloodshed of the civil war after Charles I's execution. The print portrays a world 'turned upside down', and depicts the fates of the rich and the poor, whilst condemning the middle classes for supporting the republicans. Walker's image of Cromwell is as the devil: he stands above the jaws of hell. The words "Inspiratio Diabolica" mark him as the anti-Christ, uprooting the natural order for evil ends. Words next to him invert Scripture: "kill and take possession"; or show him as devious, saying "that which is expedient is honourable." Britain's political arrangements are symbolised here by a mighty oak tree which is deep-rooted, strong, and has grown slowly. The 'fruits' of the tree include the Magna Carta, guaranteeing Britons' liberties; and the 'Eikon Basilike', a book of Charles I's political views. Helping to destroy the oak are two groups, who represent what were then called the 'middling sorts'.
Their unprincipled greed has allowed some of them to occupy a grand house in the background. By contrast the lower orders are labelled as "fatted for the slaughter" like sacrificial animals. They are drinking merrily, unaware of their impending fate.

UNKNOWN ARTIST / JOHN OUERTON

"The Cats' Castle Bisieged and Stormed by the Rats' c1665

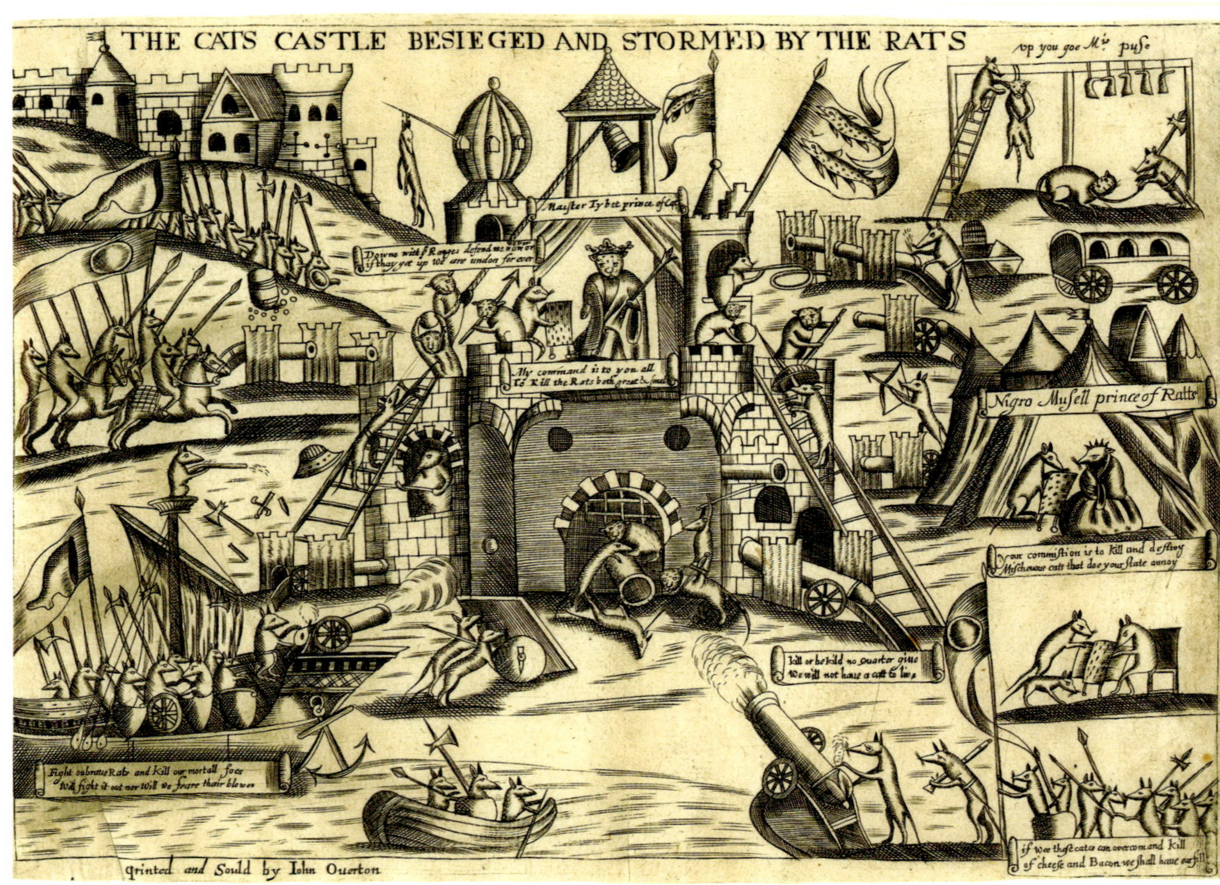

British Museum

"There is a motivation during carnival time to create a form of human social configuration that lies beyond existing social forms." [1]
Mikhail Bakhtin, 'Rabelais and his World', 1965

"At last the common people [may] set up for themselves, call parity and independence liberty... destroy all rights and properties, all distinctions of families and merits." [2]
King Charles I, 1641

During 'carnival' days in medieval societies, the normal social order was suspended or reversed: the 17th century phrase was that the world was 'turned upside down'.

This work reveals a peculiar version of the world 'upside down', and was created during the civil war. It is plausible that the print was made for readers who wished for a return to order from the inversions of wartime: one similar edition reads "This image refers to all those who are subject to their superiors."[3] The historian Christopher Hill argues that "popular revolt was for many centuries an essential feature of the English tradition [but] the middle decades of the 17th century saw the greatest upheaval that has yet occurred in Britain... from, say, 1645 to 1653, there was a great overturning, questioning, revaluing of everything in England... The crucial difference between "foolery" in medieval times and the mid 17th century was the genuine threat that it might allow the social order to be permanently overturned, rather than act as a safety valve releasing tensions."[4] One writer, Gerrard Winstanley, reported that "The old world is running up like parchment in the fire... freedom is the man that will turn the world upside down... making the earth a common treasury [by overthrowing] that Beast, kingly property."[5]

1.Bakhtin (Indiana: Indiana UP: 1984 edition), p280
2. In Christopher Hill, 'The World Turned Upside Down', (London: Penguin) 1971, p24
3. http://www.bpi1700.org.uk/printsMonths/august2007.html
4. Hill, ibid, p13-14
5. Hill, ibid, p14

'If at first you don't succeed' 2008

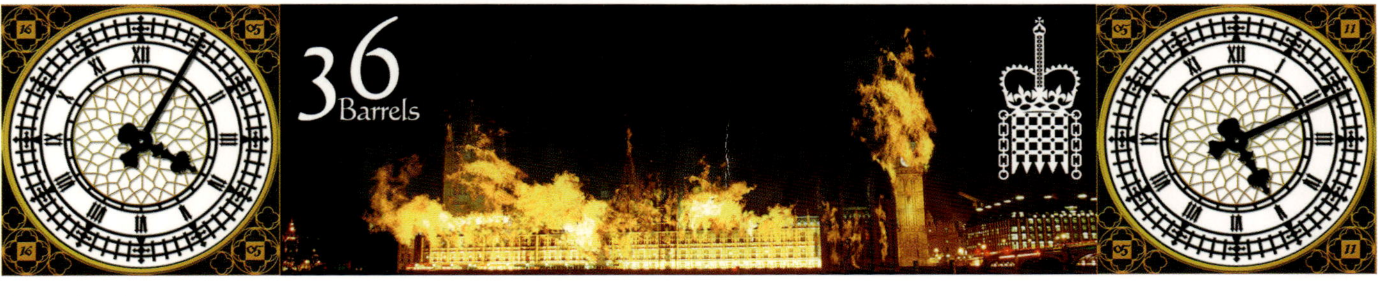

Courtesy the artist

"A foreign observer sees only the huge inequality of wealth, the unfair electoral system, the governing-class control over the press, radio and education, and concludes that democracy is simply a polite name for dictatorship... [but] British democracy is less of a fraud than it sometimes appears." [1] **George Orwell, 'England, Your England', 1941**

How could we begin to imagine a fully-fledged, alternative social order in the future? One answer is to look back at the history of dissent. Misteraitch's work draws upon the long history of radical protest against social injustices to envisage an alternative political system. Much of Misteraitch's work adapts the messages of advertising or 'official' media, like Her Majesty's Post, to upend their meanings. Here a special effect from a Hollywood film is overlaid over a tourist image of London. The two small images at either side point to the date of Guy Fawkes' attempted gunpowder plot: 1605. The artist describes himself as a 'Bastardiser of the Queen's Post' and many of his works come in the form of life-size stamps, or posters. His works are intended to be infiltrated into everyday life. Instead of carrying the Queen's head, they carry what the artist sees as more democratic insignia, appropriate to the 21st century.

1. Quoted in David Runciman 'Behind the Masks', The Guardian Saturday Review May 17 2008

JOHN LECESTER / JOHN HANCOCK **'England's Miraculous preservation Emblematically Described, Erected for a Perpetuall Movement to Posterity' 1646**

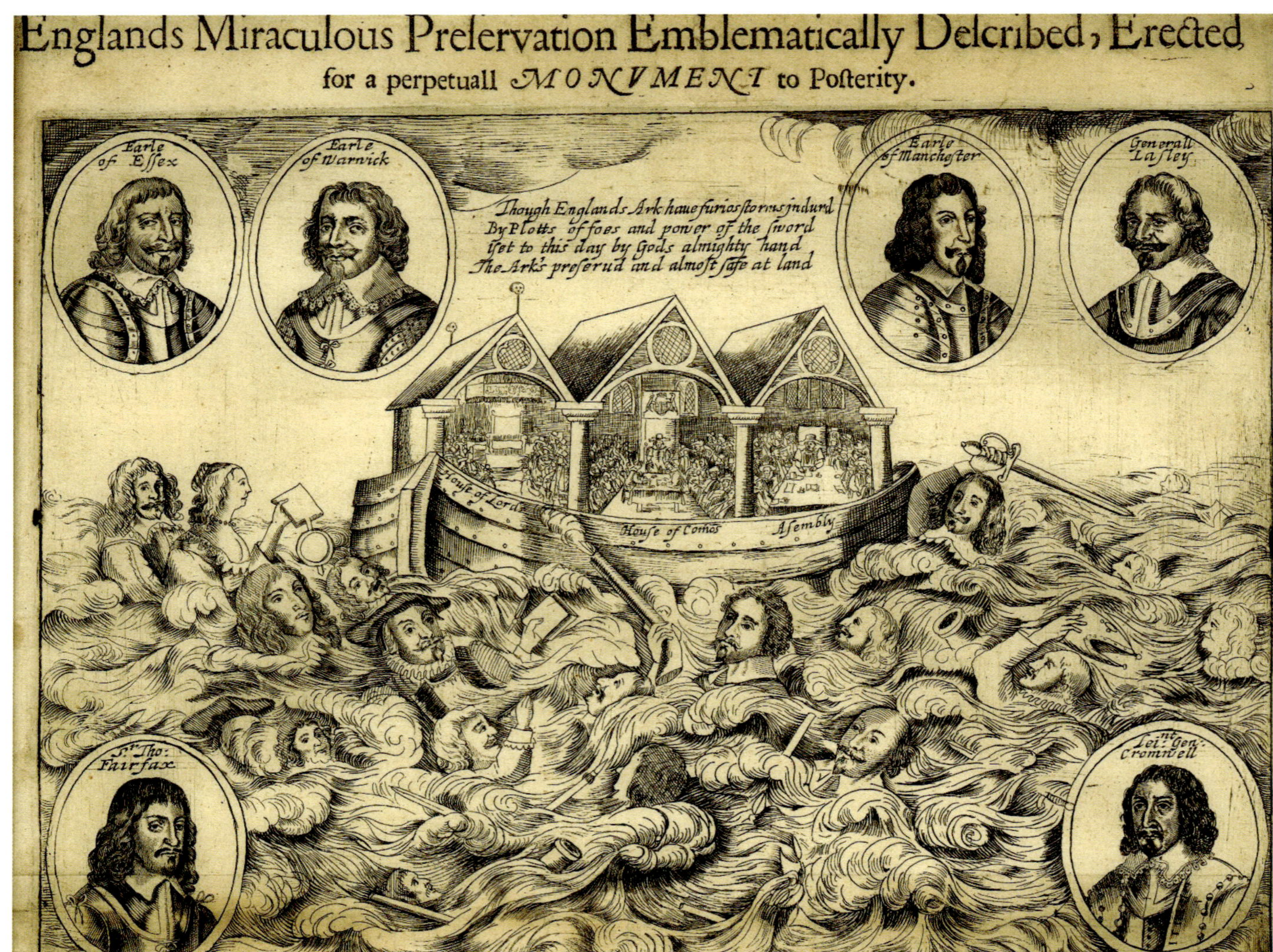

British Museum

"Britain retains intact an elaborate, formal system of rank and precedence, culminating in the monarchy itself, which means that prestige and honour can be transmitted and inherited across the generations."[1] **David Cannadine, 'Class in Britain', 1998**

This work is believed to be the first picture of Oliver Cromwell to be printed. A ship in difficult waters represents both the nation and the State, as it contains parliament. The purpose of the print, created in the civil war, was to credit Cromwell with the safe stewardship of the 'ship of state'. The text explicitly describes the houses of parliament as 'England's Ark'. This 'ark' protects the traditions of liberty through the 'flood' of the civil war. Inside the ark are the three 'Houses' of State: the House of Commons; the Assembly of Divines; and the House of Lords, which has an absent throne as the print was made after King Charles I's execution. The division between the House of Lords and House of Commons was made in the 14th century. The accompanying text reads: "Though England's Ark have furious storms endured / By plots of foes and power of the sword / yet to this day by God's almighty hand / The Ark's prefer'd and almost safe at land."

1. Cannadine 1998, p22

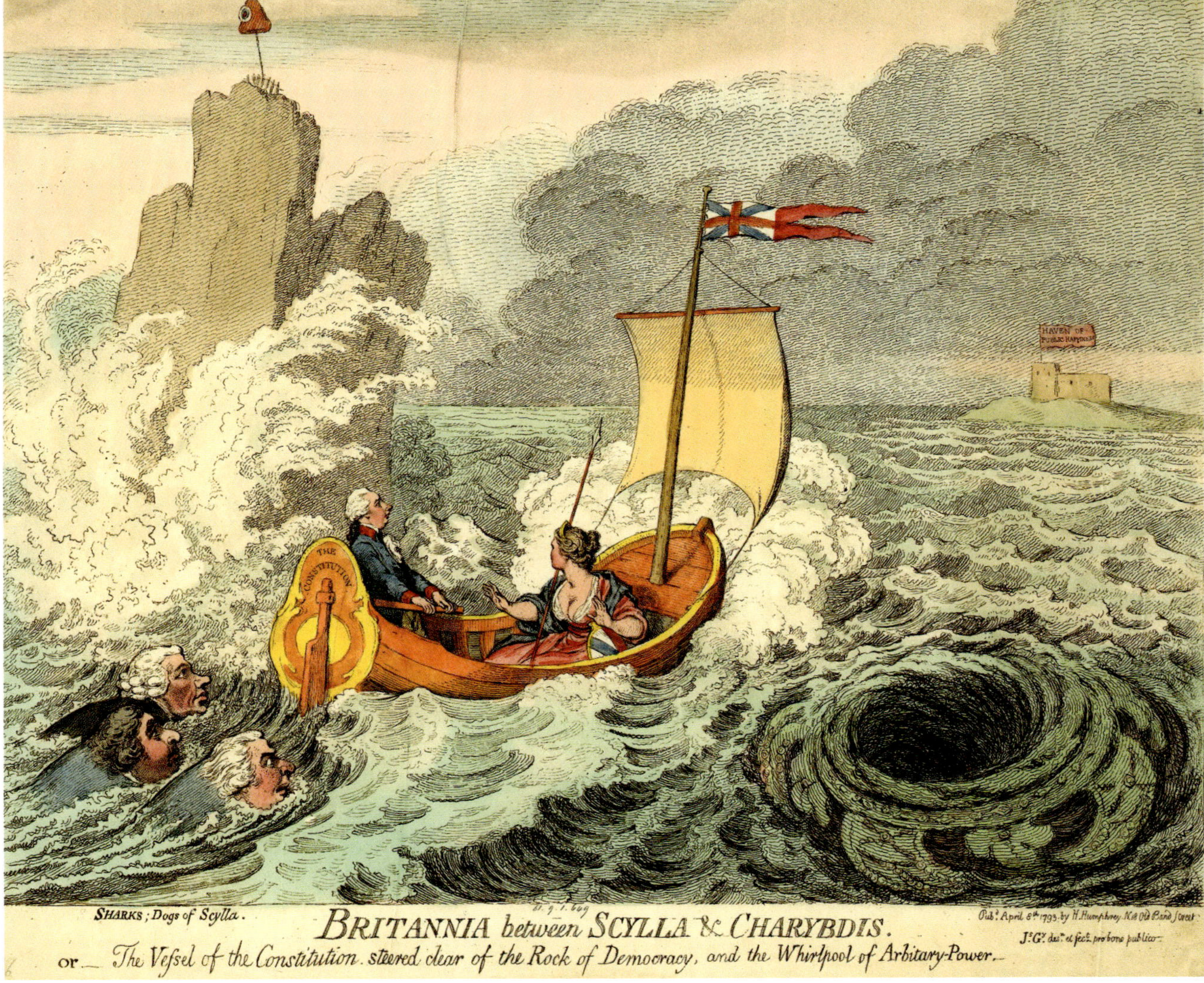

'The Vessel of the Constitution steered clear of the Rock of Democracy and the Whirlpool of Arbitrary Power' 1793

"Inequality has lived through centuries of this culture. Continuity is no accident. Social custom, like habit, economizes human effort... Continuity normally presupposes consensus. Change typically results from conflict." [1] **AH Halsey 'Social change in Britain', 1986**

Gillray's print combines two well-known images: the nation as personified by 'Britannia', and the constitution as the 'ship of state'. Prime Minister William Pitt, steers his ship on a sensible and safe middle course away from the twin threats of 'democracy' and absolutism. Democracy is appropriately on the left, topped by the symbolic Revolutionary 'cap of liberty', with rocky shores threatening to break up the boat. Radicals wore a simple cap to symbolise their universal equality in contrast to aristocrats' enormous and expensive wigs. To the 'right' is an upside-down Turkish crown, a symbol of absolute monarchy which acts as a vortex sucking all wealth and power towards it. Headwear marked out clear political positions at this time, when the terms 'left' and 'right' came into being. Finally, To the rear are the 'sharks' of Whig politicians Richard Brinsley Sheridan, Charles James Fox, and Joseph Priestly. 'Democrat' was frequently used as a term of abuse in caricature, and 'democracy' seen as a grave threat to the nation. Gillray's image of the common-sense-and-compromise middle path taken by the British remains apt. Britain maintains both a monarchy and a parliamentary democracy, and almost uniquely has no formal written constitution.

1. Halsey, 1985, p1

UNKNOWN ARTIST

The Embleme of Englands distractions as also of her attained, and further expected Freedome, & Happiness' 1658

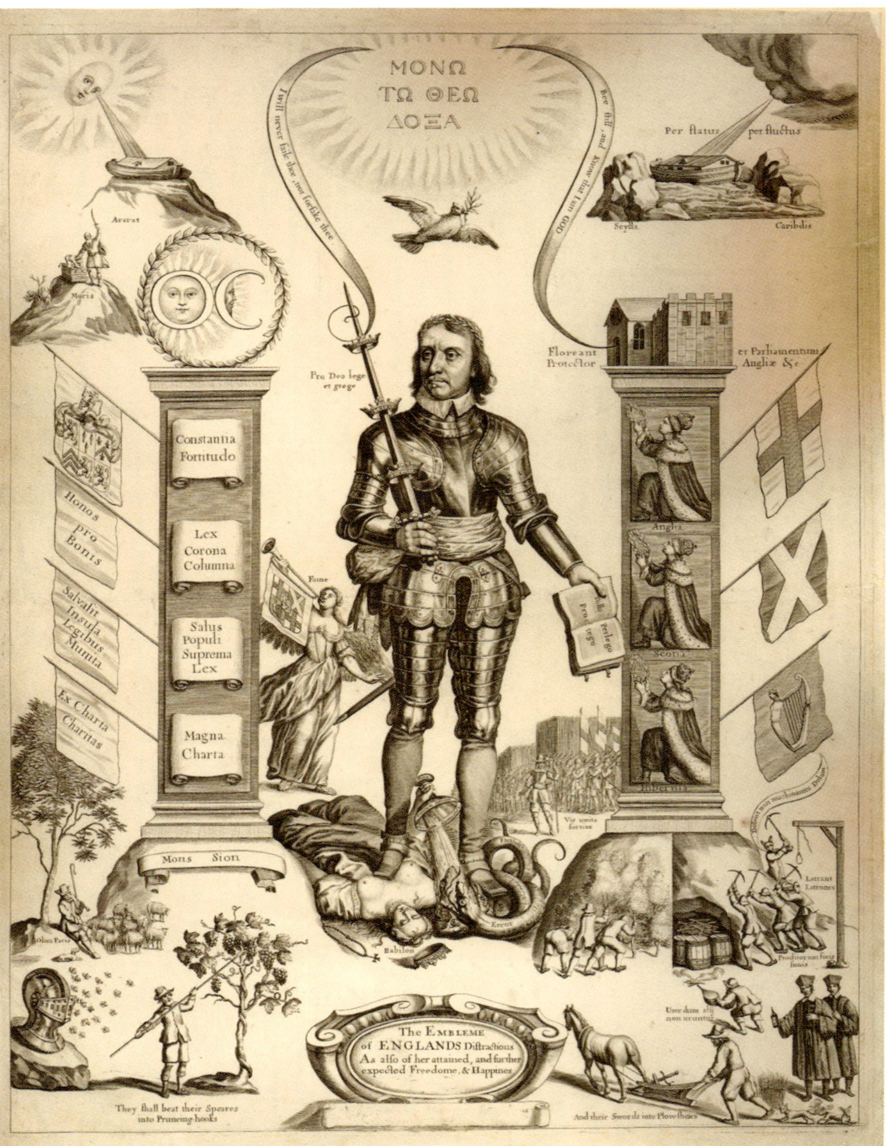

British Museum

"There is a beauty of order in society... as when the different members... have all their appointed offices, place and station."[1] Jonathan Edwards, 1740s

This print celebrates Oliver Cromwell as Lord Protector, a post he held until 1658 after refusing to become England's monarch the year before. As this image suggests, though, the Protectorate gradually adopted the trappings of a Monarchy: Cromwell resembles his predecessors as head of state in every respect. By 1657 he was usually addressed as 'your Highness' and his inauguration resembled a royal coronation: he wore purple velvet and ermine robes and carried a golden sceptre. This picture is filled with traditional emblems with no attempt to create a new pictorial language for the new regime. In the top-right is 'the ship of state', where Noah sails his ark safely between the twin dangers of Scylla and Charbydis.
On the top-left, having been carefully captained, the ship has reached benign territory. The scrolls on the left are the founding blocks of England's political constitution – the Magna Carta and Rule of Law. The small figures on the right-hand column represent the nations of England, Ireland and Scotland.

1. Quoted in Cannadine, 1998, p36

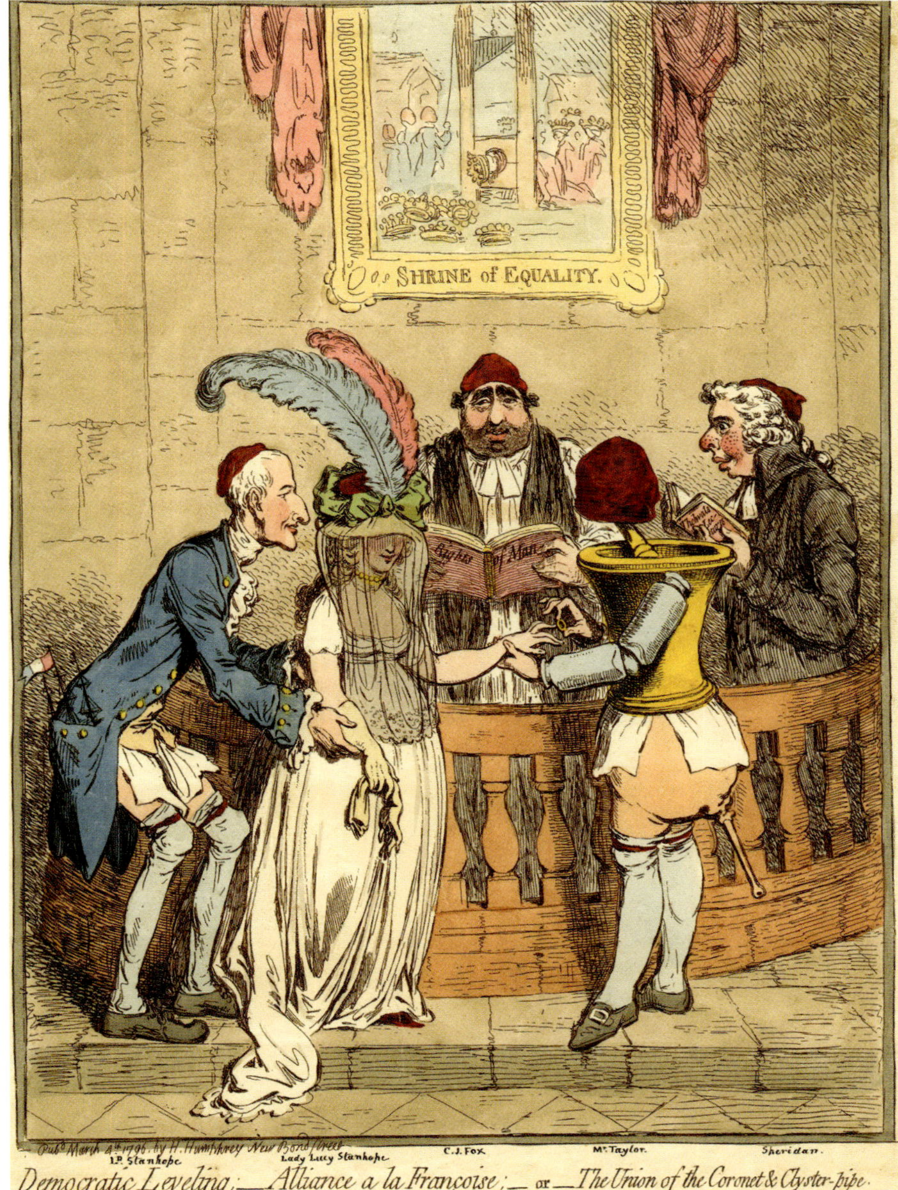

Working Class Movement Library, Salford

"The social ties and ligaments [are]... unalterable relations which Providence has ordained. [They rely on] generous loyalty to rank, proud submission... [and] principles of natural subordination."[1]
Edmund Burke, 'Reflections on the Revolution in France', 1790

Gillray's prints throughout the 1790s poured scorn on British politicians who supported the French Revolution and 'democracy'. His work echoed Burke's conservative views. This print parodies key figures in Whig circles. The scene is the marriage of the surgeon Thomas Taylor to the sixteen-year old heiress Lady Lucy Stanhope. Next to her are her father, the peer Earl Stanhope, and parliamentarians Charles James Fox and Richard Sheridan. Despite his elevated title, Stanhope promoted novel and radical causes and helped lead the London Revolution Society. He supported free elections, press freedom, and the idea that political authority should derive from the democratic will. He was satirised in popular prints as 'Citizen Stanhope', partially because of the contradiction between his democratic principles and his title. He was in a minority. Historian Roy Porter argues that, even after the Revolution, "few questioned that there should be some natural order of high and low. Differentiation was the key to society... the social hierarchy was a basic fact."[2] Samuel Johnson, for example, believed that "fixed, invariable rules of distinction of rank" were God's will, despite his own considerable social mobility.

1. Quoted in Cannadine, 1998, p55
2. Roy Porter, 'English Society in the 18th Century, 1982 ,(London: Penguin) pp15-16

RUTH EWAN

'All Things Are Common' 2008

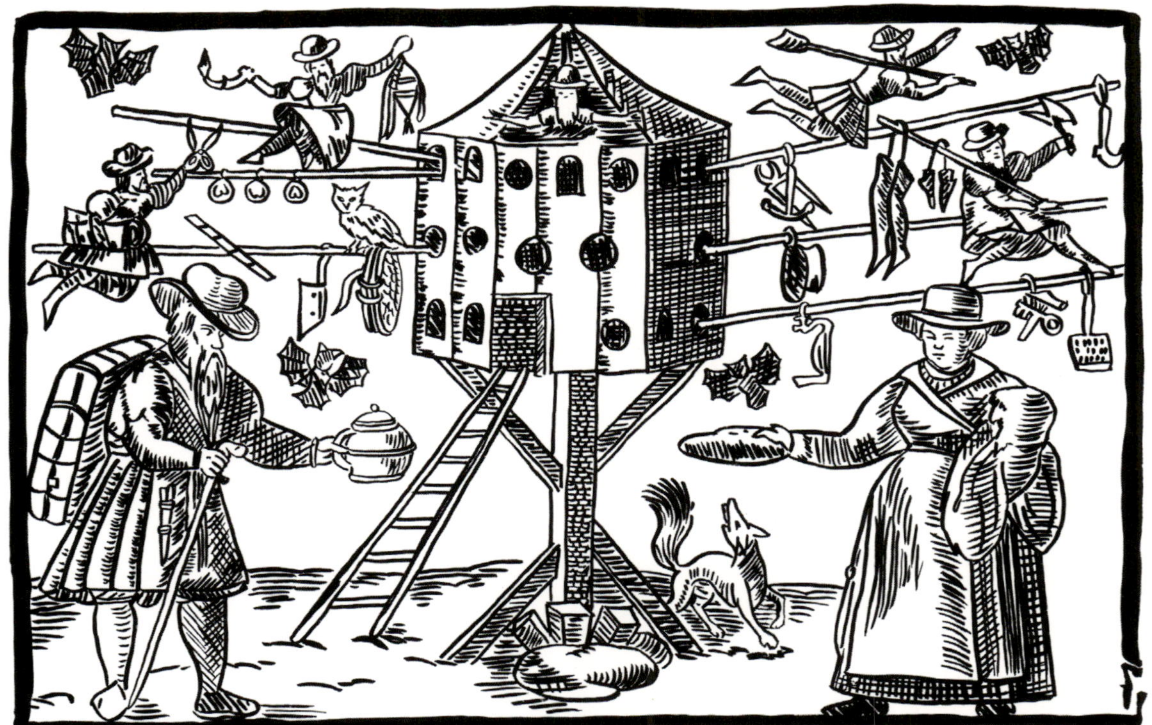

Courtesy the artist and Ancient and Modern, London

"The institutions of [social] reproduction are the family and the school."[1]
AH Halsey, 'Social Change in Britain', 1986

Ewan is interested in how we learn to 'be ourselves', and in what ways 'popular culture' can be a force for progessive social change. Most often, Ewan's works are realised by others. Her posters unearth competing pictures of the social order from the past, to ask questions about the present. The image itself is from a 17th century print. The original was created by conservatives to criticize radicals' unrealistic ideas of universal equality. A house on stilts is built against natural laws: a flight of fantasy which is a 'castle in the air'. At the time many believed a group called the Anabaptists wanted to abolish private property and all hierarchies. Modern socialists including Friedrich Engels adopted the Anabaptists as their precursors, as preachers of a new egalitarian social order. In 1626 the preacher William Gouge wrote in an instructional pamphlet called 'Of Domesticall Duties', which noted that Anabaptists "teach that all are alike and that there is no difference betwixt masters and servants."[2] One Anabaptist battle cry was "omnia sunt communia": 'all things are common'.

The print here is by a schoolchild: Ewan asked a class to create their own version of the print, to test how far they could imagine an entirely different social structure than their own. The prints are presented to be taken away by gallery visitors, both as though they were 'speculative propaganda' for a future society, and as though they were 'common property'.

1. Halsey, 1986, p23
2. Quoted in Hill, 1972, p35

HUBERT-FRANÇOIS GRAVELOT

'The State Packhorse' c.1732–1745

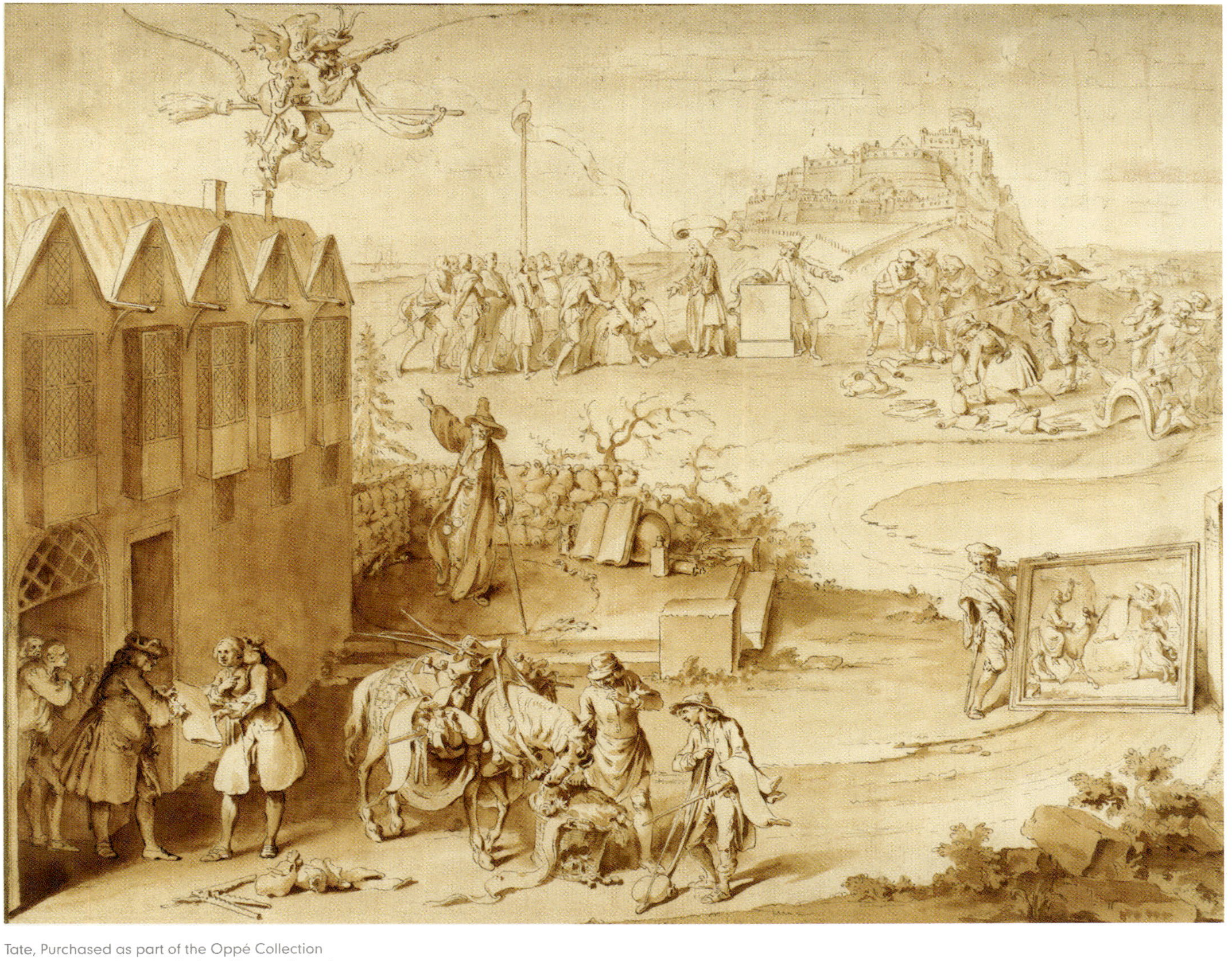

Tate, Purchased as part of the Oppé Collection with assistance from the National Lottery through the Heritage Lottery Fund 1996

"Sovereign power rests in my person alone. To me alone belongs all legislative power. Public order in all its entirety emanates from me."[1] King Louis XV, 1766

"England is different in every respect from the rest of Europe."[2] Casanova, 1750s

Though Gravelot was born in France, he was working in London when he made this lampoon of the state. But which state? The costumes here appear to be French, suggesting he was likely to be thinking of the large and powerful French state rather than the British model of government. By the mid-eighteenth century, the two were very distinct. France had an enormous, centralized bureaucracy managing the nation from Paris. Britons had a small state, leaving them to commercial activity, and indeed an independent 'middle-class' grew rapidly at this time. As Prime minister Horace Walpole noted when first travelling abroad, "I had discovered that there was nowhere but in England the distinction of middling people."[3]

Though France's population was nearly three times larger than England's, it was heavily taxed and administered: the French people became a beast of burden for the state, rather than the other way around.

1.Quoted in Mark Steel, 'Vive La Revolution', 2003, (London: Scribner) p14
2. Quoted in Porter, 1982, p7
3. Porter, ibid, p X

GERHARD RICHTER

'Elizabeth I' 1966

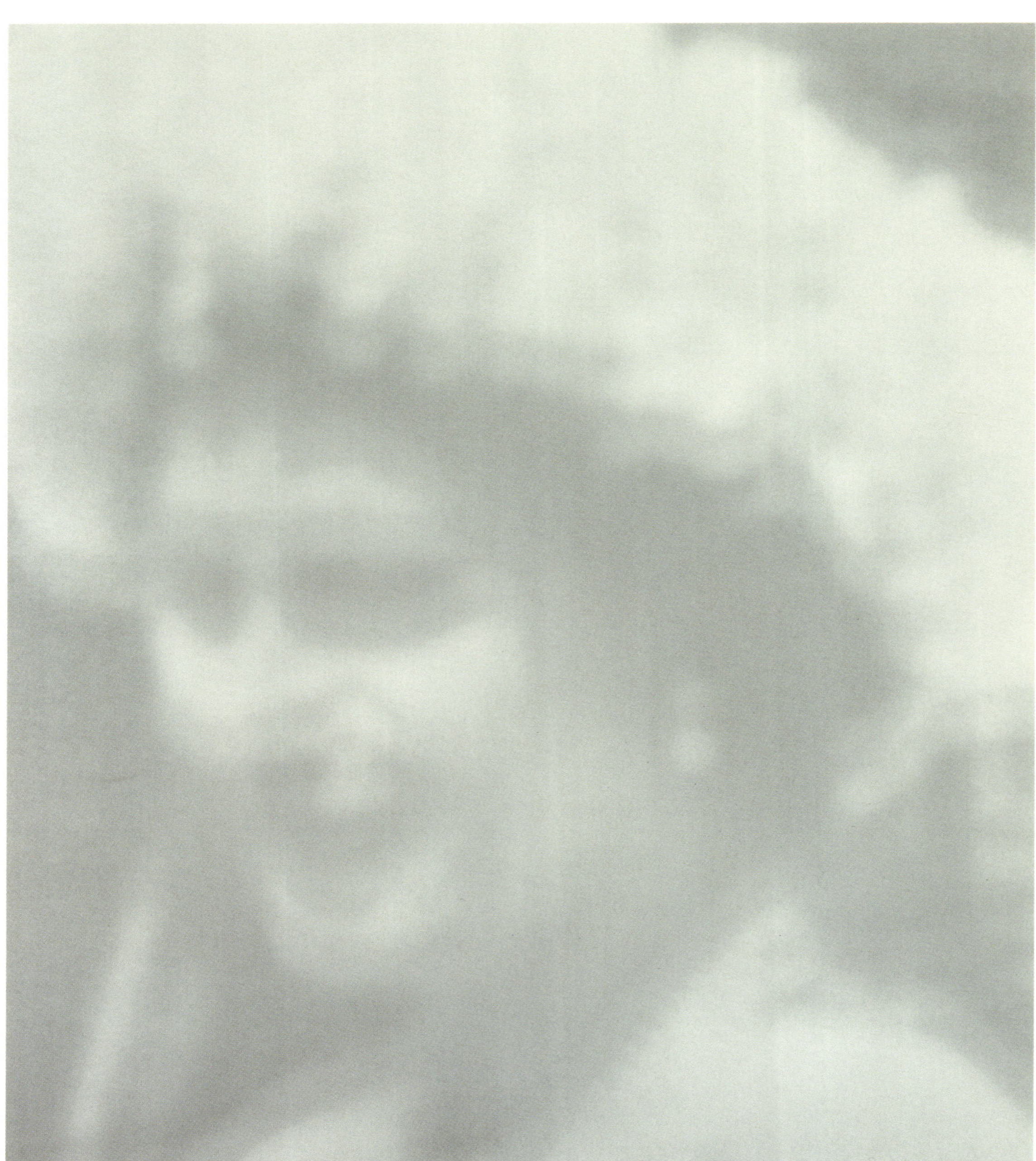

Photograph ©Tate, London, 2008; courtesy the artist.

"Above all things our royalty is to be reverenced, and if you begin to poke about it, you cannot reverence it. Its mystery is its life. We must not let daylight upon magic... The fancy of the mass of men is incredibly weak; it can see nothing without a visible symbol; and there is much that it can scarcely make out without a symbol... The best reason why Monarchy is a strong government is that it is an intelligible government. The mass of mankind understand it, and they hardly anywhere in the world understand any other."[1] **Walter Bagehot, 'The English Constitution', 1867**

Making a portrait of the Queen that proves to be an interesting artwork is an intractable problem, and one artists from Andy Warhol to Lucian Freud have tackled. The Queen's image is, after all, on every banknote, coin, and stamp: we see it daily. The monarch is the most widely deployed visual symbol for the nation, and their image has a unique symbolic value. Gerhard Richter's solution to creating a new image of the Queen was to defer our ability to 'read' it. The photographic source was a little-known press picture, and its treatment obliterates the Queen's features entirely. The image is almost a test of whether the monarch would be recognisable without any defined features present. Richter has kept his own political position opaque, simply noting that his works are "images without glory".[2]

1. Quoted in Tod and Wheeler, 'Utopia '1978, (London: Orbis) p237
2. Quoted in Gordon Burn, 'I Believe in Nothing', Guardian Saturday Review Sept 20 2008, p16

'The British Atlas, or John Bull supporting the Peace Establishment' 1816

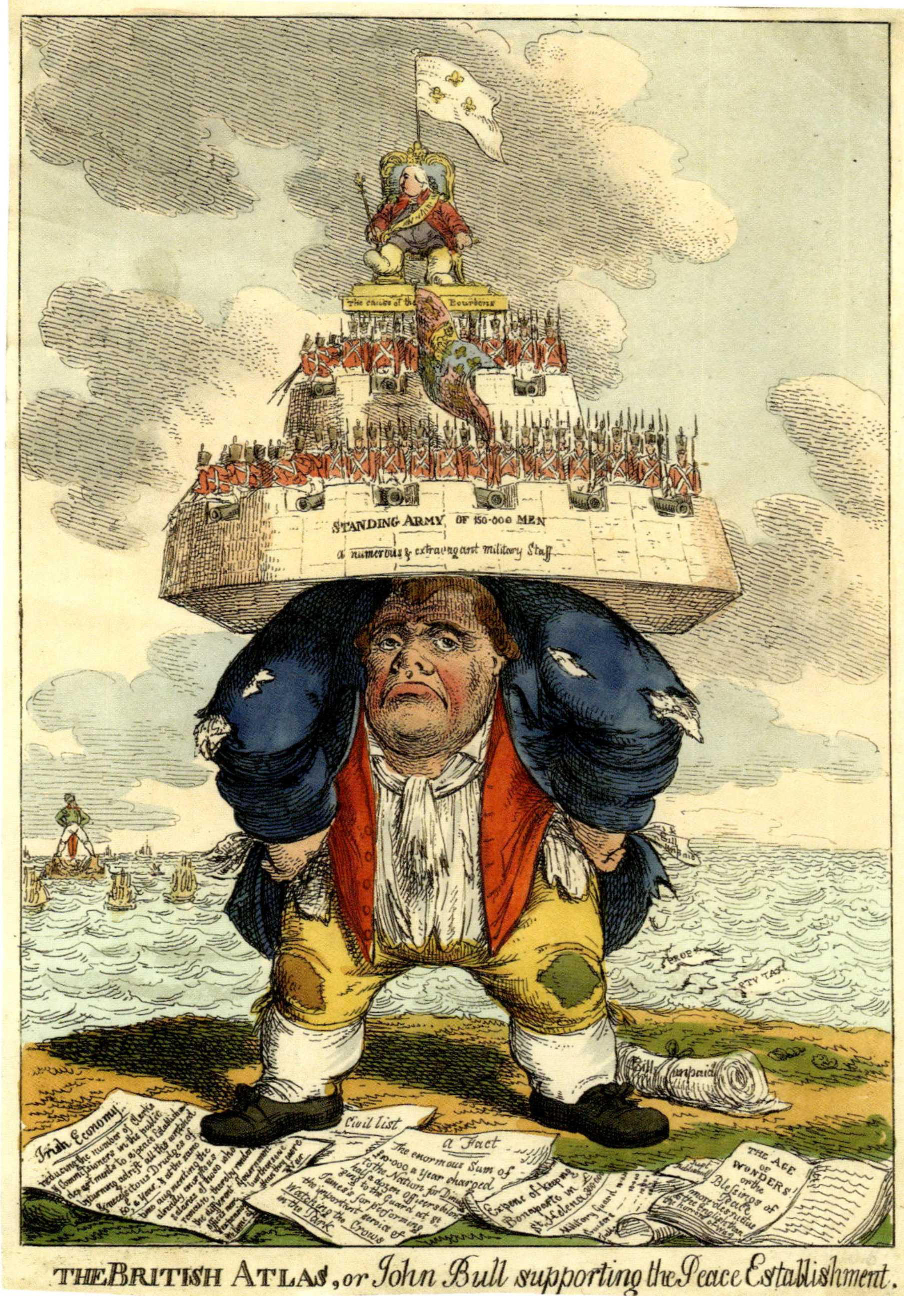

British Museum

"There is no art which one government sooner learns of another than that of draining money from the pockets of the people." [1] **Adam Smith, 'The Wealth of Nations', 1776**

Drawing contrasts between a profligate state and a longsuffering 'people' became a staple of political cartoons from the 1800s. Wililams' print is one of the most memorable ways in which it has been depicted. To fight the Napoleonic wars, Prime Minister William Pitt had to raise taxes and the national debt dramatically. 'John Bull' supports a towering pyramid of military men paid for by ever-higher taxes, and topped by the bloated Prince Regent. Napoleon stands defiant in the distance. Bull first appeared as a (bull)dog in cartoons in the 1710s, and as proud and independent. Only from the late eighteenth century was he represented as human. What makes Bull represent 'the nation?' Firstly, his very shape reflects Englishmen's idea of themselves. His well-fed torso represents the country's solid prosperity. Secondly, he is from the 'middling sort', and his physique might be said to represent the shape of England's social structure.
England had a much larger, and more prosperous commercial class than most other European countries. Its distinguishing feature was its "fat middle" to use historian Keith Wrightson's words. One writer of the time, wrote that "in most other societies, society presents hardly anything but a void between an ignorant labouring populous and a greedy and profligate nobility. But with us the space between the ploughman and the peer is crammed with circle after circle".

1. www.adamsmith.org/smith/won-b5-c2-appendix-to-articles-1-2.htm
2. In interview with the author.
3. Quoted in Porter, 1982, p49

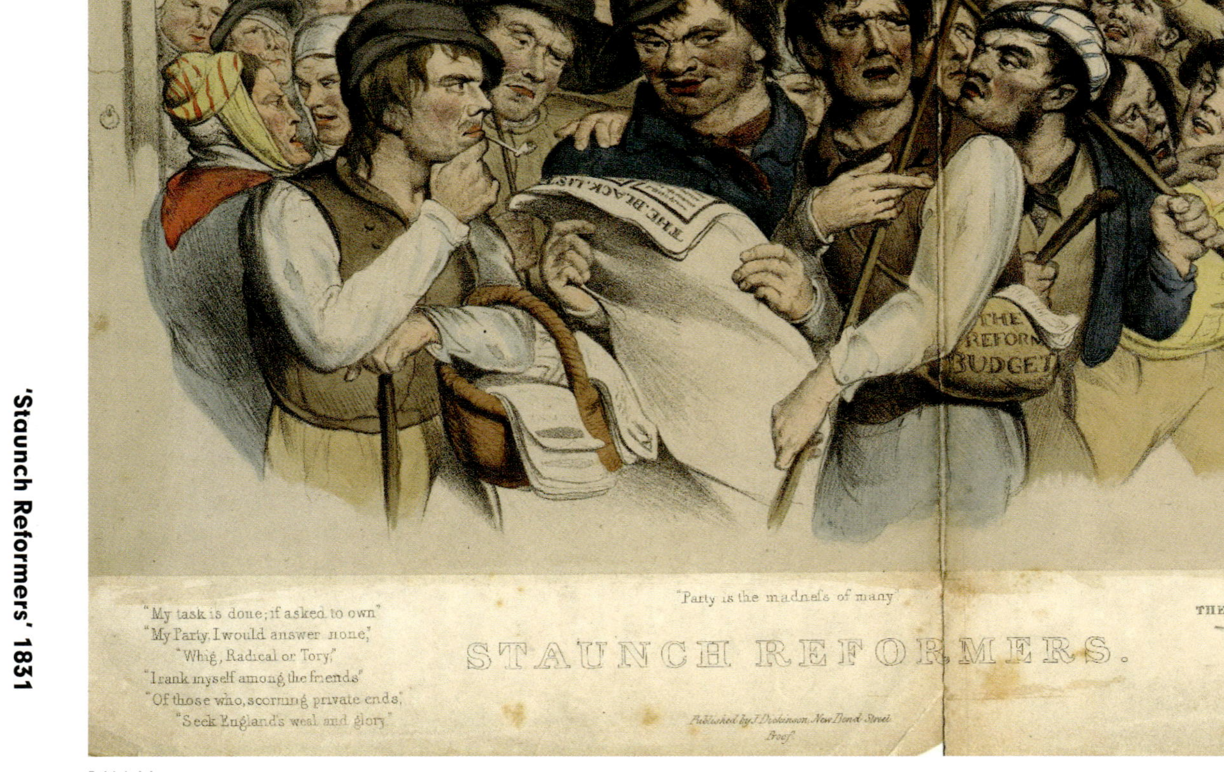

British Museum

"Those at the top of the social scale, as so often seems to be the case, have more in common with the working classes than with the middle ranks."[1]
Kate Fox, 'Watching the English', 2004

Some have seen the shape of the social order as loop rather than a pyramid, where the two ends are close whilst never meeting. This work highlights the level of working-class support for the monarchy in the 1830s.
The historian Linda Colley has noted that the print shows "the crowd and the crown" hand in hand – with the two ends of the social spectrum in imagined sympathy.[2] There are, of course, some contradictions here: the crowd fly placards supporting Tom Paine, a republican; union membership; and a 'cap of liberty' marking them as democrats.

Oddly, the monarchy is viewed as being 'above' politics and the commercial classes are the people's oppressors. As Colley has also noted, "behaving ostentatiously as loyal Britons was a way of challenging the official description of such [radical] activities as seditious. It showed that what they were doing was legitimate and positively public-spirited. It was they who were the authentic patriots... They knew that arming themselves with patriotic language and symbols could be a thoroughly pragmatic strategy." [3]

1. Fox, 2004, p315
2. Linda Colley, 'Britons', 2003 (London: Pimlico) p320
3. Colley, ibid, pp316-18

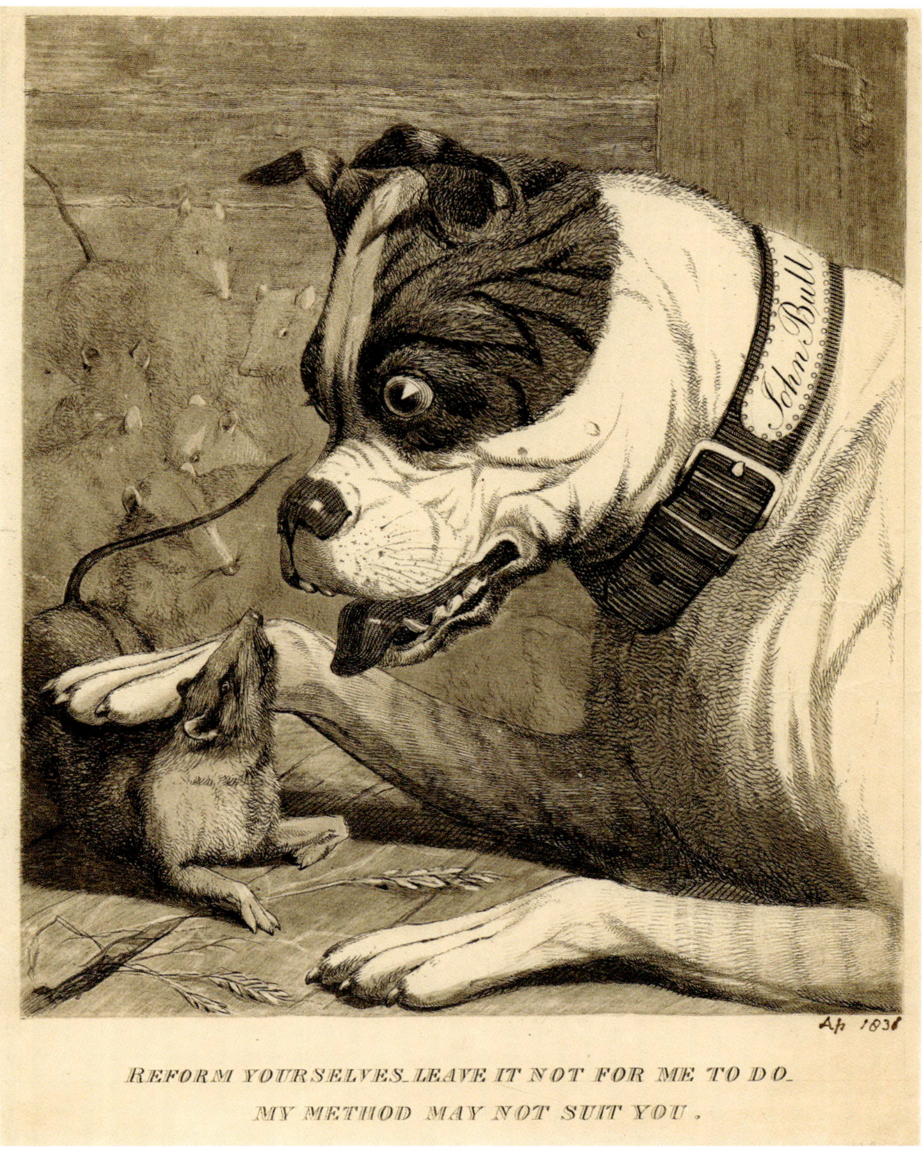

British Museum

"England is [one of] the type of deferential countries, in which the numerous unwiser part wishes to be ruled by the less numerous wiser part. The numerical majority... is ready, is eager to delegate its power of choosing its ruler to a certain select minority. It abdicates in favour of its elite, and consents to obey whoever that elite may confide in... The office of an order of nobility is to impose on the common people..."[1] Walter Bagehot, 'The English Constitution', 1867

The Great Reform Act of 1832 gave the vote to nearly 1 in 5 adult men and created new constituencies in the industrial towns. In the words of historian Miles Taylor, "In 1832, Britain shone as a beacon of democracy to the rest of the world."[2] This print supported the campaign to overhaul parliament, but is homely rather than angry: 'John Bull' is a loyal dog at the family hearth. (The figure of 'John Bull', used to represent 'the English people', was firstly developed as a dog in 1712, and was only later human.) The image expresses a polite request for managed change rather than revolution or radical action. As the historian Linda Colley has noted, "this generation of [British] radicals berated parliament for its members exclusiveness and parasitism, while continuing assiduously to petition it... They retained, most of them, a gut belief in the fundamental worth of the institution even as they called for its thoroughgoing reform."[3]

1.Quoted in Tod and Wheeler, 1978, p237
2. Miles Taylor, 'Bagehot: 'The English Constitution', 2001 (Oxford: OUP)
3. Colley, 2003, pp320-1

UNKNOWN ARTIST

'Chartists' march' 1839

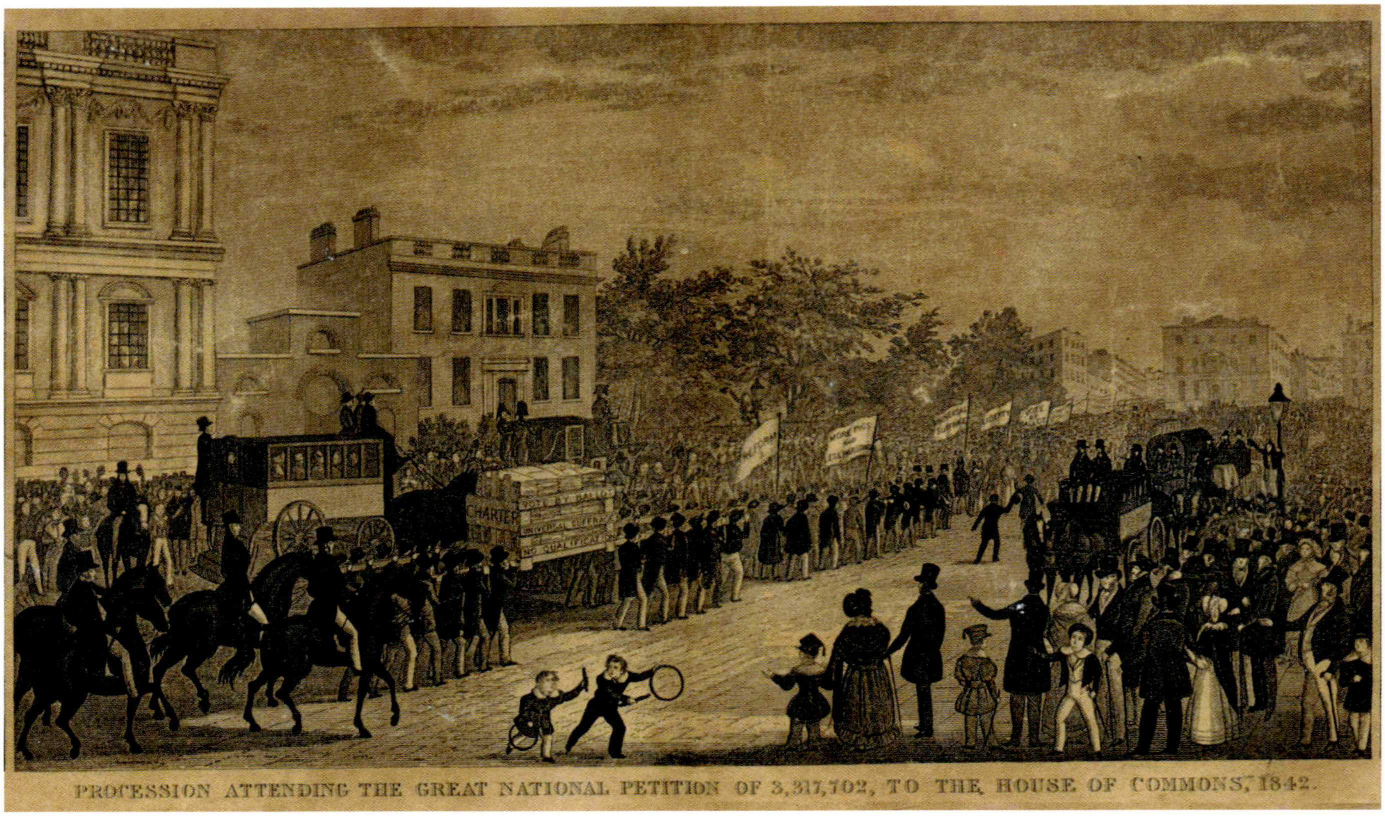

PROCESSION ATTENDING THE GREAT NATIONAL PETITION OF 3,317,702, TO THE HOUSE OF COMMONS, 1842.

Working Class Movement Library

"A spirit of combination had grown up among the working classes of which there has been no example in former times... They aspire to be at the top instead of at the bottom of society – or rather that there should be no bottom of top at all."[1]
James Bronterre O'Brien, 1831

"The emergence of class is one of the great themes, perhaps the great theme, of modern English social history."[2]
Professor Keith Wrightson, 1991

Chartism was a political movement set up by working men in the 1830s. As O'Brien argued, the idea of society as being clearly divided into 'classes' rather than estates or orders had gained widespread currency.
One Chartist leaflet of 1839 argued that "The wealth producer is made the slave to the possessors of wealth that he has laboured to create; power is transferred from labour to capital." The Chartists campaigned to reform the British electoral system, believing all men over the age of 21 should have the right to vote in constituencies with equal number of voters. They presented petitions to Parliament between 1839 and 1848 which were all rejected. This image pictures their 1839 march to Parliament to present a petition signed by 1.2m people (and three miles long) – from a population of 25m.

1. Quoted in Asa Briggs: 'A Social History of England', 1983 (London: Penguin), p202
2. Wrightson 'Estates, Degrees and Sorts: Changing Perceptions of Society in Stuart and Tudor England,' in Corfield (ed.), 'Language, History and Class', 1991 (Oxford: Blackwell) P31

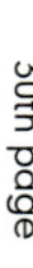

GEORGE BERNARD O'NEILL

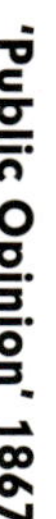

'Public Opinion' 1867

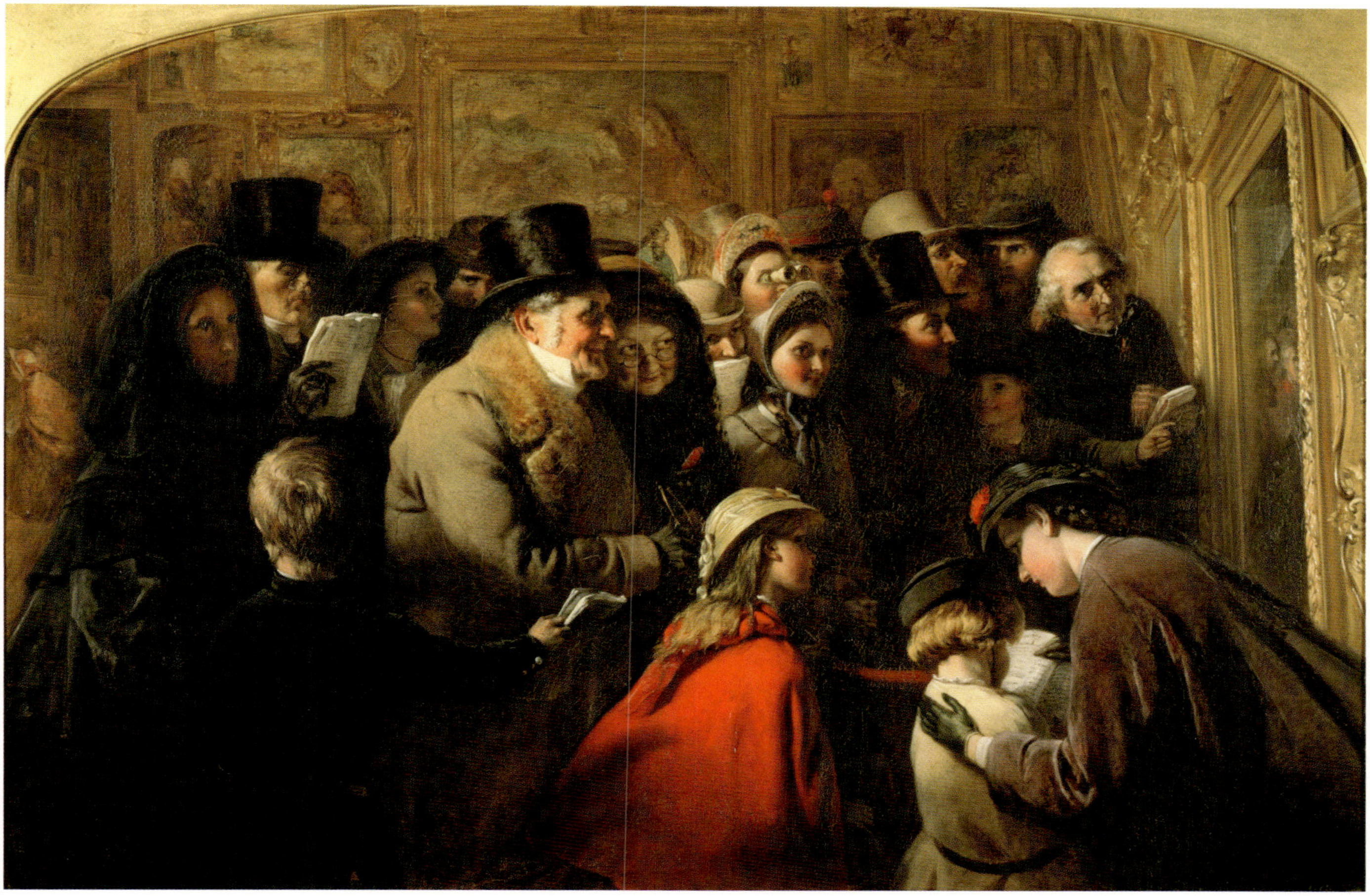

Courtesy Leeds Museums and Galleries

"Culture… comforting and lulling, serves to keep alive the bald economic determination of existence."[1]
Walter Benjamin, 'The Arcades Project', 1927-1940

Are public galleries ways of bringing people together, or are they socially divisive? O'Neill's painting tackles the problem of representing 'the public' in what were brand new types of public space, at least for most British cities. In theory the creation of new civic institutions in the 1860s extended cultural opportunities to all. In practice one aim was to 'civilise' lower social groups by exposing them to their social superiors and their pursuits. Sir Robert Peel for example argued that the National Gallery would "cement the bonds of union between the richer and the poorer orders of the state."[2]

In practice, O'Neill's 'public' are certainly not drawn from the whole social spectrum: this is not a panorama in reality. The most recent major study of Britain's gallery-going found that: "in the visual arts… patterns of consumption are stratified primarily according to status and education [rather than simply class]… Visitors to art museums and galleries are differentiated not only by their higher status and education but further by their socio-political orientations, in being, for example, generally more liberal and tolerant than others."[3]

1. Benjamin (trans 1999: Belknap / Harvard: London) p43
2. Quoted in Ferdinand Mount, 'Mind the Gap', 2005, (London: Short Books) pp225-6
3. http://users.ox.ac.uk/~sfos000/papers/poetics2007.pdf

VICTORIA KOCHOWSKI

'Queen Mao' 2008

"What is the Crown, but something set above / The jangle and the jargon and the hate / Of strivers after power in the State / A symbol, like a banner, for men's love?" **'A prayer' for Princess Elizabeth in 1947, by John Masefield, Poet Laureate**

The first lines of John Masefield's poem rehearse a traditional justification for the head of state to be a sovereign monarch: that they are 'above' competing interests, and are a symbol of unity and continuity. One dictionary definition of a 'sovereign' is "one who exercises supreme, permanent authority, especially in a nation or other government".

No-one in recent history deserves this epithet more than Mao Tse-Tung, 'Chairman' of the People's Republic of China from 1954. Kochowski's image here can be easily misread. It is not an attempt to equate two different types of political rule, but a means to picture the past and the future.
Her merging of the British and Chinese currencies into one image represents the countries with global economic hegemony from both 19th and 21st centuries.
The artist's work is based on the idea that power is based on both the global reach of a nation's currency and of its culture. This includes the dissemination of its totemic images so that they become universally familiar. Kochowski's question is: will English be supplanted by Chinese as the world's language for business and cultural production, in a generation's time?

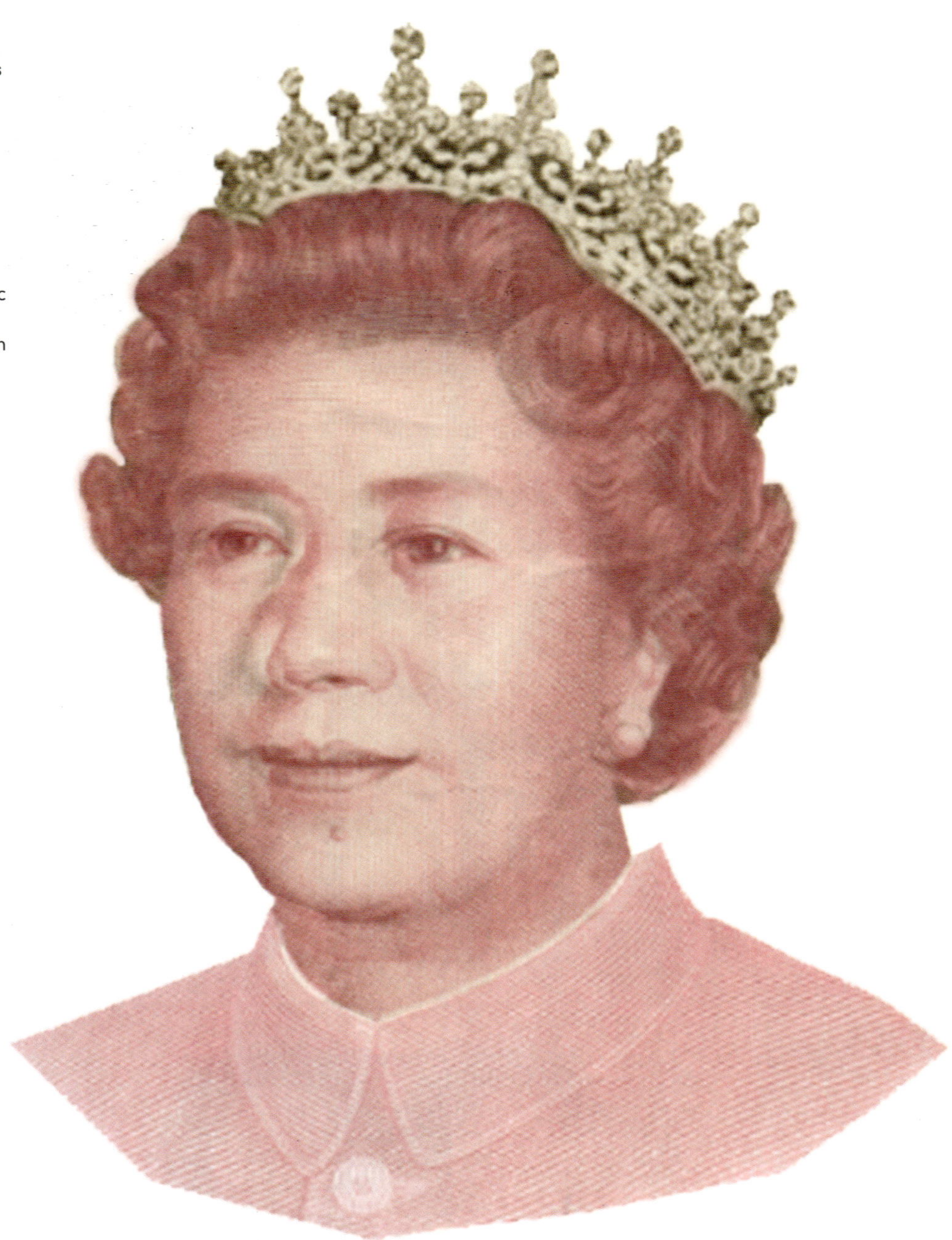

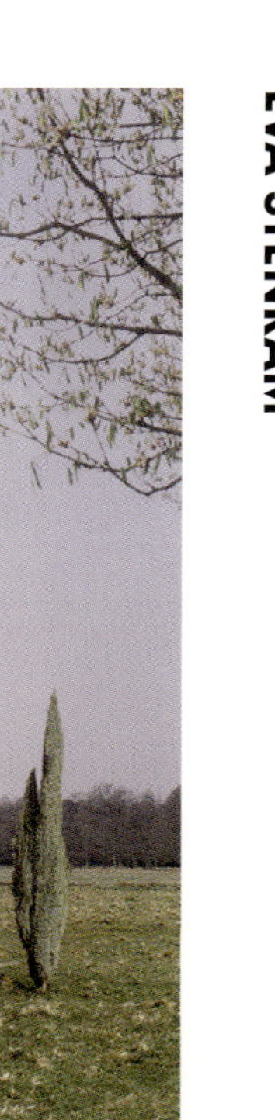

Courtesy the artist

EVA STENRAM

'The Royal Estate' 2003

"Property Ladder: a cunningly devised social system which divides people into two classes: the smug and the damned"[1]
AA Gill, Sunday Times, 2006

How do we correlate different types of buildings with different social ranks? The British class system is often seen as being embodied in peoples' houses and their materials: stone for the rich; brick for the middle; concrete flats for the poor. The architecture critic and supporter of Prince Charles, Nikos Salingaros, has argued that "architecture is... the hierarchical ordering of artificial structures".[2] Eva Stenram starts with the proposition that buildings reflect social hierarchies to stage a thought experiment.

What would it look like if we 'cross-bred' the 'top' and 'bottom' of the hierarchy of buildings, by merging the homes of the poorest and richest people? 'The Royal Estate' maps the facades from each British Royal palace – Windsor House, Holyrood House, Kensington House, Sandringham House, Balmoral House, Buckingham Palace and St James's House – onto a council estate of seven tower blocks. Nevertheless, she notes that Buckingham Palace is the size of a 'middle-rise' council estate: it is six storeys tall and has 775 rooms.

1. Sunday Times Culture July 16 2006, p34
2. http://zeta.math.utsa.edu/~yxk833/Charles.html

DANIELA ROSSELL

Four untitled works from the series 'Rich and Famous' 1999–2002

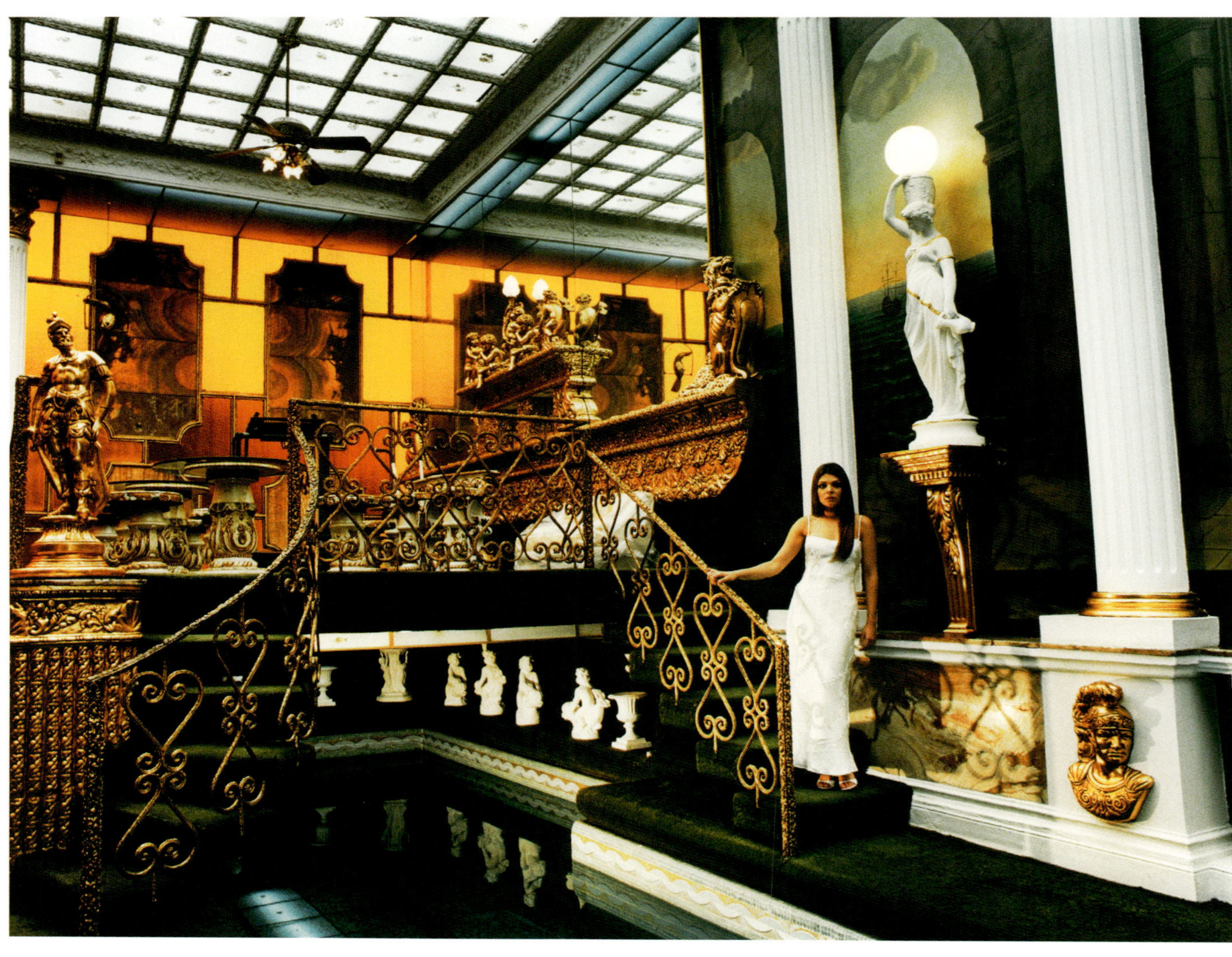

Tate, Presented by the Latin American Acquisitions Committee 200
Photograph © Tate, London, 2008; courtesy Greene Naftali Gallery, New York. 3

"The fury after licentious and luxurious pleasures is grown to so great a height that it may be called the characteristic of the present age."[1]
Henry Fielding (1707-1754)

How do the relationships between power, wealth and taste differ between parts of the world? Daniela Rossell's series 'Rich and Famous' reveals Mexico's social elite in their homes. Who would live in a house like this, we might ask? Whilst the images appear satirical, the sitters all chose their own settings, costumes and poses: this is how they wish to be seen. On one level, the works are self-portraits which the artist's role has been simply to release the camera's shutter. Rossell's works function through the assumption that our tastes and social position are not those of her sitters, but she asks wider questions about how taste has evolved in different nations. For historian Simon Schama, modern Western tastes derive from a bourgeois Protestant ethos – the "embarrassment of riches". High status is connoted by deferred gratification rather than overt displays of wealth. Accordingly, Protestant nations associate high rank with astringency or abstinence from indulgence; Catholic ones less so. However, many of the sitters here are actually related to members of the sadly misnamed Institutional Revolutionary Party (PRI), which effectively ruled Mexico from 1929-2000.

1. Quoted in M. Dorothy George, 'Social Change in Graphic Satire', 1967, (NYC: Walker) p21

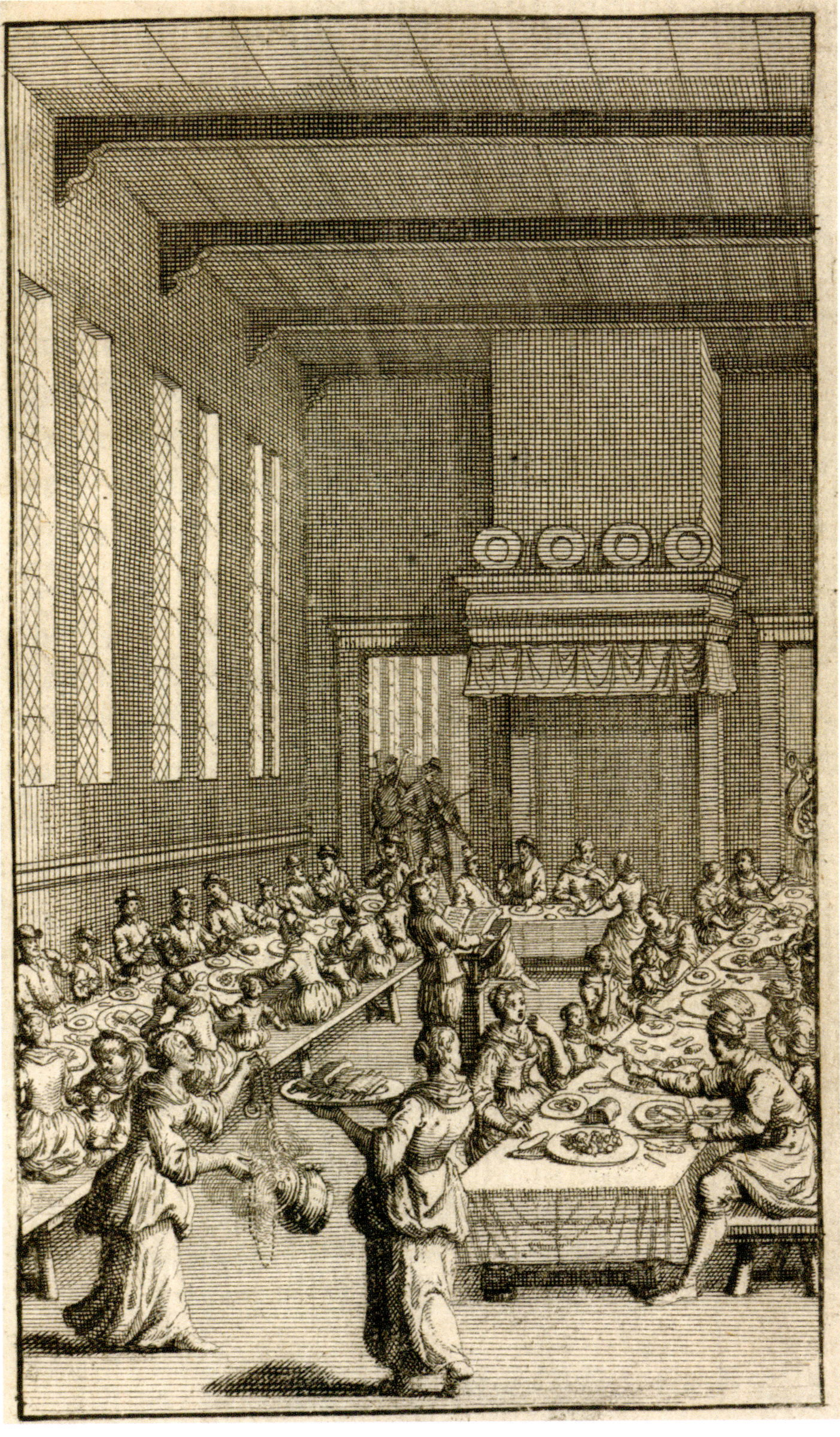

British Library

THOMAS MORE

'Communal living' from 'Utopia' 1715

"Besides agriculture, which is so common to them all, every man has some peculiar trade to which he applies himself, such as the manufacture of wool, or flax, masonry, smith's work, or carpenter's work; for there is no sort of trade that is in great esteem among them. Throughout the island they wear the same sort of clothes without any other distinction, except what is necessary to distinguish the two sexes, and the married and unmarried. At the hours of dinner and supper, the whole Syphogranty [team of magistrates] being called together by sound of trumpet, meet and eat together"[1] From 'Utopia'

This image was created to visualise More's imagined social order in 'Utopia'. It is a vision in which every aspect of life is both produced and consumed collectively. Moreover, no particular trade "is in great esteem" above any other: all work is viewed as of equal importance in making sure society runs smoothly. In this miniature paradise, everyone only works six hours a day so that they can learn from one another and contribute the collective life of society in other ways.

1. http://www.bl.uk/learning/histcitizen/21cc/utopia/more1/communal1/communal.html

MARKUS VATER

'Tradition, Family, Property' 2008

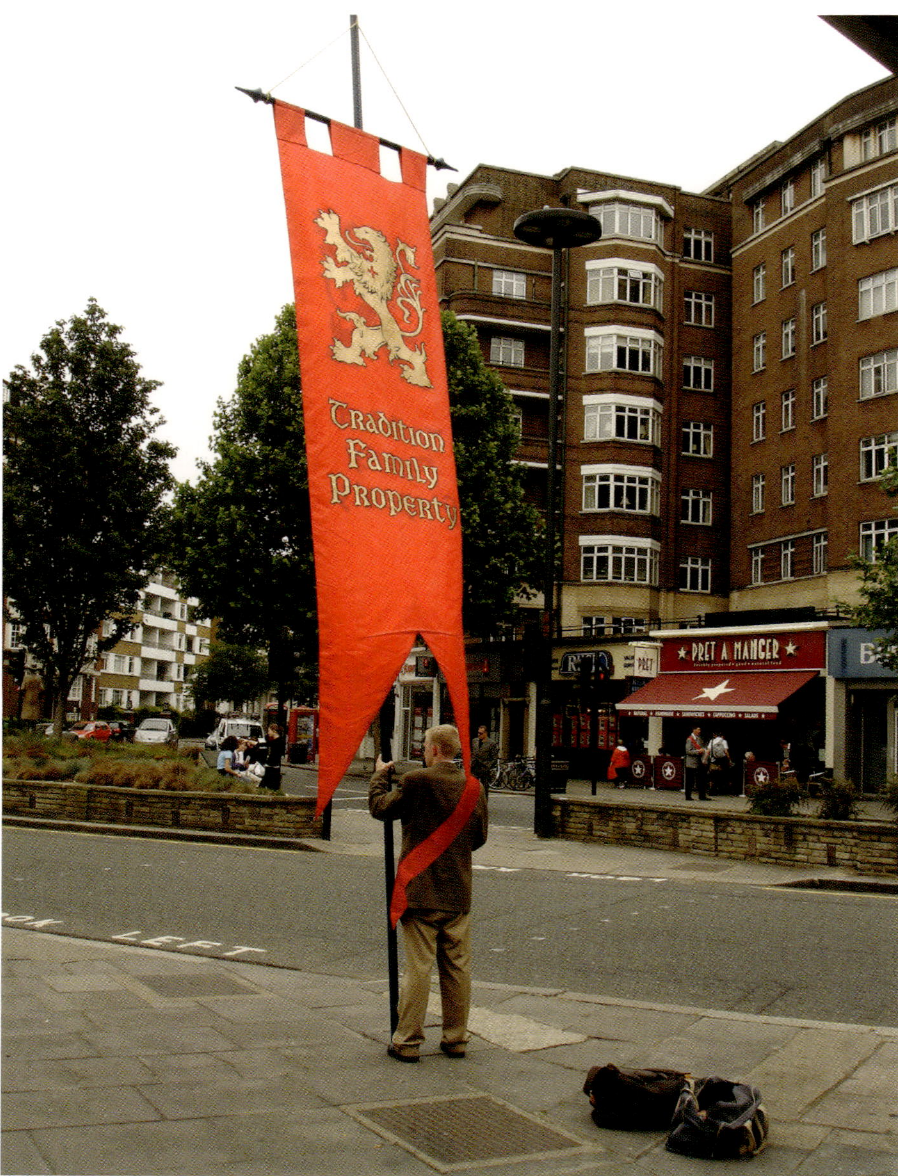

Courtesy the artist and Vilma Gold, London

"Consciousness begins with disobedience"
William Blake

Markus Vater's image is a documentary record of an unexpected sight on the streets of South Kensington, which pictures a protest group campaigning to reform the social order. London SW7 is one of the most expensive postcodes in the world to live in, and its residents are unfamiliar with the sight of pressure groups armed with banners taking to the streets. Most pressure groups are from the left, broadly speaking; this one is a delightful exception, advocating the virtues of private property to some of the richest people in the world. Vater's work usually visualises philosophical propositions rather than ones about society, but it is always based on unpicking the myths we hold dear about our place in the world.

PICTURING GEOGRAPHIES:

'INEQUALITY IS A SPATIAL MATTER'

PICTURING MYTHOLOGIES:

'NO THEM, ONLY US'

"Inequality is a spatial matter."[1]
Professor Daniel Dorling, University of Sheffield

What are the ways in which we organise our 'imagined communities' in space, and what are the stories that we tell ourselves to explain or justify the differences between us? This section contrasts two types of image. The first type of image here are maps that allow us to see the world in new ways. Some allow us to imagine places in which social relations are totally different to our own, like Thomas More's Utopia. This is the earliest work here, from 1516. Others allow us to visualise what our own position is within our society, or see what place in the world each country has – what economic power it commands over others, or how many resources it possesses. Social hierarchies are played out in space, both locally and globally: the images here make clear what those hierarchies are, and show how where we live or were born affect our life-chances. Making maps is one of the most fundamental ways we can understand how our 'imagined community' is ordered.

In England in particular, what Doreen Massey has called our "geographical imaginary" is unavoidably connected to class and status. Place and social ranking are indubitably connected; geography and stratification are unavoidably linked in how we classify others. Most people still intuitively correlate dialect and class; a 'regional' accent is one associated with any region other than the south-east. More tangibly, the economic niche we occupy is circumscribed by where we live, and is certainly affected by our place of birth. In turn, the price of our houses reflects the economic niche we have managed to occupy.

Where do we imagine the category of 'them' ends and that of 'us' begins? If maps provide scientific ways of viewing the world, the second type of image appeals to our imagination. Broadly speaking, all of the artists here make an image of a worldview in which our differences are explained. The problems they tackle are: What are the stories and myths that describe the differences between us, and tell us what each group in our community is and does? Secondly, how can we show these myths? Allegories and emblems have long provided artists with the means to symbolise beliefs, and many of the images here use these traditional means of expression. The section contains the second earliest work in the exhibition: the 'great chain of being' made in 1579. It pictures a world in which every living thing has its place: the ranking of things is immutable and agreed on by all. It is the ultimate expression of Benedict Anderson's phrase in the book 'Imagined Communities', that "in the minds of each [member] lives the image of their communion".[2] Each of us has a mental image of our relation to others: it often takes an artist to make it real or bring it into focus.

1. In interview
2. http://en.wikipedia.org/wiki/Imagined_Communities

THE CHALLENGE: UNDERSTANDING GLOBAL INEQUALITIES

"Throughout the world, people who are vulnerable and socially disadvantaged have less access to health resources, get sicker, and die earlier than people in more privileged social positions. Health equity gaps are growing today, despite unprecedented global wealth and technological progress."

You can say it, you can prove it, you can tabulate it, but it is only when you show it that it hits home. There is a long history of using illustrations to help spread new medical scientific ideas. Anatomical imagery, for example, is at least 500 years old. That imagery allowed us to look inside human beings and, among much else, showed us just how much of the brain was dedicated to visual understanding.

We now know that health relies as much on the anatomy of society as on the anatomy of our bodies. And we are just beginning to learn that an unequal human world is also more likely to be a sick world. How, though, can we better understand the distribution of resources around the world, and of where most people are sick and die early as compared to people in more privileged positions? How can we fathom the extent to which equity gaps are growing despite unprecedented global wealth and technological progress? Drawing images is one way to engage more of our imagination to help understand the extent and arrangement of world inequalities in health.

The science of the make-up of world human anatomy – cartography – has a similar history to that of anatomical drawing. Gerardus Mercator's wall maps of 1569 were produced just 14 years after the second edition of Andreas Vesalius's humani corporis fabrica. And just as Vesalius's images helped guide the scalpel through flesh, Mercator's maps helped guide ships across the oceans. But these products of the enlightenment were not just simple guides. The images they produced helped change the way we thought about the world. In the long run they helped us learn to be less superstitious, but also presented a very mechanical, inhuman image of both person and planet. Mercator's projection is the one you still see when the weather is described on television. The Mercator projection is a useful projection to carry with you if you wish to sail around the planet. It is not, however, that useful for showing, for example, how diseases are spread amongst the population. To show such spread, a world population cartogram is a far better base map.

The Mercator projection is the worst of all the well known global map projections to use to depict disease distributions because it stretches the earth's surface to the most extreme of extents and hence introduces the greatest visual bias. On a Mercator projection, area is drawn in ever expanding proportion to how near territory is to the poles. Thus, on such a projection, India appears much smaller than Greenland, whereas India is in land area alone over seven times larger than Greenland.

The human eye–brain system is far better equipped to judge the relative values of objects by the size of the area that each object occupies rather than to translate shades of colour into rates and then imagine what they imply. The new world population cartogram published in Nature in 2006 produced by Mark Newman shows the world with land area drawn in proportion to the population. Unlike previous cartograms, this one is produced by software which approximates the image to the best unique world cartogram (that which distorts the least on the surface of the sphere whilst still scaling areas correctly). One criticism of older algorithms has been that they produce an "area correct" but somewhat arbitrary solution with an end result that often reflects the initial projection used. For any given distribution there are an infinite number of cartograms that can be drawn with area in proportion to that distribution, but only one which also minimises distortion.

Looking further into the human anatomy of this small planet, in addition to adding more subjects to map, we could begin to think of how to move beyond the nation-state as our means of categorising people. There is much more that could be done. However, what I think matters most are the new ways of thinking that we foster as we redraw the images of the human anatomy of our planet in these ways. What do we need to be able to see — so that we can act?

As a species we are just beginning to learn that unprecedented global wealth and remarkable technological progress does not result in the reduction of inequalities in health, nor in a decline in human suffering, nor in an enlightened and glorious new age. An anatomically correct technical image of the planet or the human body is not enough for us to learn how to better live with each other, nor to see other individuals or distant large groups of people as human. But new ways of depicting the world and people can change how both it and we are seen; possibly for the better. Traditional illustrative anatomy, just like scientific cartography, can de-humanise. The human body was first clearly laid bare in ink for the beginnings of modern surgery in 1543, and the coastlines of the continents were first consistently exposed on paper for crude mercantile trade in 1569. For almost all of the last five centuries these "scientific" human and world views have shaped our thinking in one particular direction. They have suggested purely technical fixes, implied we were enlightened, and reinforced a world view that progress simply requires more detailed understanding rather than re-thinking, new imagination, and greatly expanded empathy. The maps in Worldmapper, a collaboration between researchers at the Social and Spatial Inequalities Research Group at the University of Sheffield and Mark Newman, from the Center for the Study of Complex Systems at the University of Michigan are part of a much wider attempt to see and think differently.

Daniel Dorling is Professor of Human Geography in the University of Sheffield. His recent publications include 'The Atlas of the Real World: Mapping the Way We Live' (Thames and Hudson) and 'Human Geography of the UK (Sage Publications).

THOMAS MORE / AMBROSIUS HOLBEIN

'A map of the island of Utopia' 1516

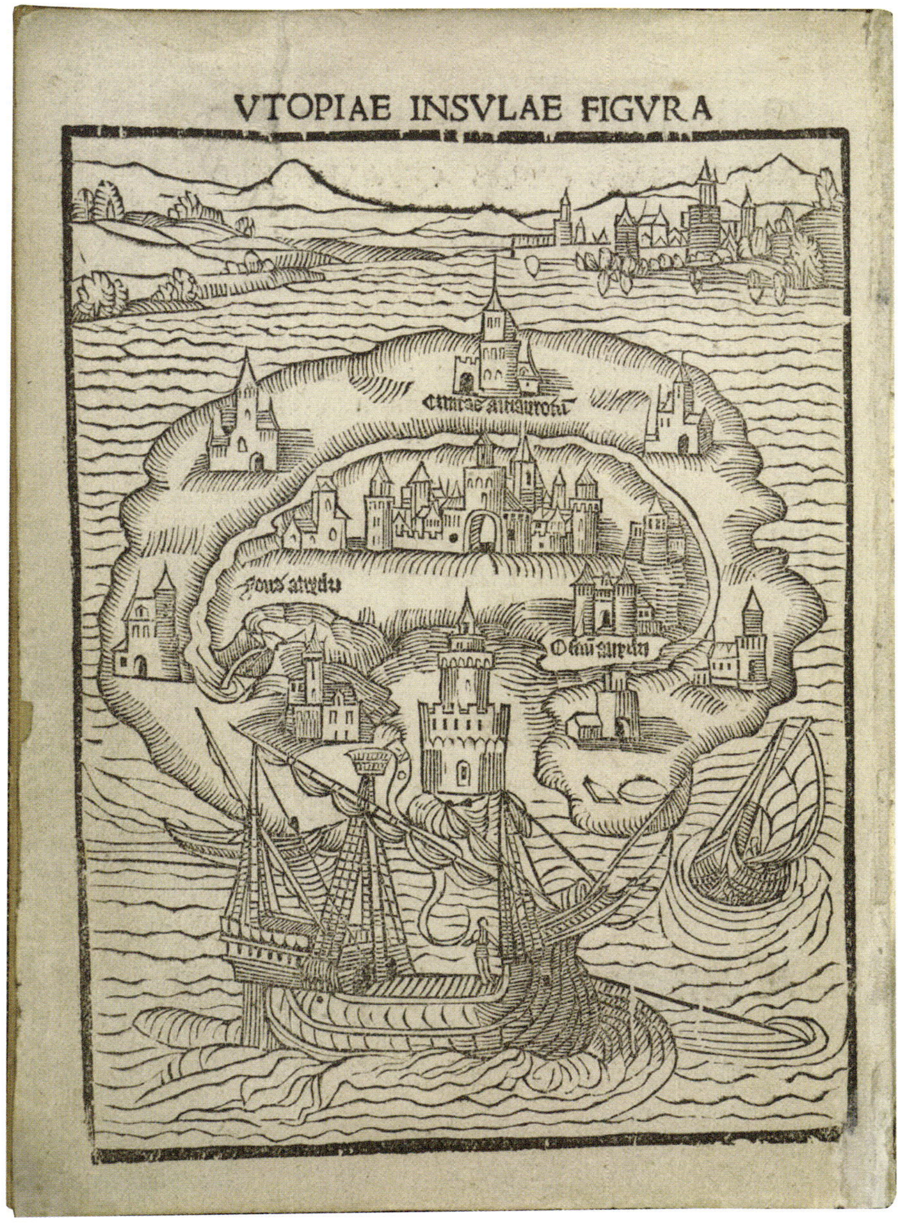

British Library

"Those who think themselves the masters of others are indeed greater slaves"[1]
Jean-Jacques Rousseau 'The Social Contract', 1762

What would a map of a place where everyone was equal look like? Is it even possible to visualise a place without any social hierarchies? 'Utopia' is a micro-society in which all the rules of the Tudor world were upended. 'Utopia' is an island – a world small enough to imagine in its entirety: "the island of Utopia is in the middle just 200 miles broad". On the island, all goods are collectively produced and shared. All meals are eaten communally and sociability and equality of manners as well as economic means is encouraged. More contrasts the Anemolians, a people on a nearby island, with the Utopians. For the latter "gold and silk" were "the playthings of children" and to be despised; wealth was shared equally and status symbols despised. More's vision is of an almost communist society in which there are no hierarchies, and work is undertaken collectively. It is possible to think that More believed that rulers enjoyed imagining they were powerful personally, whilst he knew they simply occupied *positions* of power.

1. ebooks.adelaide.edu.au/r/rousseau/jean_jacques/r864s/book1.html

UNIVERSITY OF SHEFFIELD

Map asset-poor households in Britain, 2001

"We do dwell in different zones, more than ever... most of us are perfectly pleased that the lower classes should be reasonably prosperous and healthy, so long as we don't have to see them or hear them... In practice, the lowest class is 'cabined, cribbed, confined' to its physical and social ghetto."[1]
Ferdinand Mount, 'Mind the Gap', 2004

How far does where you live affect how much you earn? The average weekly wage for UK employees was £447 in 2006, but in London it was 30% higher, and in the north-east which has the lowest average wages, 10% lower.[2] The Social and Spatial Inequalities Research Group (SASI) at Sheffield University have devised a method for picturing how the wealth of the country is distributed geographically, and how relative poverty is concentrated in particular areas. Their images are part map, part graph. In the 'cartogram' (part diagram, part cartography) each hexagon represents 100,000 people – roughly the number in a parliamentary constituency. The shape of the nation is distorted to reflect human geography, to show where people are clustered. London and Glasgow are the primary areas where deprivation is concentrated. The map reveals an extremely clear north-south divide: outside of greater London, almost nowhere in the south of England has high densities of asset-poor households. What such a map cannot picture are factors beyond geography like gender: men's average earnings remain a quarter higher than women's.

1. Mount, 2004 (London: Short Books) pp283, 314-5
2. www.statistics.gov.uk/pdfdir/ashe1006.pdf

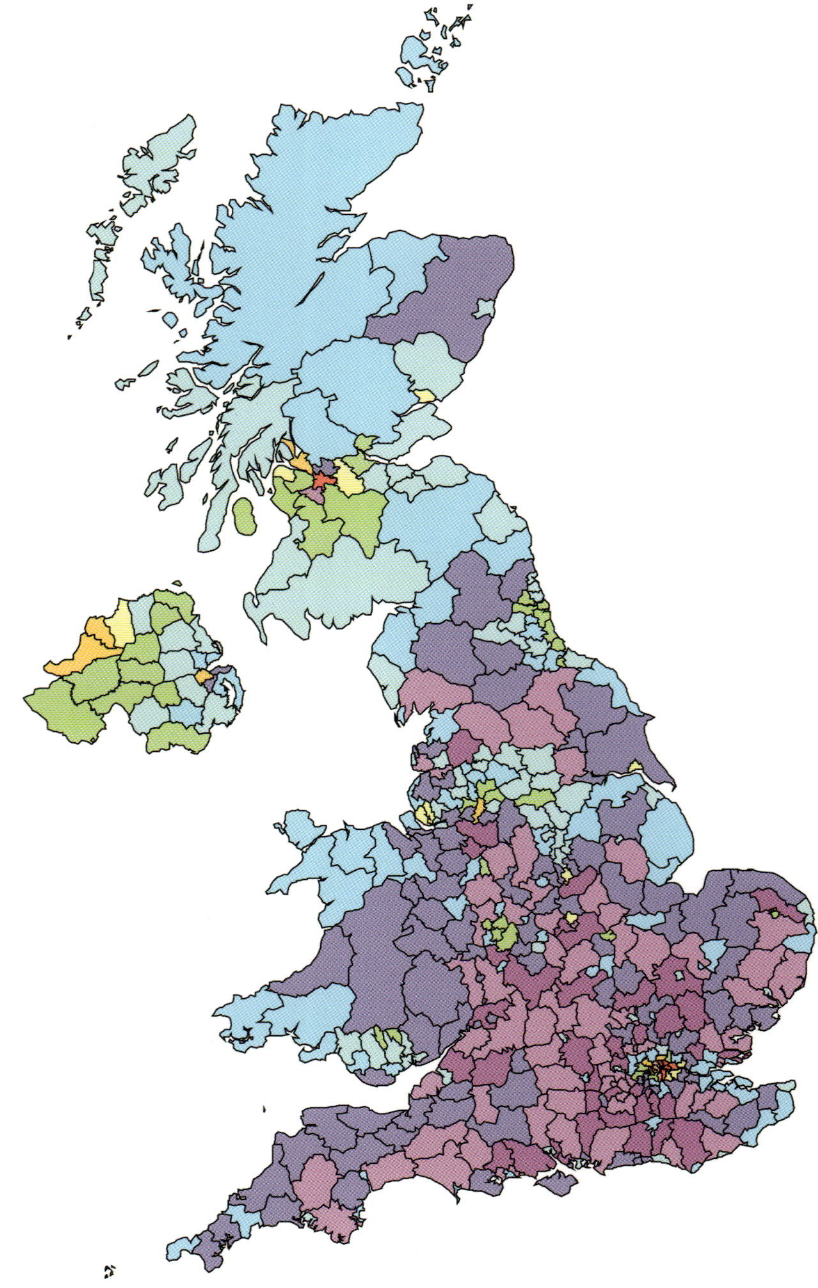

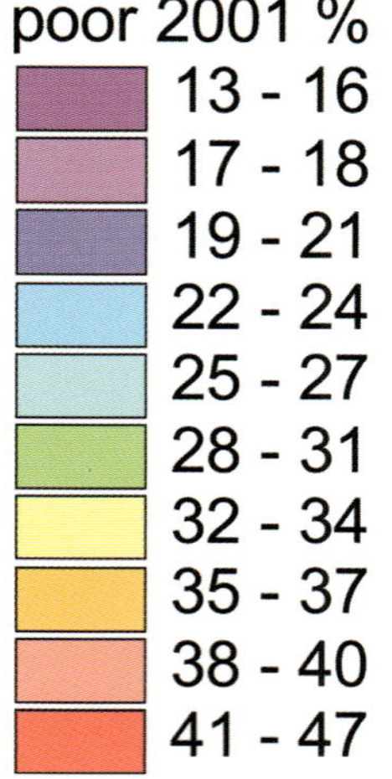

Map of levels of asset-wealthy household in Britain, 2003

"The fact that house prices are rising so fast in London and the south east than they are in general or in the north means that homeowners in the south are making money hand over fist. That contributes to national levels of inequality."[1]
Professor Doreen Massey, 'Is the World Really Shrinking?' 2006

The SASI team's map of "asset wealthy" households shows very clearly that, seen at a national level, there is a 180' arc west of London – through the 'home counties' – where wealth is most densely concentrated. According to the World Bank, the UK's total net wealth is roughly £6 trillion: housing accounts for £3.5 trillion of this wealth, and this map allows us to see, to some extent, where that wealth lies spatially. In former industrial areas like the north-east, parts of Yorkshire, and south Wales, only a small minority of households have accumulated substantial savings as capital and liquid assets over their and their predecessors' lifetimes. There are other less obvious conclusions to be drawn. Coincidentally, there are approximately 60 millions Britons on a land mass of roughly 60 million acres. But we live in some 24 million households, which are built on just 1/20 of the land. Britain is, then, a very urbanised country: but the preconditions of this concentrated human geography have included the ownership of land by very few hands over a very long term. One estimate is that 70% of the land is owned by 1% of the population.[2] According to some contentious estimates, just 6,000 landowners own about 40 million acres – some two thirds of the whole country.[3] The Crown Estate alone is believed to own the equivalent of a whole county.[4]

1. http://www.open2.net/freethinking/oulecture_2006.html
2. www.poverty.org.uk/L02/a.gif
3. Ibid
4. Quoted by Tim de Lisle in 'Intelligent Life', Autumn 2008 (London: The Economist), p11

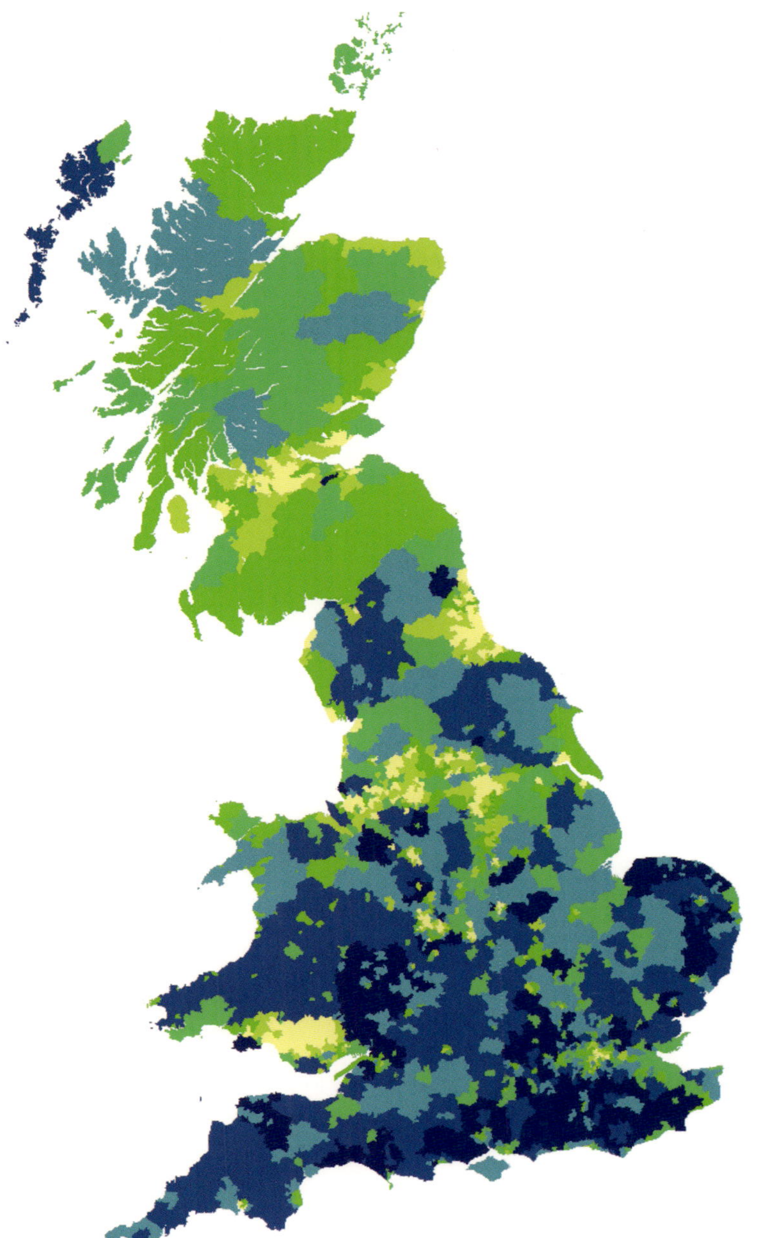

% Wealthy 2003

- 0 - 10
- 11 - 20
- 21 - 30
- 31 - 40
- 41 - 50
- 51 - 60
- >60

UNIVERSITY OF SHEFFIELD

The 'Football League' of British cities: an index of quality of life

"The UK is disproportionately important [in human geography] in being the setting for one of the longest running social experiments in the world... People in the UK, over a long period of time, have had to behave and be controlled in a very consistent way to keep the suburbs nondescript, the inner cities mostly poor, the home counties most affluent and the peripheries peripheral."[1]
Professor Daniel Dorling, 'Human Geography of the UK', 2000

How can we compare the standard of living which each town and city in Britain offers? The University of Sheffield's geography department uses five equally weighted measures of well being. They are: life expectancy, education measured according to percentage of the population with university degrees; the proportion of the population out of work and claiming Job Seekers Allowance or Income Support; the levels of relative poverty – the number of people earning under 60% of the national average salary; and average house prices.[2] The table reveals a startling north-south divide. In the north, only York scores highly. Liverpool is in a 'league' all of its own. All 10 places where you are most likely to be relatively poor and poorly educated, and stand a higher chance of being unemployed or in low-income work, and even suffer an early death, are in smaller northern towns and cities.

1. Dorling, 2000, p179
2. Dorling, 'Inequality in Britain 1997-2006', pp353-361

		Average housing price '03	% adults with a degree 2001	% poverty 1999-2001	% working age claiming JSA/IS 2003	Average score 2003
Champions League	Cambridge	244862	41	29	5.1	82.3
	Aldershot	238991	22	17	3.7	81.9
	Reading	211794	26	20	4.7	81.5
	Oxford	255181	37	30	6.1	80.9
Rest of Premiership	Crawley	205506	19	22	4.8	79.8
	Bournemouth	214296	17	21	7.1	79.1
	York	147513	23	25	5.4	78.2
	Worthing	186992	16	20	6.4	78.0
	Brighton	212361	29	27	9.3	77.6
	Southend	186481	13	19	7.5	77.6
	London	283387	30	33	10.3	77.5
	Bristol	160708	23	25	7.7	77.1
	Southampton	172585	19	25	6.9	76.9
	Norwich	138187	18	27	7.5	76.3
	Portsmouth	157145	16	25	6.6	76.2
	Milton Keynes	161625	18	25	6.6	76.0
	Swindon	150689	15	22	6.6	76.0
	Gloucester	141690	16	22	8.5	75.5
	Warrington	119668	17	23	6.8	75.1
	Northampton	135871	17	24	7.8	75.1
	Ipswich	134514	16	25	10.1	74.7
	Chatham	142374	12	23	7.7	74.2
Championship	Preston	97038	17	26	7.2	73.6
	Derby	114280	18	27	10.5	73.1
	Leeds	119262	19	32	8.9	72.8
	Nottingham	123663	18	28	9.8	72.7
	Telford	115722	13	27	9	72.6
	Leicester	124812	17	28	11	72.6
	Blackpool	103656	13	24	8.9	72.5
	Plymouth	118978	13	28	9.8	72.4
	Hastings	163128	15	25	13.4	72.3
	Luton	143698	14	28	9.7	72.2
	Wakefield	110407	14	28	9	72.1
	Peterborough	123089	14	28	9.5	72.1
	Coventry	111165	16	28	10.9	72.0
	Huddersfield	97815	15	29	8.7	71.6
League 1	Manchester	119569	19	30	11.6	70.9
	Sheffield	96328	16	33	10.4	70.8
	Wigan	88946	12	27	8.6	70.7
	Birkenhead	95632	13	29	12.2	70.6
	Bolton	89281	15	29	10.4	70.4
	Mansfield	94749	9	28	9.4	70.4
League 2	Grimsby	77898	10	28	11.5	70.0
	Doncaster	82267	11	30	10.6	69.8
	Birmingham	122794	14	33	12.8	69.7
	Stoke	78834	11	29	10.3	69.7
	Newcastle	111220	16	34	12.8	69.2
	Barnsley	79492	10	32	10.8	68.9
	Rochdale	92523	14	31	12.2	68.8
	Burnley	55879	12	31	10.7	68.7
	Bradford	75919	13	33	11.5	68.6
	Middlesbrough	81760	12	32	13.1	68.4
Conference	Sunderland	91322	12	34	12.4	67.8
	Blackburn	70969	14	30	12.7	67.8
	Hull	72374	12	33	17.1	66.0
Conference North	Liverpool	87607	14	36	18	64.7

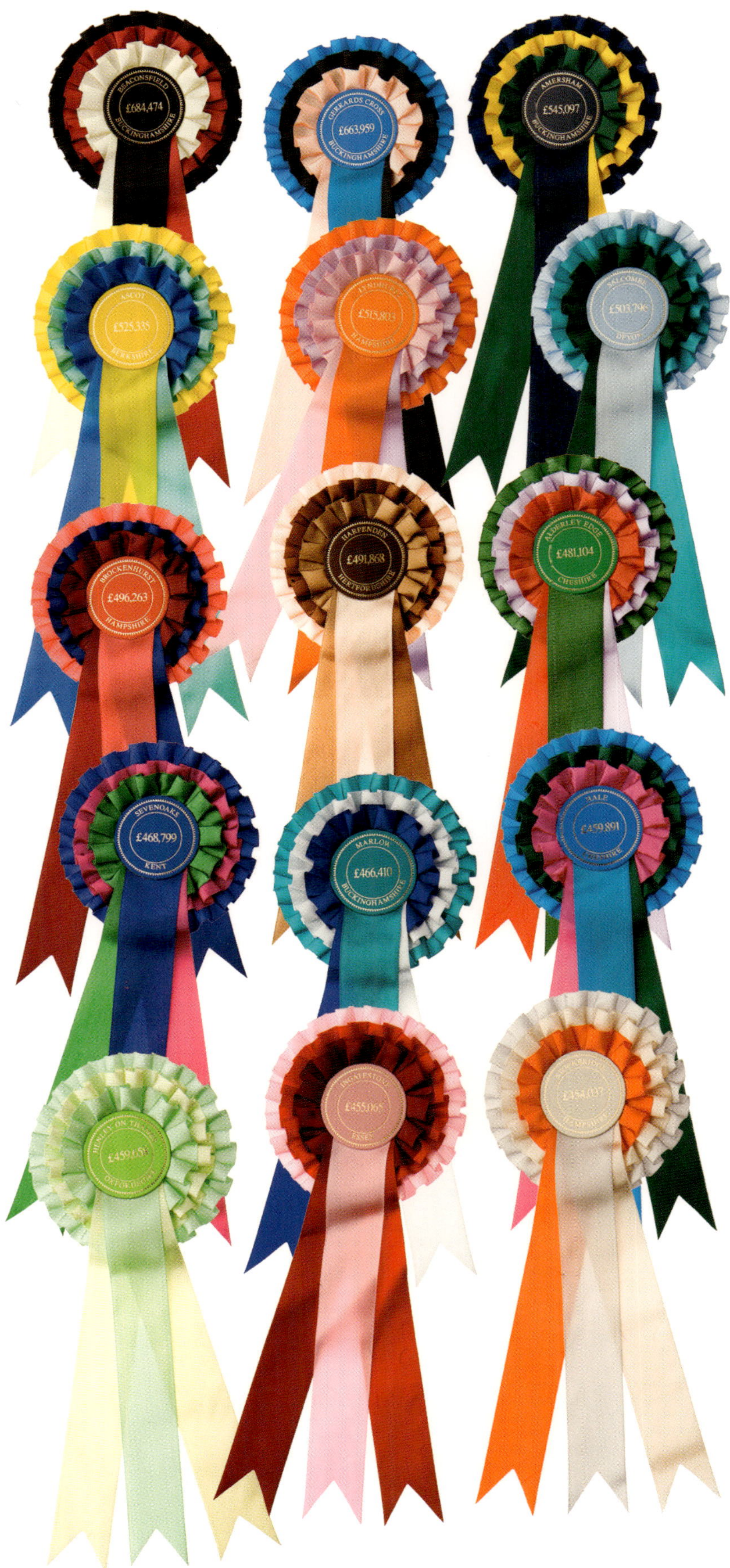

Where are the richest parts of the UK? And how far does wealth make people happy? The Daily Telegraph's survey of non-metropolitan areas are ranked on average house prices.[1] It is a cliché of the English property market that the older a property the better an investment it is: many still agree with the sentiment expressed by academic Peter Bromhead that "much of what is most pleasing in English society has been left to us by pre-industrial society." [2]

Accordingly many of the most expensive parts of the UK to live in are in rural or suburban areas in the south-east.

Almost none of these locations, however, are in the 'happiest' places in the country according to a new study by the British Household Panel Survey and Dr Dimitris Ballas of Sheffield University and Dr Mark Tranmer of Manchester University.[3]

The BHPS asked 10,000 people every year to estimate their own well-being based on the standard of living their location offered them. Eight of the ten 'happiest' places are in Scotland and the north of England, such as Manchester, Nottingham and West Lothian. There are no overlaps between the top 10 places on the two lists.

1. http://www.telegraph.co.uk/property/main.jhtml?xml=/property/2008/04/19/nosplit/prichtown10-01.xml
2. Peter Bromhead, 'Life in Modern Britain', 1971 (London: Longman), p11
3. http://news.bbc.co.uk/1/hi/health/7584321.stm

image by Ben Branagan & Gareth Holt

UNIVERSITY OF SHEFFIELD

"We are looking at social divides far more important than those reflected merely by income... Poverty and wealth and fundamentally about being excluded from society or included in it."[3]
Professor Daniel Dorling, 'Poverty, Wealth and Place, 1968 to 2005', 2007

"The poorest 20% of the population in the United Kingdom have an income comparable to that of the poorest 20% in the Czech Republic, a far less wealthy country... Where you live can limit or assist your life chances from the cradle to the grave... Britain is becoming increasingly segregated across all ages by class, education, occupation"[2]
Professor Daniel Dorling and Dr Bethan Thomas 'Identity in Britain: A Cradle to Grave Atlas', 2007

The historian Roy Porter has asked the question of a previous age, "how far was there a segregative geography of rank?"[3] Researchers at Sheffield University have asked the same question of our own time, believing "the clearest way in which social polarisation is expressed is through geographical manifestations."[4] Thomas and Dorling's research illuminates what the patterns are that determine our life chances. The UN defines a household as being in 'relative poverty' if it has an income lower than 60 per cent of the median average level. According to this definition, 21 per cent of children and pensioners, and 14 per cent of all adults lived in households below the poverty line in 2007.

1. Porter, 1982, p45
2. http://sasi.group.shef.ac.uk/publications/identity.html
3. http://www.jrf.org.uk/knowledge/findings/housing/2077.asp
4. Phil Rees and Daniel Dorling, 'A Nation Still Dividing, 1971-2001', 2003 pp1287-1313

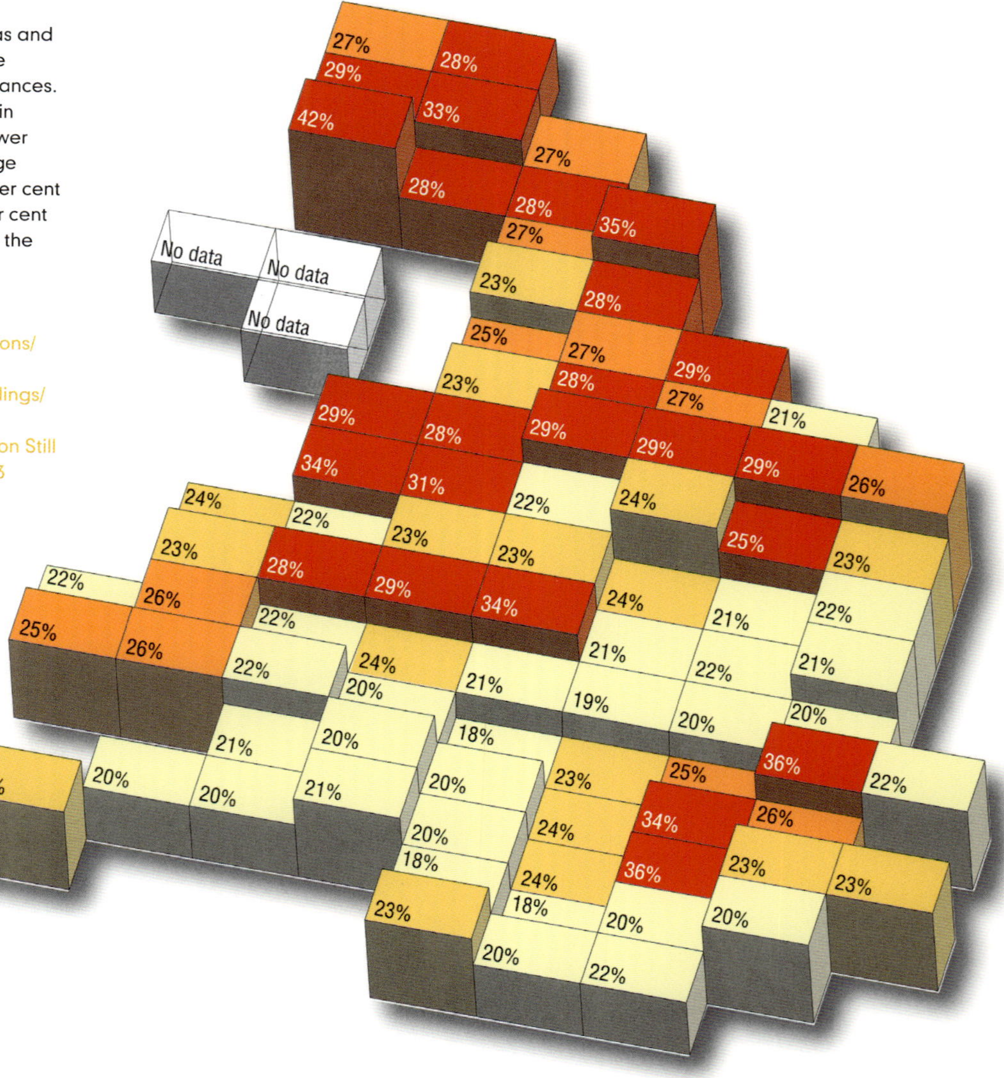

Cartogram of Britain's poverty levels in 2000 by United Nations definition

THE FINANCIAL TIMES

'If Britain's regions were countries...' 2008

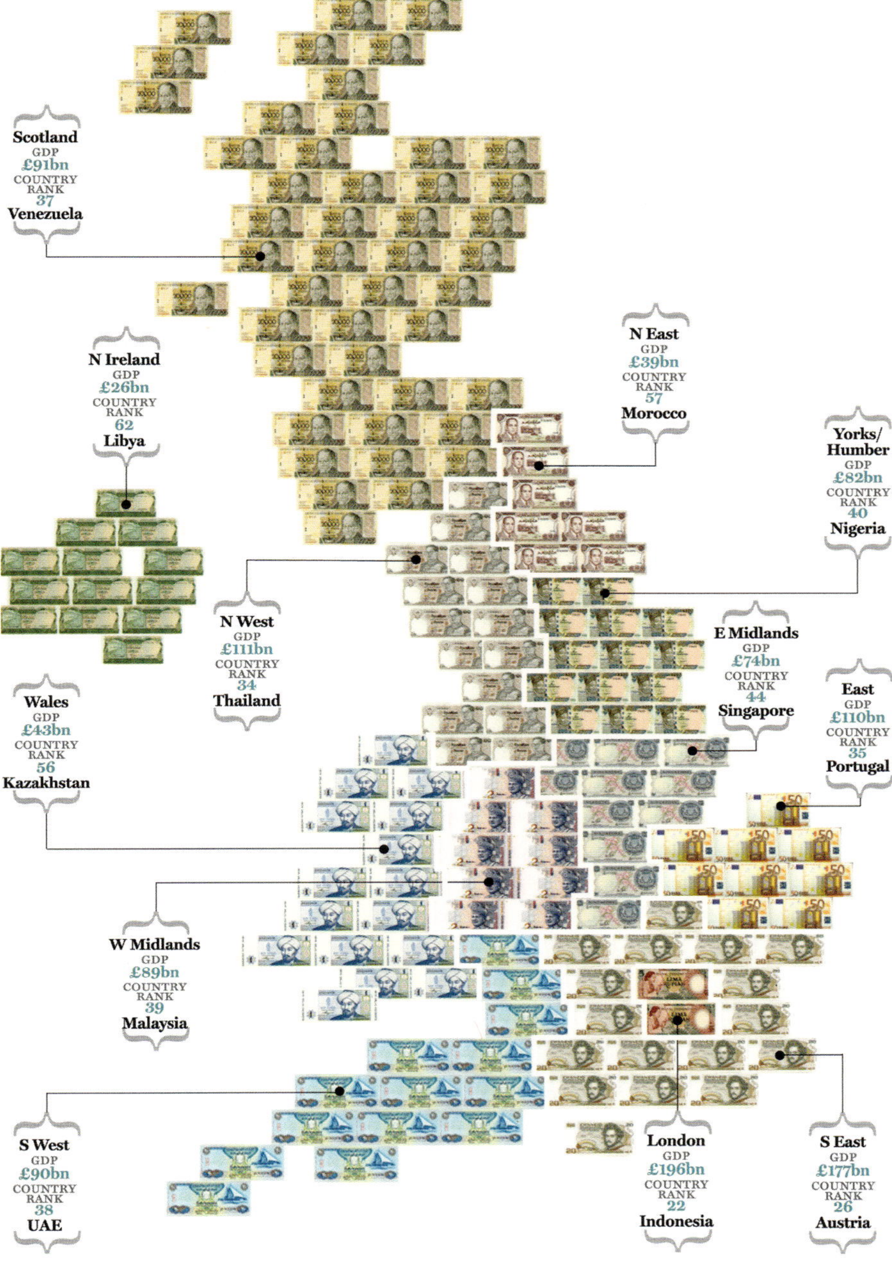

"Regional inequality does not begin and end with such measures as per capita income, GDP or unemployment, important as these are. It both reflects and is fuelled by a massive democratic deficit beyond the capital and the self-referential elites that congregate there."[1]
Doreen Massey, 'World City', 2007

The Financial Times presents a provocative proposition: imagine that the different regions of the UK were separate countries. What would their place in the pecking order of world economic powers be? Subdividing the country into smaller units highlights either what relative contribution each makes to the national economic story, or how subordinate different regions are to the power of the south-east, depending on your view. The FT's image makes clear that, despite national inequalities, the average Briton has a much greater economic power than the majority of people in the world today. The image reminds us that in global terms, as journalist Andrew Marr has said, "To be born British is still a fantastic stroke of luck."[2]

1. Massey 2007 (Cambridge: Polity) p159
2. http://www.telegraph.co.uk/portal/main.jhtml?xml=/portal/2007/05/12/nosplit/ftmarr112.xml

Courtesy Financial Times

CHARLES BOOTH

'Descriptive Maps of London Poverty' 1898–9

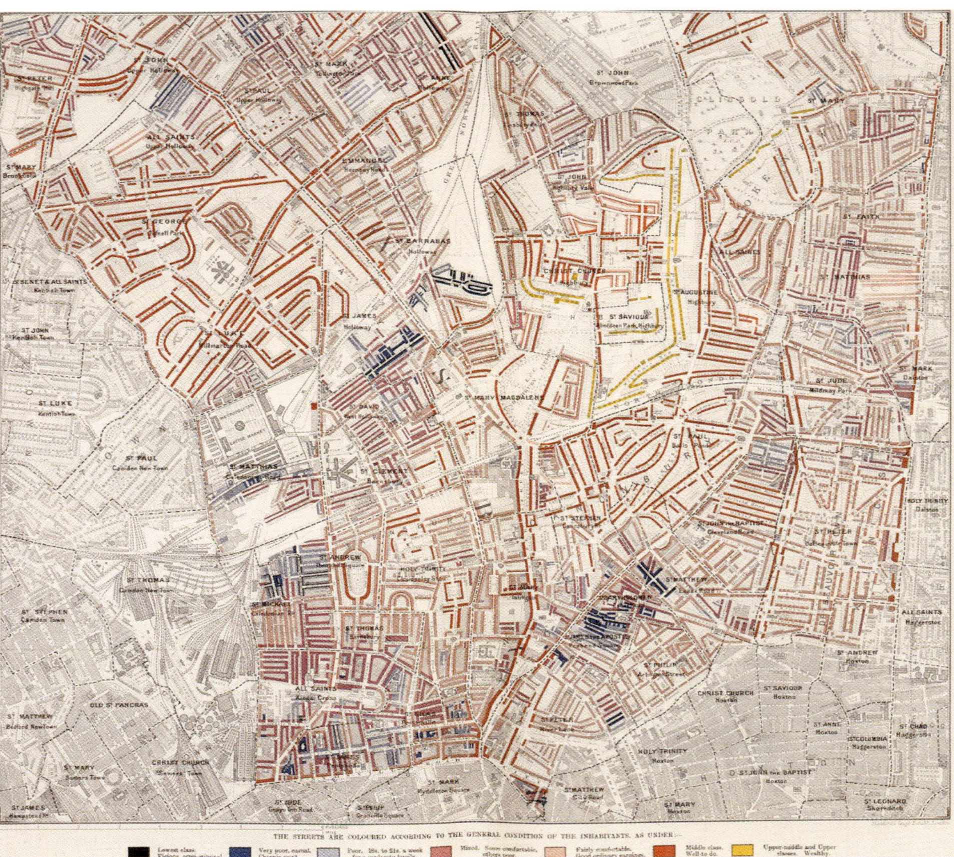

The Library of the London School of Economics and Political Science

"Outside the countryside, most cities, towns, suburbs and even streets which were rich or poor a century ago are in much the same relative position now."[1]
Daniel Dorling, 'Human Geography of the UK', 2000

Charles Booth's 12 maps of London classified every street into one of seven categories, from rich in gold to "semi-criminal" in black. His maps show how as Doreen Massey argues, that "geography is the space of the social": how inequalities are manifested spatially. Booth was one of the very first 'social scientists' and began making a social survey of the city to disprove the idea that poverty was widespread. He ended up concluding that he and his contemporaries had massively underestimated the extent of poverty, after two decades of research and 17 published volumes. Booth invented his own scheme of classification to cope with the problem of who earned and did what across the whole of London, then the world's biggest city. Each group was subdivided, so that the working class had six subsections reflecting regularity of work and income: 'high-paid labour'; 'regular standard earners'; 'small regular earners'; 'intermittent earners'; 'casual earners'; 'the lowest class'. Booth estimated that of 900,000 citizens, 11,000 were in the very lowest class, "semi-criminal".

1. Dorling, 2000 (London: Sage) pp176-7

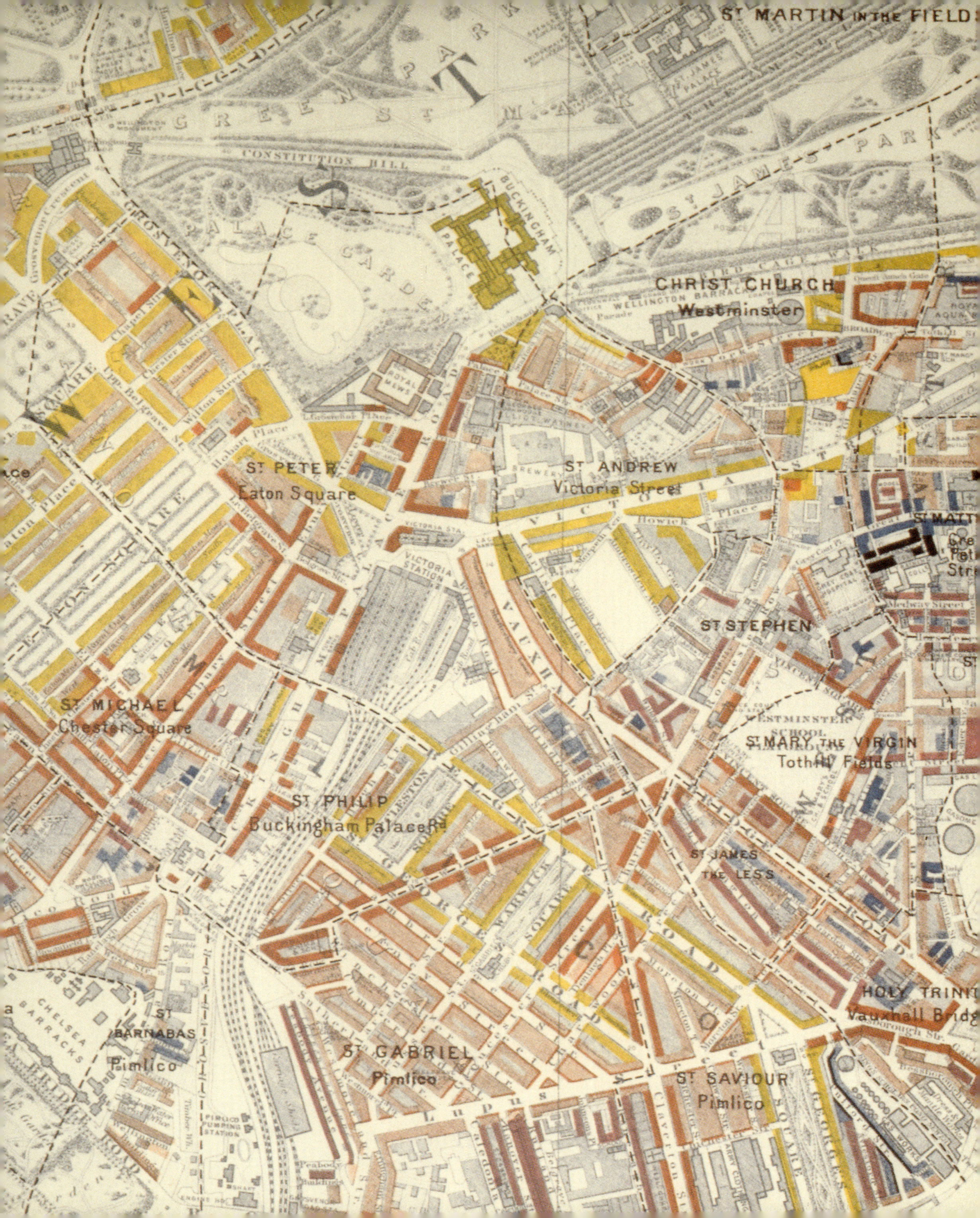

ST MARTIN IN THE FIELDS
GREEN PARK
CONSTITUTION HILL
BUCKINGHAM PALACE
PALACE GARDEN
ST JAMES'S PARK
CHRIST CHURCH
Westminster
ST PETER
Eaton Square
ST ANDREW
Victoria Street
VICTORIA STATION
ST STEPHEN
ST MICHAEL
Chester Square
ST MARY THE VIRGIN
Tothill Fields
WESTMINSTER SCHOOL
ST PHILIP
Buckingham Palace Rd
ST JAMES THE LESS
HOLY TRINITY
Vauxhall Bridge
ST BARNABAS
Pimlico
CHELSEA BARRACKS
ST GABRIEL
Pimlico
ST SAVIOUR
Pimlico

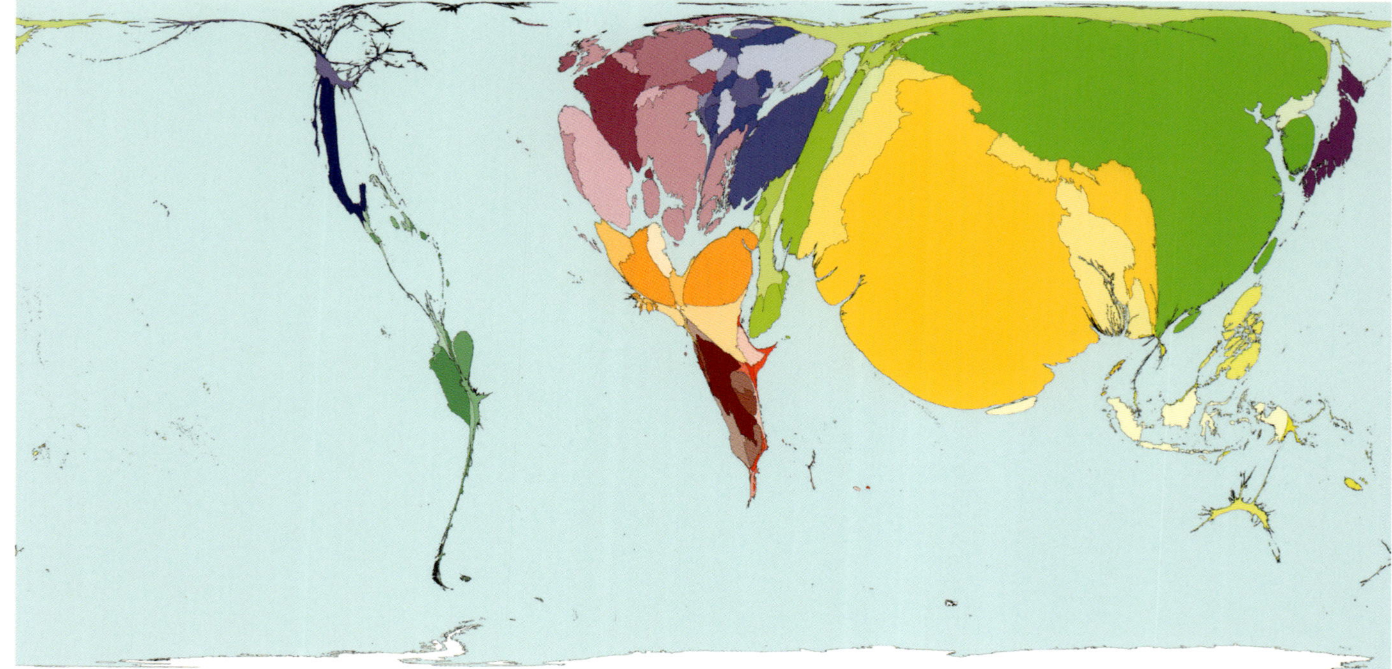

Global Wealth Distribution in 1AD

"How can we fathom the extent to which equity gaps are growing despite unprecedented global wealth and technological progress? Drawing images is one way to engage more of our imagination to help understand the extent and arrangement of world inequalities."[1]
Professor Daniel Dorling, University of Sheffield, 'The Challenge: Understanding Global Inequalities', 2007

Visualising how wealth is distributed across the globe is an intractable problem. The 'Worldmapper' project, online at www.worldmapper.org, shows countries by relative sizes to graphically reveal the extent of the inequalities between them. The SASI team have created maps over a long timeframe from economists' best estimates. They reveal how far the global economic order has changed. Of course, nations' boundaries have shifted: the sizes here reflect the estimated economic output of the geographical area the current-day nations represent. At Christ's birth, broadly speaking the largest economies were those with the largest and densest populations, able to support more than agriculture. Bangladesh and China are thought to have been the richest parts of the globe.[2]
By 1500, European territories were some of the world's richest; Central and South-eastern Africa were the poorest.[3]

1. http://medicine.plosjournals.org/perlserv/?request=get-document&doi=10.1371/journal.pmed.0040001&ct=1
2. In the earliest map the territory size reflects the proportion of global GDP, by purchasing power.
3. In 1500 and 1900 maps the territory size shows the proportion of global GDP in US dollar, by purchasing power.

Maps by Mark Newman, data by Daniel Dorling, text by Anna Barford, quality control by Ben Wheeler, website by John Pritchard, postes by Graham Allsopp .

Global Wealth Distribution in 2015

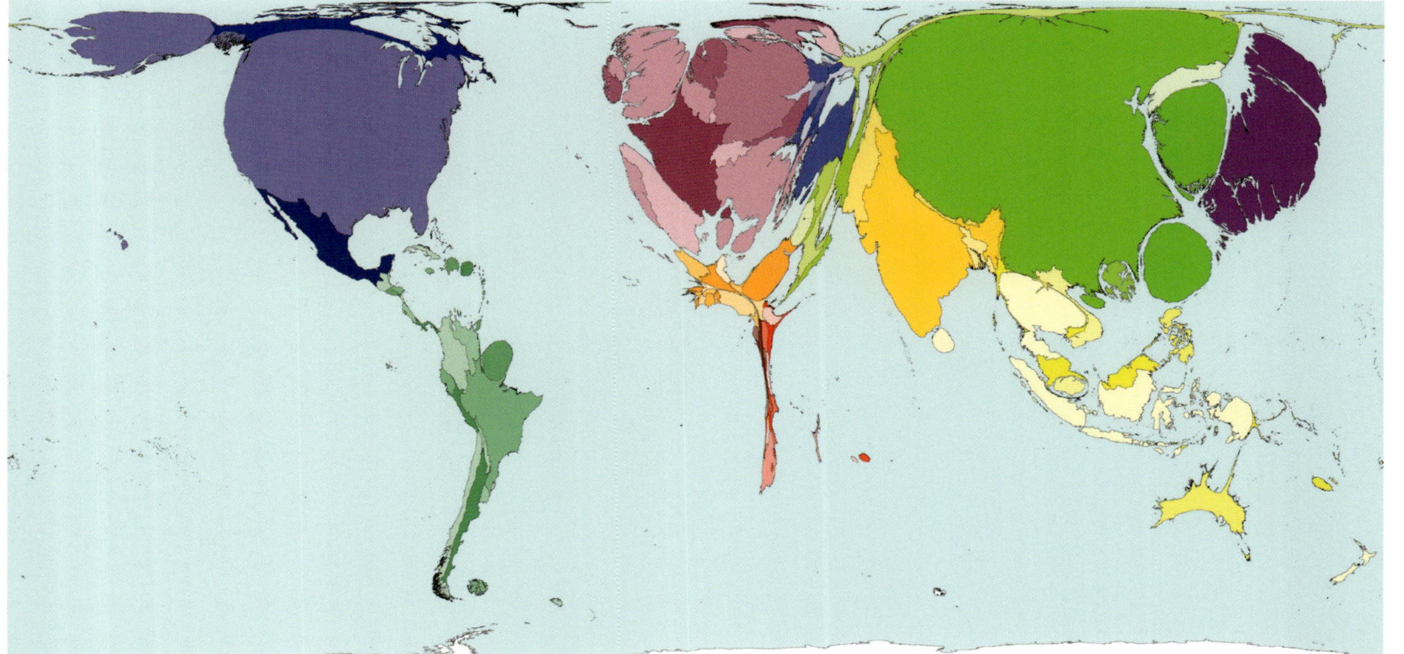

Who will occupy the biggest place on the global stage in the near future? In the present day, the countries that have the disproportionately largest economies in relation to their populations are Luxembourg, Norway and Switzerland; those with the smallest are Ethiopia, Burundi and the Democratic Republic of Congo.[1] This map extrapolates recent rates of economic growth to predict what nations' relative positions will be in less than a decade, In 1960, China only commanded one twentieth of the world economy; it is likely that it could recoup its position of 1AD in creating a quarter of the world's wealth very soon. In terms of accumulated wealth rather than economic output, the World Bank estimates that nearly half is concentrated in just 12 of the world's 300 countries. Whereas Africa has only just over 3% of the world's wealth, despite a population three times that of the whole EU.

1. The 2002 map shows territory sizes as proportions of global wealth as GDP. The 2015 map shows the proportion of worldwide GDP by purchasing power, estimated from current growth rates.

UNIVERSITY OF SHEFFIELD

Global income distribution: numbers of people living on under $10 each day, 2002

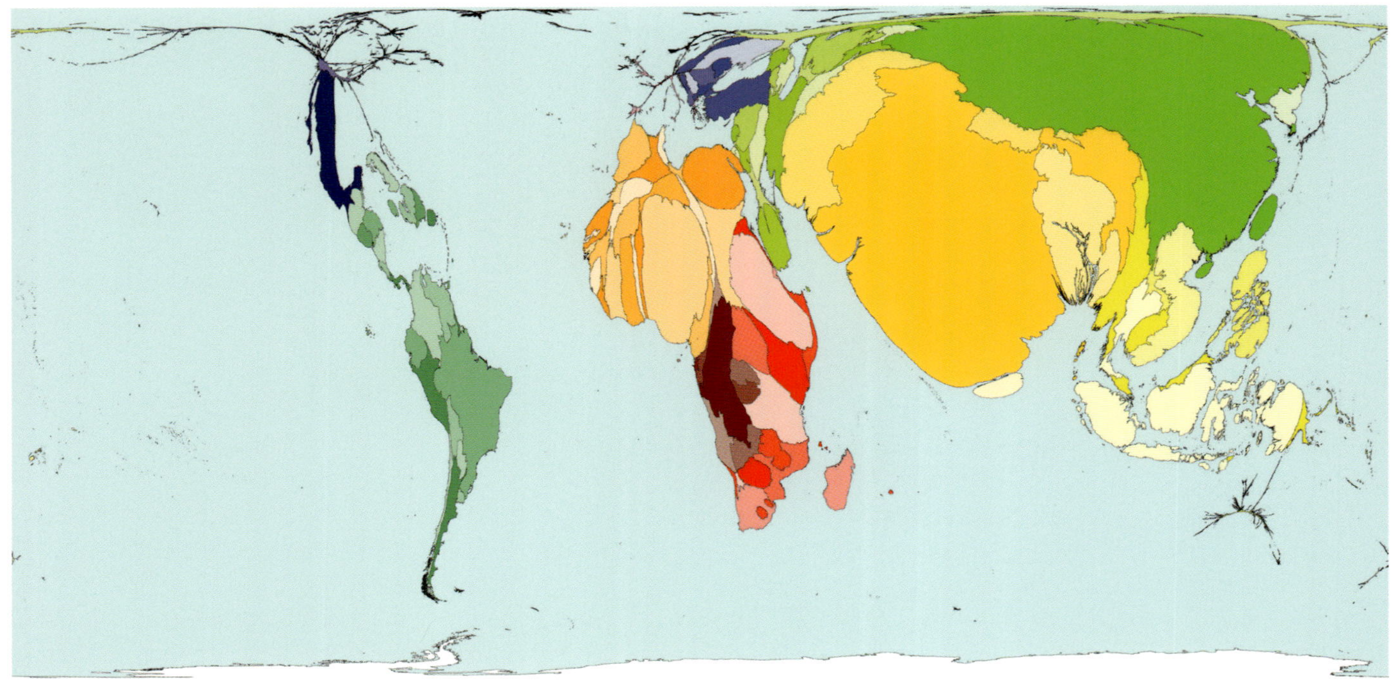

The map here created by researchers at Sheffield University reflects the number of people living on less than the equivalent of what $3650 a year would buy in the USA. The map reflects personal incomes rather than nations' whole economic outputs, to allow us to measure what standards of living people in different countries really have. As costs of living differ between places, the maps account for this by showing what the authors call 'purchasing power parity' (PPP). In fact, earning $10 a day is very far from the lowest levels of income in the world. In 2002, two in every five people were living in a state of poverty which threatened their survival: on less than the equivalent of just $2 a day. Nearly 1000 million of these were living on under a dollar a day. Taking the base measure of global poverty as '$1-a-day' has been criticized in some quarters. However, it helps illuminate the sheer distance between the levels of health, nutrition, and education that people in different countries can expect. Almost 95% of households in Africa are encompassed by this map; less than 1% of those in Western Europe are.

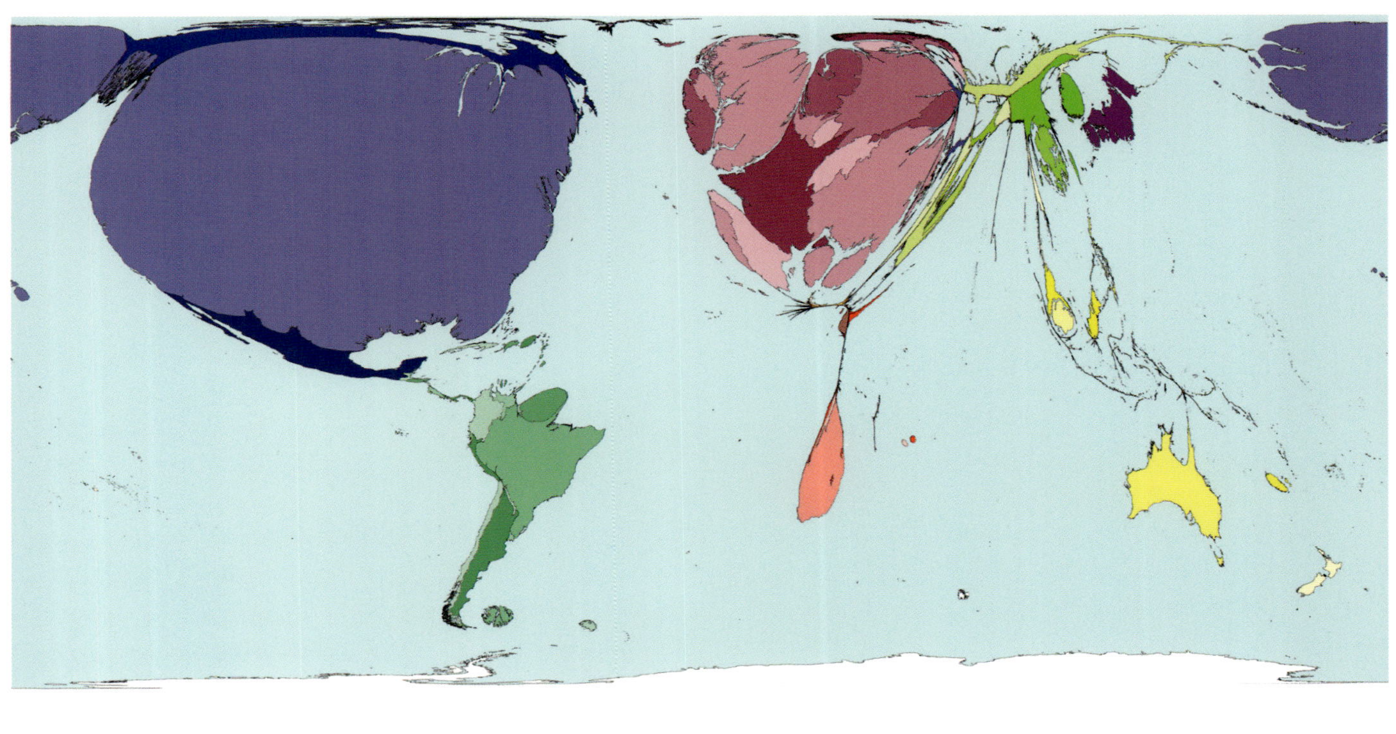

UNIVERSITY OF SHEFFIELD

Global income distribution: numbers of people living on over $200 each day, 2002

Researchers at Sheffield University have established a global comparison for a very high level of income: more than $200 per day, or $73,000 a year when adjusted for national 'purchasing power'. In 2002, only 53m people in the whole world had such incomes. Well over half of these – 31m – lived in the largest industrialized nation, the USA. In fact, only the US, Western Europe and Japan have more than a tiny proportion of people earning over $36,500 a year ($100 a day). In these industrialised areas, around 1/5 – 1/6 of the population have such luxurious lifestyles. In the rest of the world, it is 1/50 of the population. Southern Asia, Northern Africa, Eastern Europe and Central Africa have the smallest proportions of high earners.

UNIVERSITY OF SHEFFIELD

Cartogram of Britain by the dominant social grade of people aged 25–39, 2005

"England is [still] a patchwork of almost hermetically sealed sub-worlds, in which class as much as race is a crucial factor."[1] **Julian Baggini, 'Welcome to Everytown', 2007**

What does Britain's occupational structure look like? The economy is inseparable from the country's geography. The two determine what opportunities are open to us, and what our differing social roles and even incomes are likely to be. This map reveals what the single largest social groups are in each part of the country, when judged by type of employment. The country is divided up into hexagons representing 100,000 people (the size of a parliamentary constituency, roughly speaking). Each reflects the dominant type of work available in the area, though 'A', 'B', and 'C1' are grouped together ('A' is only 3% of the population). Unsurprisingly, there are strong correlations between this cartogram and the maps of wealth and poverty created by the same team. Enormous swathes of the south of England are dominated by 'AB/C1's – white-collar, middle-class workers. At and past the Midlands, only small parts of the country's economy are clearly based upon skilled white-collar jobs. And only in parts of Glasgow are 'D' and 'E' groups – unskilled manual workers, casual labourers, and those reliant on the state – in the majority.

1. Baggini, 2007 (London: Granta), P64

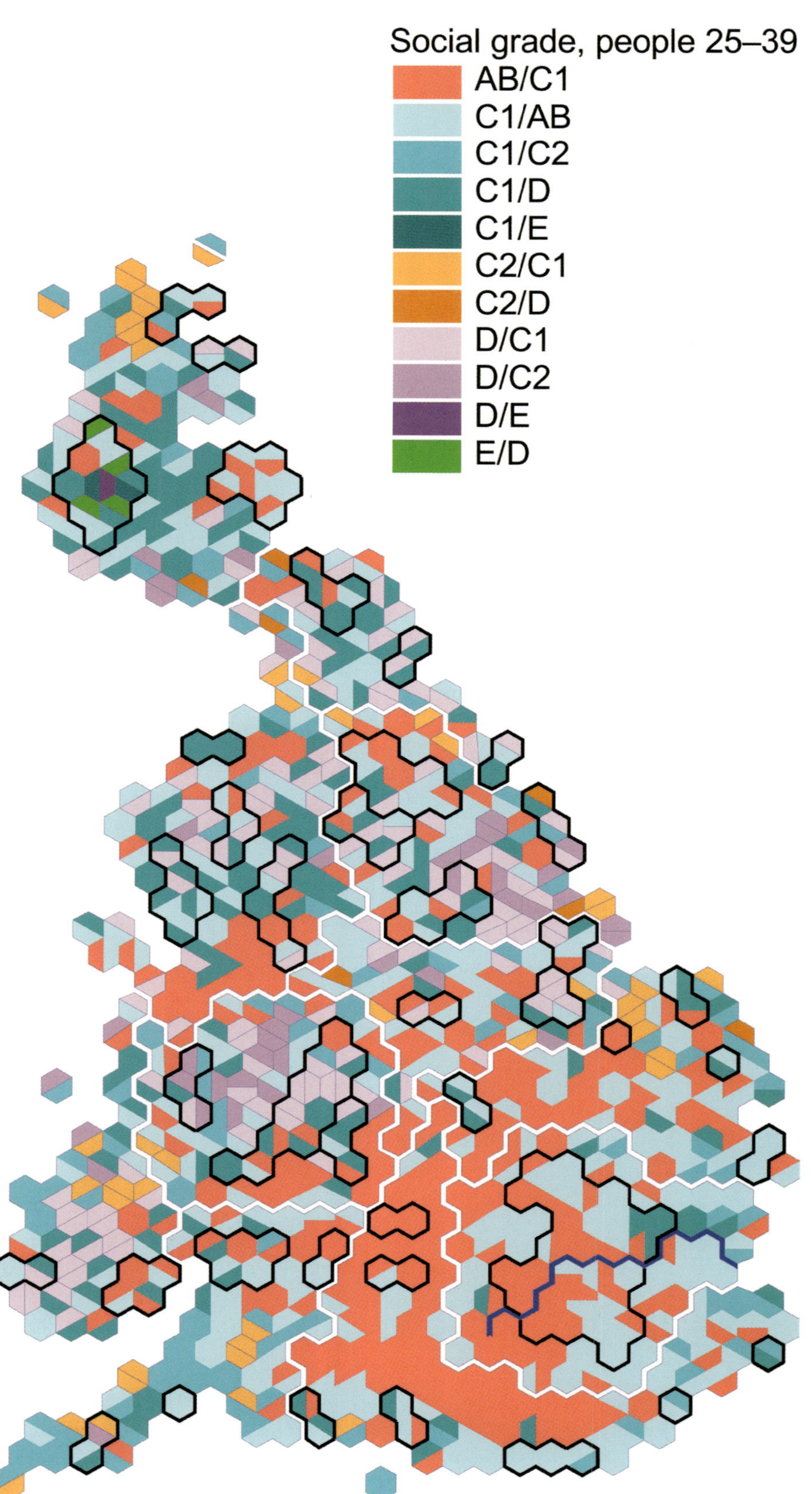

Levels of inequality of every European Union member, 2008

image by Ben Branagan & Gareth Holt

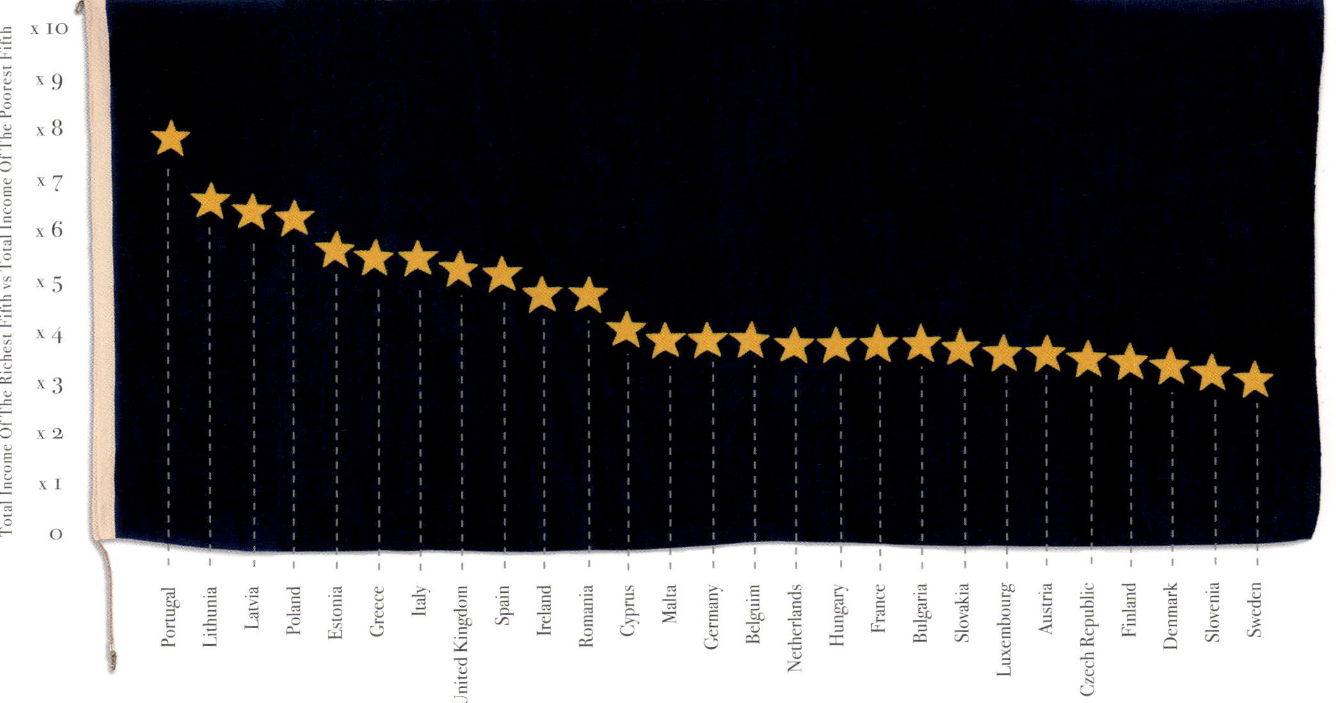

"The pursuit of equality itself is a mirage. What's more desirable and more practicable than the pursuit of equality is the pursuit of equality of opportunity."[1]
Margaret Thatcher, speech in New York, September 15th 1975

Which European country has the most equitable income distribution, and which has the most unequal? In Britain, the fifth of the population with the highest incomes earn more than five times someone in the lowest fifth. In Portugal, the top 20% earn over eight times more than poorer citizens. In Sweden, the gap between rich and poor is at its lowest, with the former earning only three times that of the latter. The levels of inequality reflect nations' traditions and values: whether liberty and competition are more valuable than social justice and solidarity. Researchers at Sheffield University have found that of all the industrialized nations, Japan has "the richest poor people". In other words, poorer groups are least disadvantaged relative to the rest of the population.

1. http://www.margaretthatcher.org/speeches/displaydocument.asp?docid=102769

THÉOPHILE STEINLEN

'Britannia in the arms of death' 1894

"Competition is the completest expression of the battle of all against all which rules in modern civil society. This [is a] battle, a battle for life, for existence, for everything... capital... is the weapon with which this social warfare is carried on"[1]
Friedrich Engels, 'The Condition of the Working Class in England', 1845

Many writers from Engels onwards have argued that imperial expansion is the logical result of a capitalist and class-based social structure. The imperial powers' relations might well be encapsulated by the military strategist Carl von Clausewitz's phrase that "war is politics continued by other means."[2] The academic AH Halsey has also argued that "British nationalism and the social hierarchy are intertwined": that large parts of our built environment and housing stock, which still determine our relative social positions, were built with the proceeds of colonial trade.[3] In 1894, the British Empire stretched over almost a third of the world's land mass: 14m square miles were administered from one small island. The French satirical magazine 'Le Rire' present the consequences of this from the opponents' side. Britannia is here the bride of the angel of death, bringing misery and mortality to the world. The second implication is that Britain's commercial hegemony is nearing its end.

1. www.marxists.org/archive/marxworks/1845/condition-working-class/index.htm
2. http://en.wikipedia.org/wiki/Carl_von_Clausewitz
3. Halsey, 1986, p1

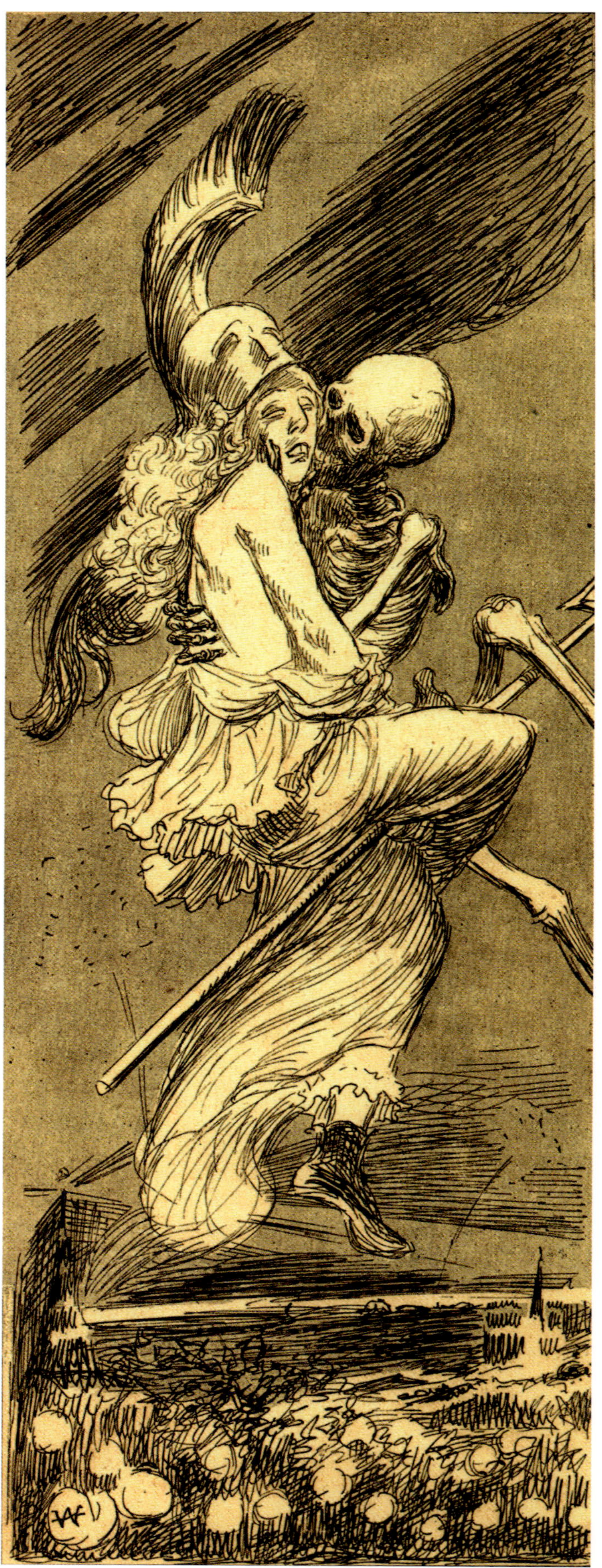

'Britannia in the arms of death' from the magazine 'Le Rire' ('Laughter') Collection Sunderland Libraries

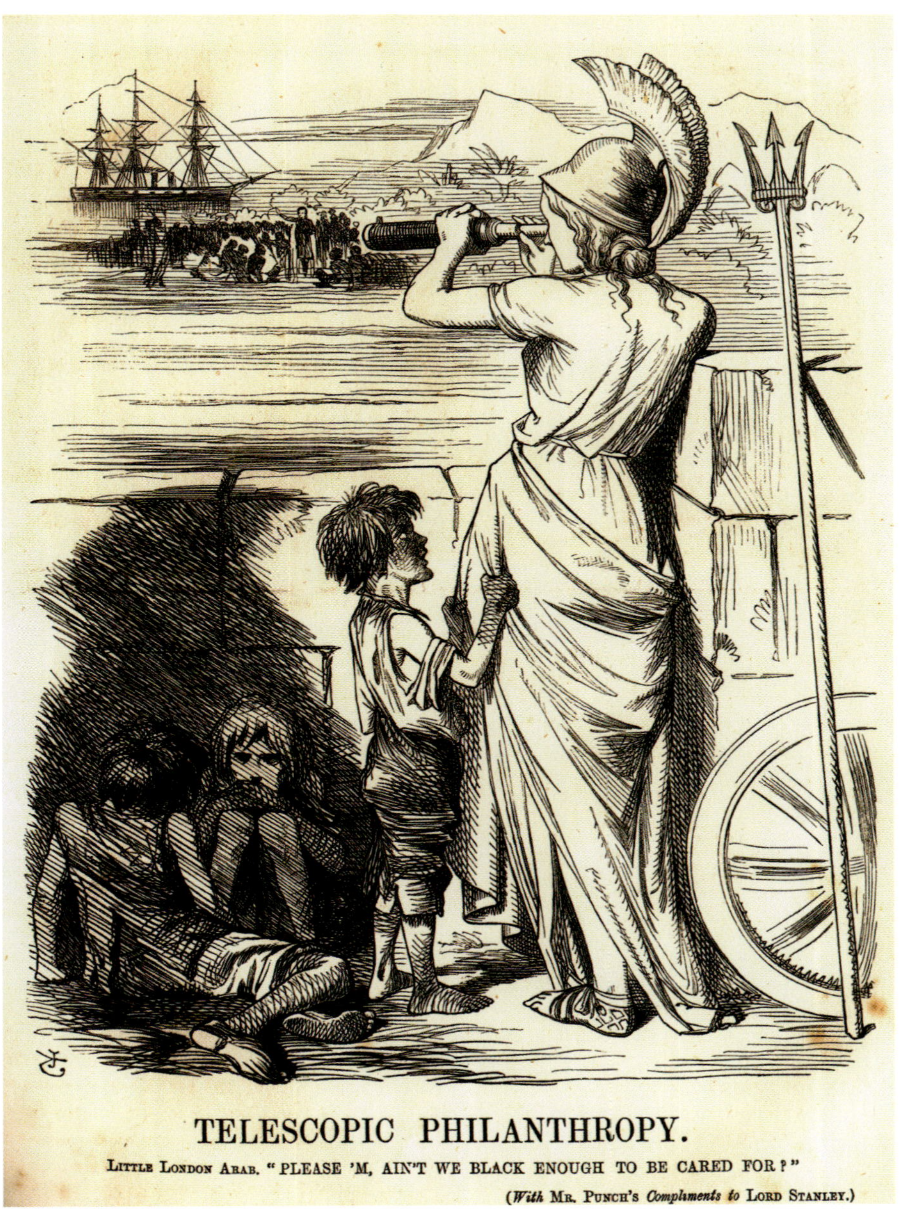

'Telescopic Philanthropy', from 'Punch'

"And this also,' said Marlow suddenly, 'has been one of the dark places of the earth'."[1] **Joseph Conrad, 'Heart of Darkness', 1899**

This print asks: how well do we know our own countrymen? It predates, but echoes Joseph Conrad's description of men on the Thames estuary, looking out to sea and to the distant locations of trade, investment, and plunder. Tenniel's print was made in response to a particular speech to Parliament, by Lord Stanley, who advocated 'domestic' philanthropy. Stanley argued that the rich should invest at home to improve the lot of their countrymen rather than investing overseas: "If we wanted to spend a million a year in civilising savages, there was a population within five miles of the House of Commons that stood as much in need of civilisation as the Africans, and had been quite as much neglected."[2] It has been argued that Tenniel gave the boy features from a classical statue to indicate his ethnic superiority, and to invite his readers' sympathy. Others depicted the underclass as being from another continent: Henry Mayhew saw himself as a "traveller in the undiscovered country of the poor... of whom the public had less knowledge than of the most distant tribes of the earth."[3]

1. en.wikiquote.org/wiki/Heart_of_Darkness
2. http://projects.vassar.edu/punch/linden.html
3. http://www.lib.cam.ac.uk/Exhibitions/whole_island/captions.html

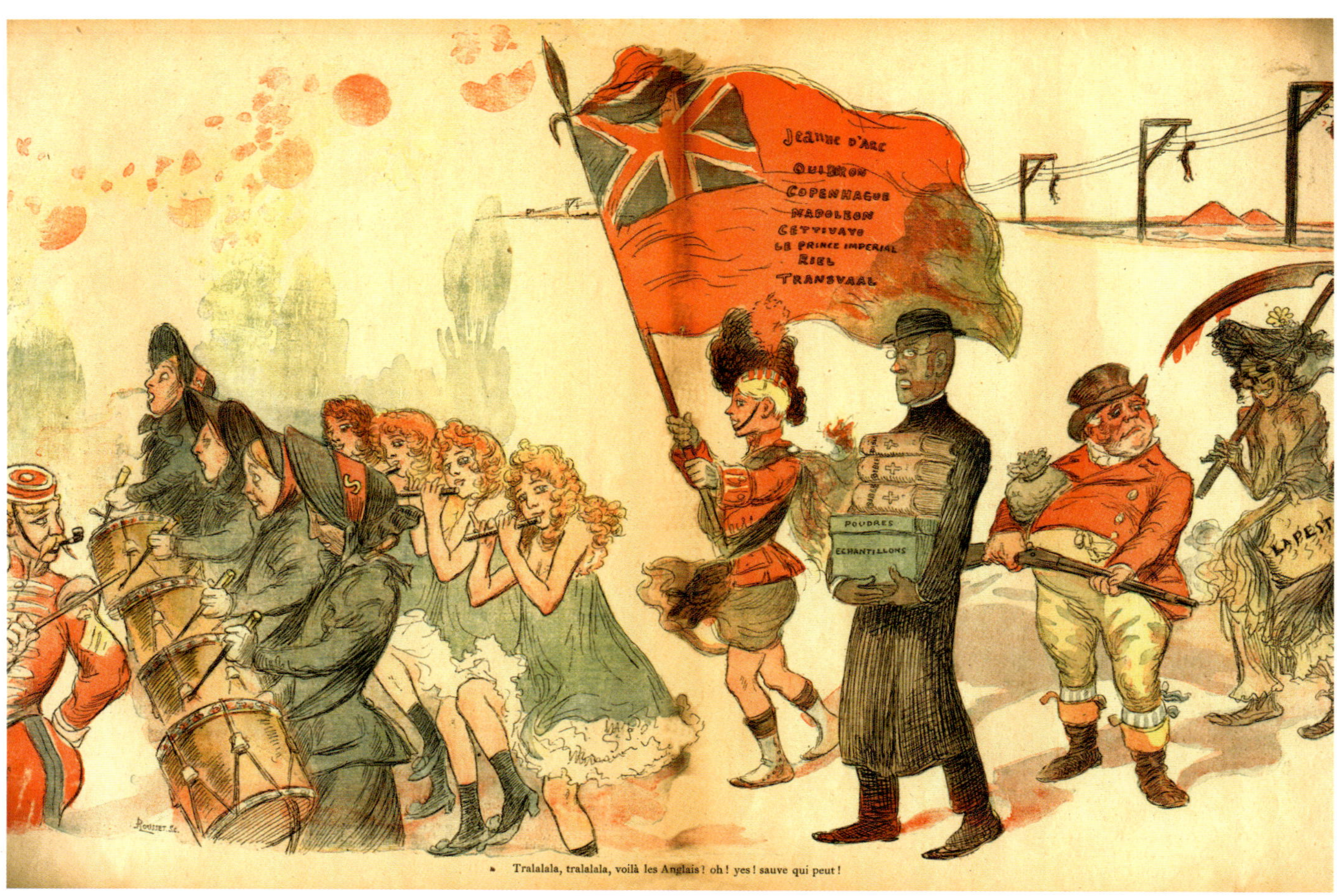

'Les English', from the magazine 'Le Rire' ('Laughter'), 1894. Private collection

"The French wish not to have superiors, the English wish to have inferiors."[1]
Alexander de Tocqueville, 1830s.

"What should they know of England who only England know?"
Rudyard Kipling, 'The English Flag'

The French satirical magazine Le Rire here compares France and England's values and social structures. This image neatly illustrates the historian David Cannadine's idea that when the French "put their social structures on public display, they have parades (which are intrinsically egalitarian), whereas the British have processions (which are innately hierarchical)."[2] It paints a picture of the politics of 'bread and circuses', which enabled the labour force to work ever harder and sustain ever higher levels of production. The image of society as a kind of march or convoy, with 'leaders' at the front and the least fortunate eventually 'catching up', is often repeated by those who promote the virtues of the free market. The fact that a skeletal figure marked 'the plague' closely follows John Bull suggests that the spread of the British Empire around the globe was far from benign.

1. http://www.cs.princeton.edu/~chazelle/politics/france.html
2. Cannadine, 1998, p53

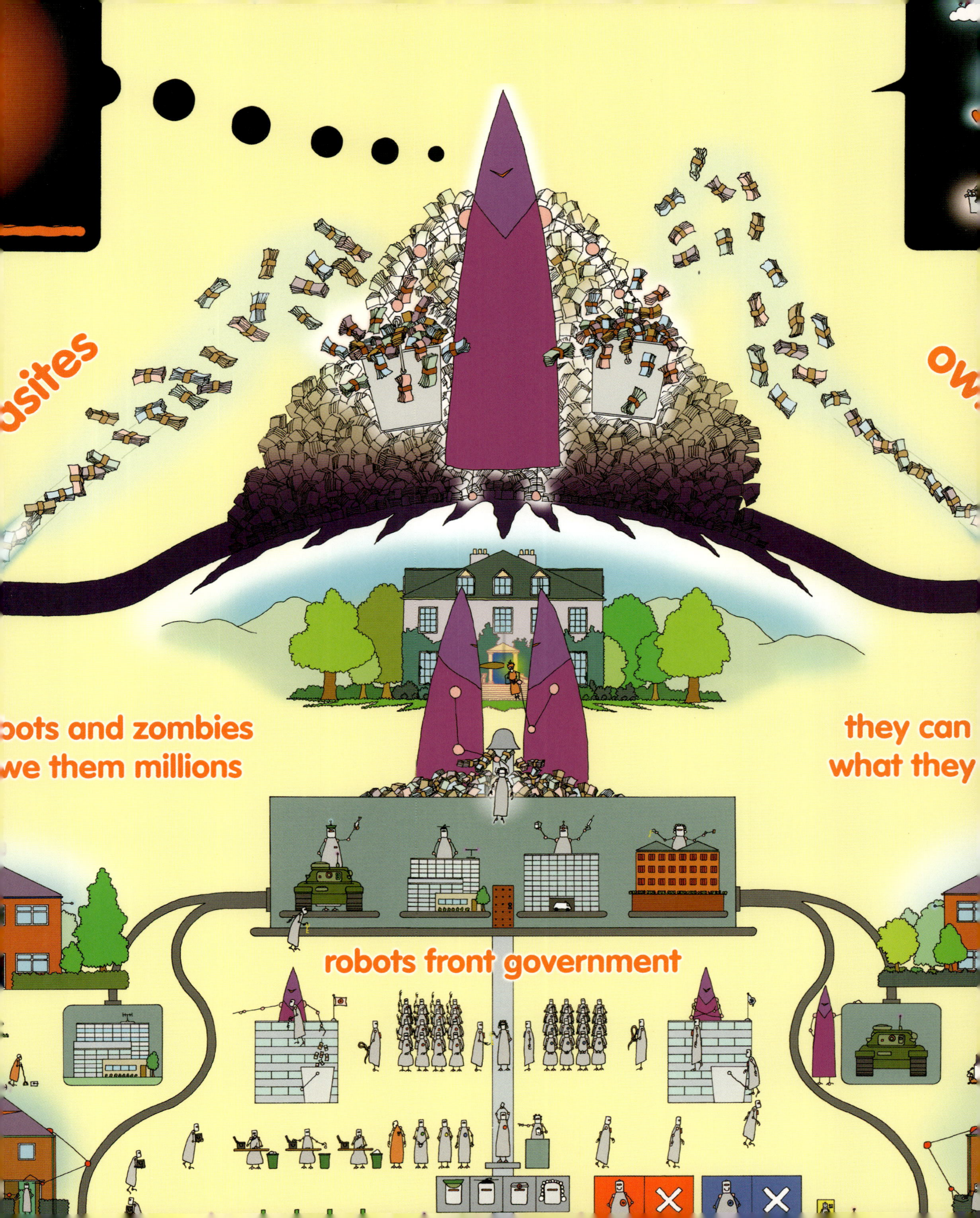
asites
ow
ots and zombies
we them millions
they can
what they
robots front government

'The great chain of being' 1579

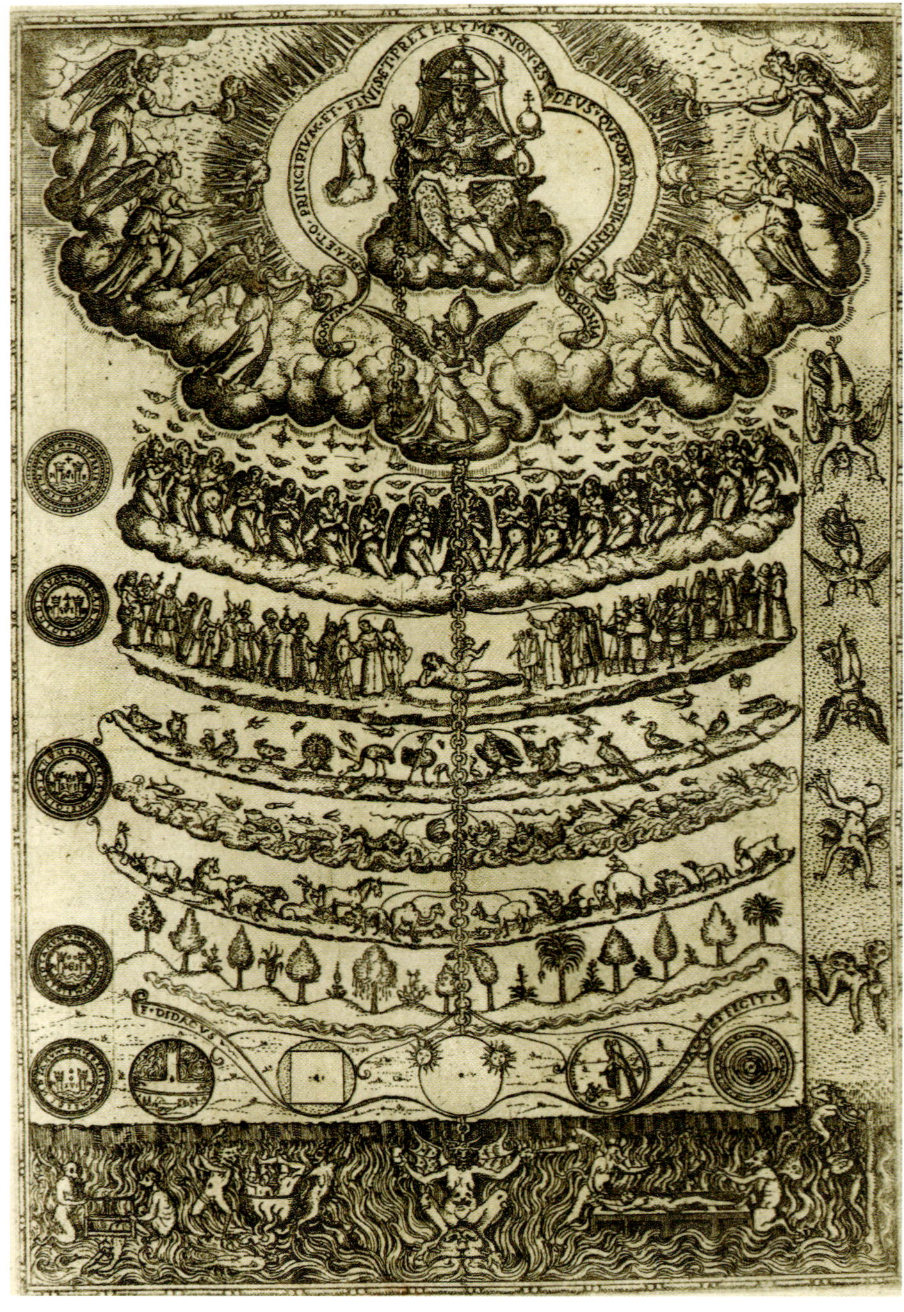

From 'Rhetorica Christiana', 1579

"In the course of His providence, [God] has thought good to appoint various orders and degrees of men here upon earth...[ranked] according to the stations which it hath pleased God to allot them."[1] Thomas Broughton, 1746

The Elizabethan worldview was that all living things were not only linked, but could be ranked in hierarchical order. One writer argued that "from the Mushrome to the Angels", all life is "linkt with adamantine chaines".[2] This is the most single famous image of late medieval times to depict that idea. An enormous chain literally runs from the bottom of creation to the spiritual apex, God. Social differences were viewed as 'rungs' on this vertical axis. The King is in the highest position as God's representative on earth, followed by aristocratic lords, down to the peasantry. Early modern England, however, saw considerable social mobility, and most people knew it. Only a few left accounts of who were seen as the key groups, though. One, a country parson called William Harrison, claimed that "We in England divide our people commonly into four sorts as gentlemen, citizens or burgesses, yeomen, and artificers or labourers."[3] Within this scheme, the crucial distinction is that of gentility: the crucial threshold that of not undertaking manual labour. Indeed 'gentlemen' included everyone from titled nobles to professionals: some 5% of the population.

1. Quoted in Cannadine, 1998, p26
2. Samuel Ward in 'The Life of Faith', 1621-2: http://etext.virginia.edu/cgi-local/DHI/dhi.cgi?id=dv2-50
3. http://www.bartleby.com/35/3/1.html

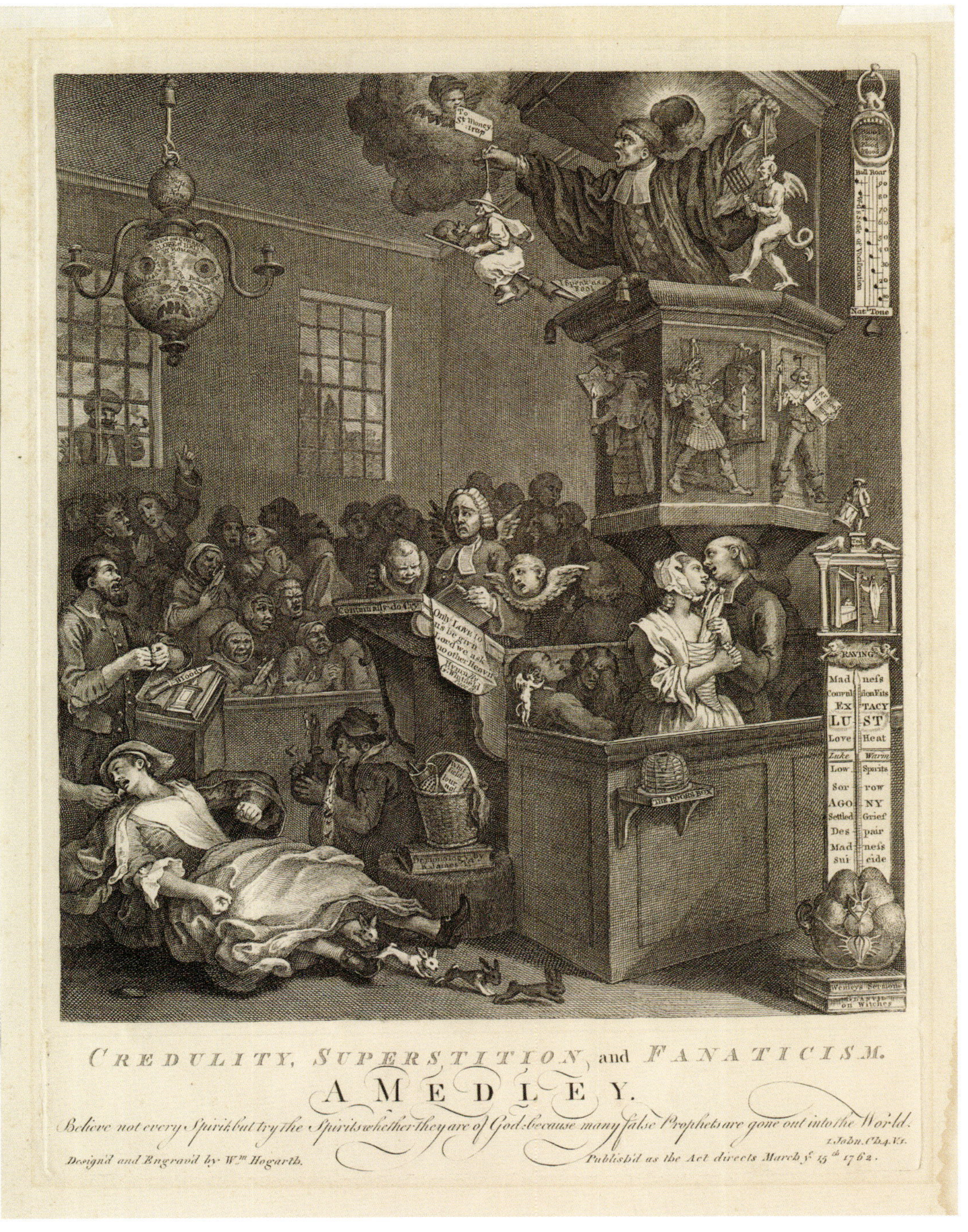

Collection Sunderland Libaries

"Mankind are happier in a state of inequality and subordination."[1]
Dr Johnson (1709-1784)

This gloriously titled print depicts a microcosm of England in which the leaders are the priests, and the congregation duped by their deceit. The nation is represented as a small parish church, in which we can see each other all at once. Hogarth's ingenious metaphor has been endlessly copied: Private Eye's 'St Albion Parish News' also featured the then prime minister as a vicar in charge of a crumbling parish church. Here, one preacher is surrounded by puppets of the devil and a witch, and reads a text saying "I speak as a fool." A second minister is caught in a sex scandal, thrusting a devotional icon down a girl's blouse. The majority of the flock are only too willing to be taken in by their empty rhetoric and hysteria. Why, Hogarth asks, do we want to enter into a state of willed subordination? In Hogarth's satirical world, there are only rulers and ruled, with bread and circuses for the latter.

1. Quoted in Porter, 1982, p15

JOHN GODDARD / RICHARD DEY

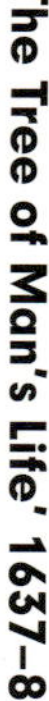
'The Tree of Man's Life' 1637–8

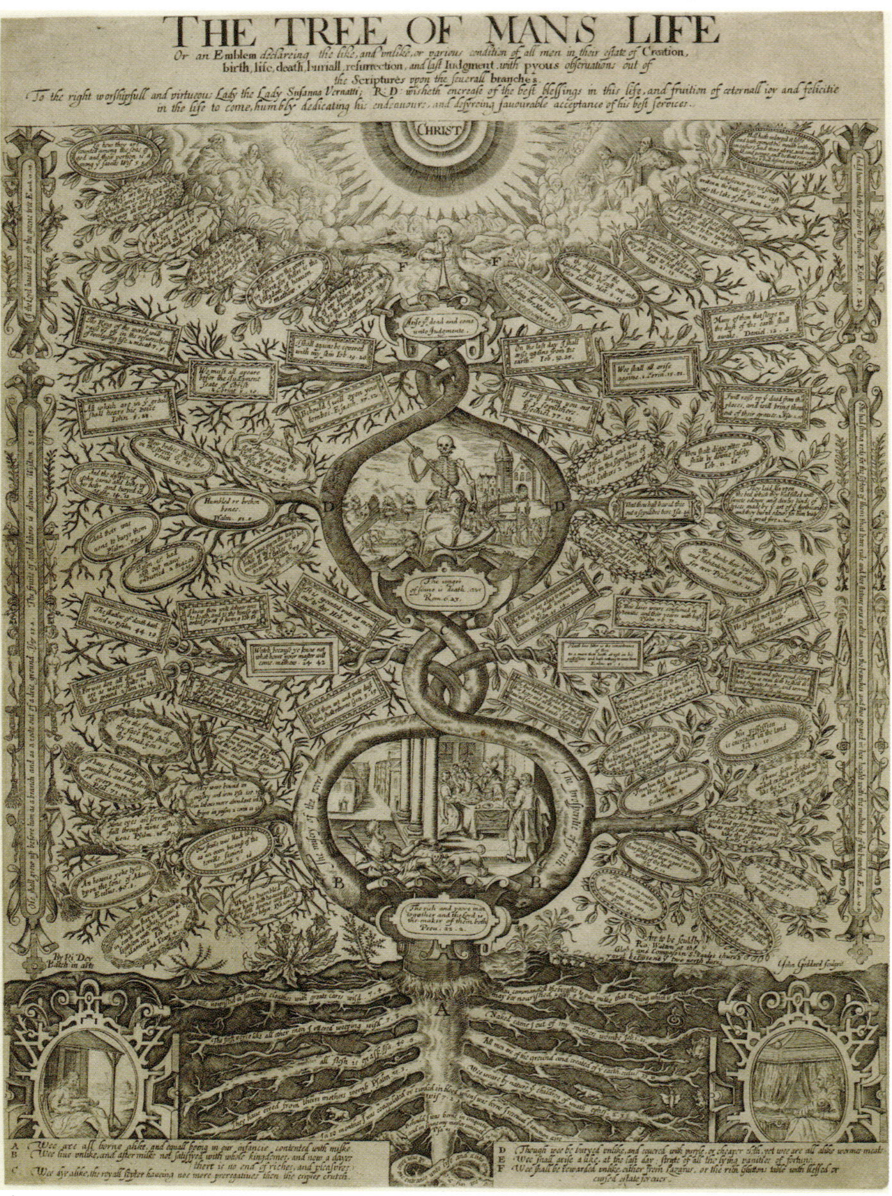

British Museum

"Religion is the only firm foundation of all power. The church and state do mutually support and give assistance to each other."[1] **Charles I, 1640s**

One of the most popular images of the nation in early modern times was 'the tree of the commonwealth'. Edmund Burke described government as developing "in the method of nature… Nothing is more beautiful in the theory of parliaments than that principle of renovation".[2] For Goddard, both an individual's life cycle and society are represented by a tree. However, the image was also used to illustrate the sum total of human knowledge: similar prints were titled 'The Order of the Universe'. The tree features Biblical texts to illustrate the six stages of man's life from birth to resurrection. The texts accept worldly iniquities whilst underscoring how trivial worldly goods are: "Wee are all borne alike, and equall being in our infancie, contented with milke / Wee live unlike, and after milke not satisfyed with whole kingdomes, and now a dayes there is no end of riches and pleasures / Wee dye alike, the royall septer haveing noe more prerogatives then the criples crutch / Though wee be buryed unlike, and covered with purple, or cheaper cloth, yet wee are all alike wormes meate / Wee shall arise alike, at the last day: stripte of all the lying vanities of fortune / Wee shall be rewarded unlike, either from Lazarus, or the rich Gluttons table with blessed or cursed estate forever."

1. Quoted in Hill, 1972, p98
2. Peter Stanlis, 'Edmund Burke and the Natural Law', 2003 (Piscataway: Transaction), p99

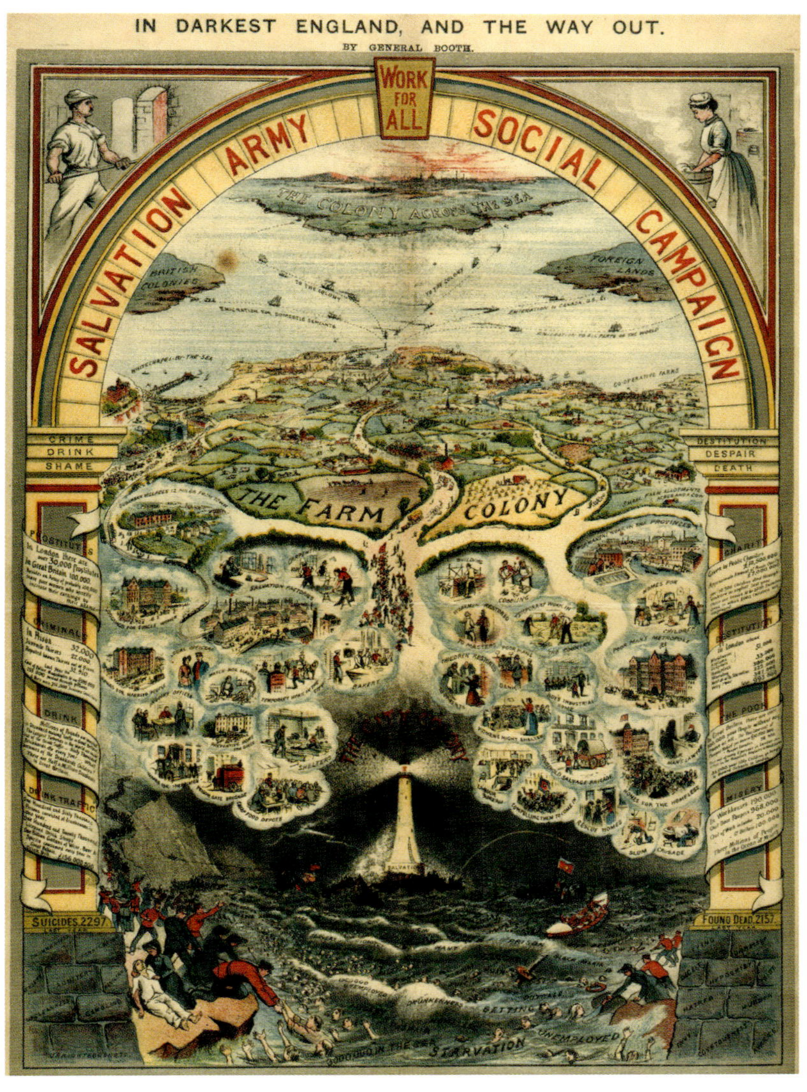

"This summer the attention of the civilised world has been arrested by the story which Mr. Stanley has told of Darkest Africa... It seemed to me only too vivid a picture of many parts of our own land... As there is a darkest Africa is there not also a darkest England?"[1]

From 'In Darkest England', chapter I: 'Why 'Darkest England'?', 1890

Writer Jonathan Raban has remarked that "to talk of 'Darkest London' was more of an understatement than an exaggeration".[2] General William Booth's book of this name was accompanied by this extraordinary print. Booth's stated aim was "the permanent deliverance of mankind from misery". The print is at once a diagnosis of social ills; a remedy for them involving resettlement, emigration, and economic restructuring; and a complete cosmology. Booth's vision is of a nation split into two moral, spiritual and economic halves: he called the drowning souls "these sinking classes". The connection between economic and moral poverty was a commonplace: one 1831 government report noted that "the reports from Sunderland exhibit a state of human misery, and necessarily of moral degradation, such as I hardly ever heard of."[3]

1. Text from www.gutenberg.org
2. Raban, 1974, p94
3. Charles Greville quoted by Donald Thomas, 'The Victorian Underworld', 1998 (London: Hodder), p13

IN DARKEST ENGLAND, AND THE WAY OUT.

BY GENERAL BOOTH.

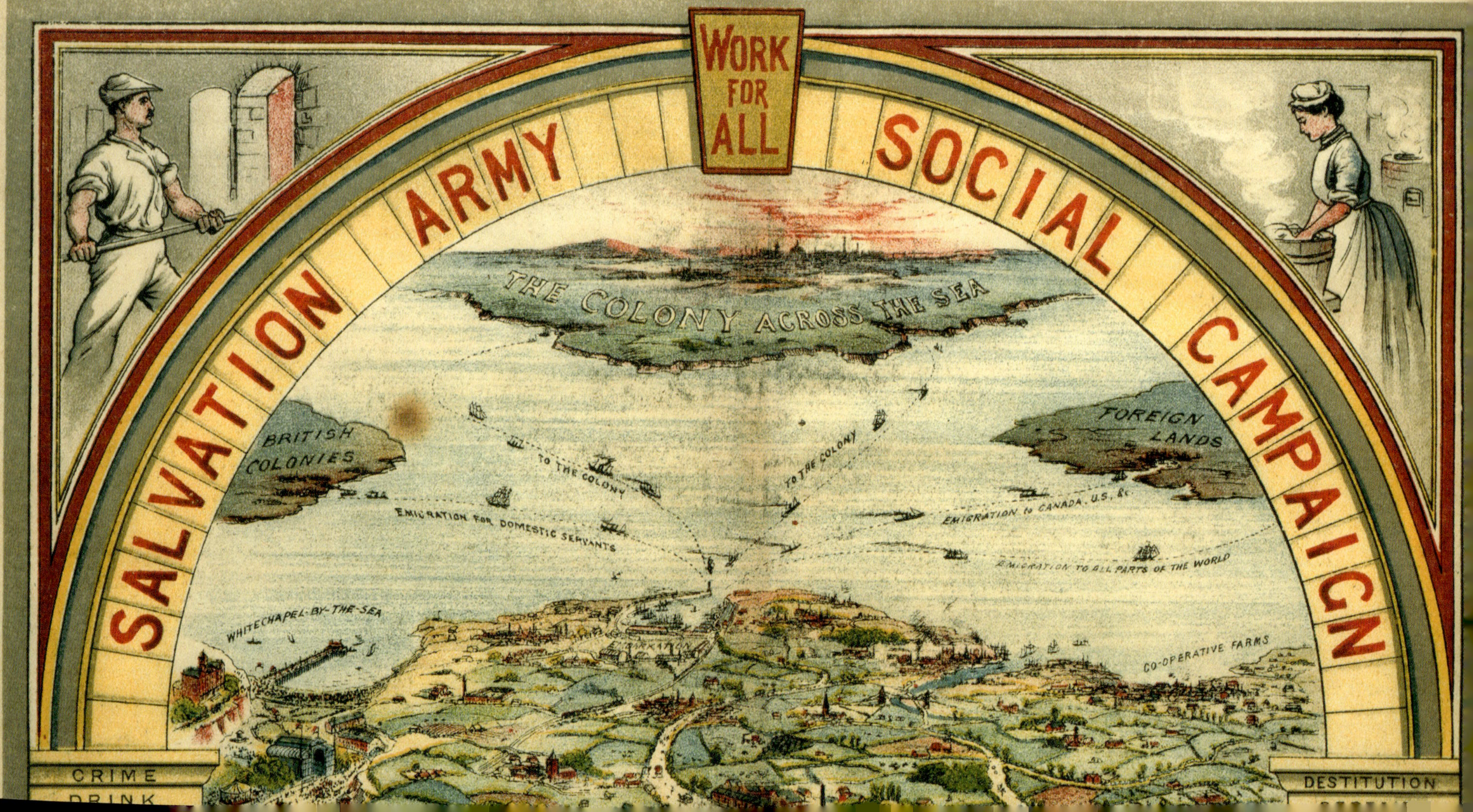

WORK FOR ALL

SALVATION ARMY SOCIAL CAMPAIGN

THE COLONY ACROSS THE SEA

BRITISH COLONIES

FOREIGN LANDS

TO THE COLONY

TO THE COLONY

EMIGRATION FOR DOMESTIC SERVANTS

EMIGRATION to CANADA, U.S. &c

EMIGRATION TO ALL PARTS OF THE WORLD

WHITECHAPEL-BY-THE-SEA

CO-OPERATIVE FARMS

CRIME

DRINK

DESTITUTION

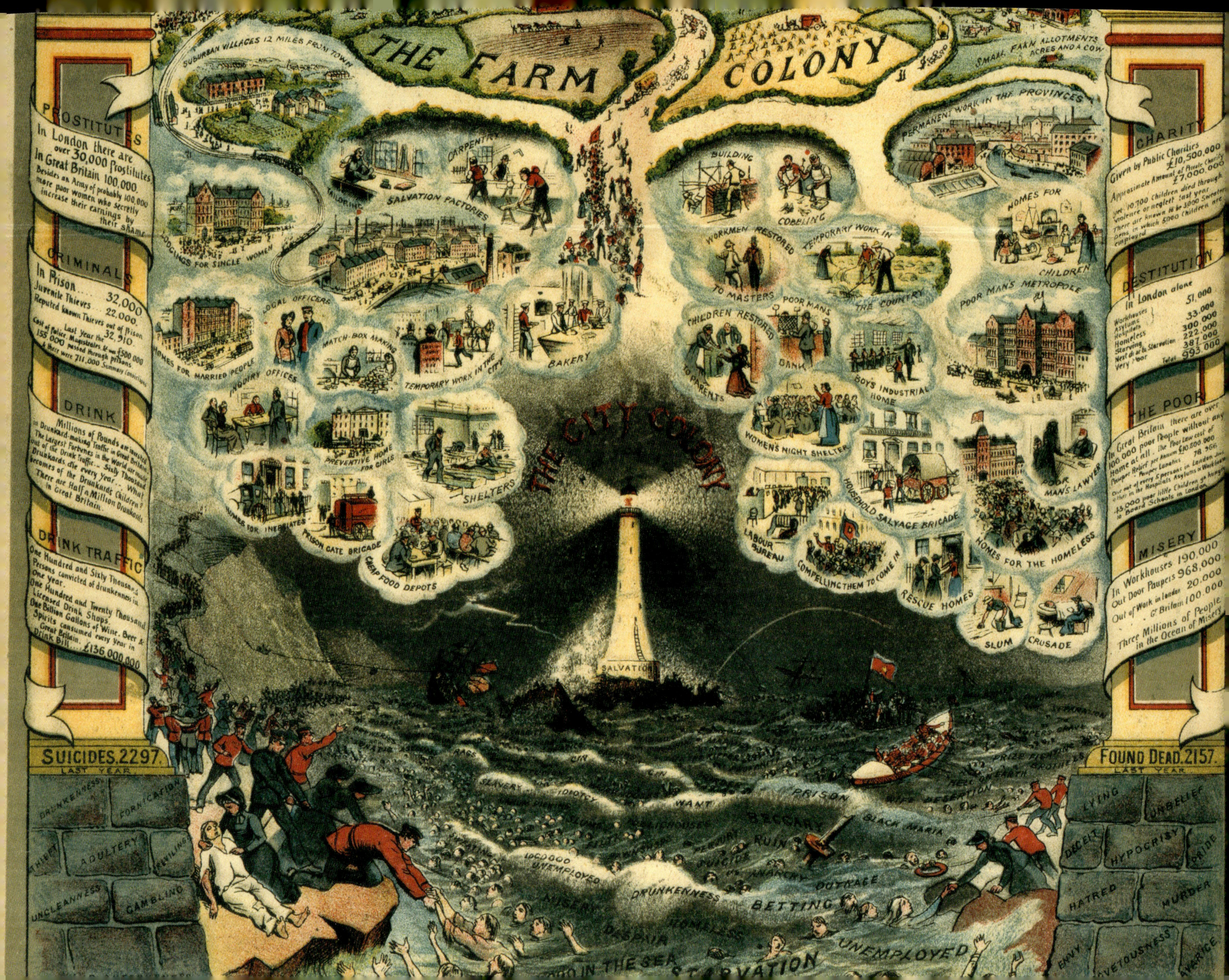

THE FARM COLONY
SUBURBAN VILLAGES 12 MILES FROM TOWN
SMALL FARM ALLOTMENTS 3 ACRES AND A COW
PERMANENT WORK IN THE PROVINCES
SALVATION FACTORIES
CARPENTRY
BUILDING
COBBLING
LODGINGS FOR SINGLE WOMEN
WORKMEN RESTORED TO MASTERS
TEMPORARY WORK IN THE COUNTRY
HOMES FOR CHILDREN
POOR MANS METROPOLE
HOMES FOR MARRIED PEOPLE
LOCAL OFFICERS
MATCH-BOX MAKING
TEMPORARY WORK IN THE CITY
BAKERY
CHILDREN RESTORED TO PARENTS
POOR MANS BANK
BOYS' INDUSTRIAL HOME
INQUIRY OFFICES
PREVENTIVE HOME FOR GIRLS
SHELTERS
WOMENS NIGHT SHELTER
HOUSEHOLD SALVAGE BRIGADE
POOR MAN'S LAWYER
HOMES FOR INEBRIATES
PRISON GATE BRIGADE
CHEAP FOOD DEPOTS
LABOUR BUREAU
COMPELLING THEM TO COME IN
RESCUE HOMES
HOMES FOR THE HOMELESS
SLUM CRUSADE
THE CITY COLONY
SALVATION
PROSTITUTES
In London there are over 30,000 Prostitutes
In Great Britain 100,000.
Besides an Army of probably 100,000 more poor women who secretly increase their earnings by their shame
CRIMINALS
In Prison.... 32,000
Juvenile Thieves... 22,000.
Reputed known Thieves out of Prison 32,910.
Last Year the Cost of Police, Magistrates, &c was £500,000
155,000 passed through prisons.
& there were 711,000 Summary Convictions
DRINK
Millions of Pounds are invested in Drunkard-making Traffic in Great Britain. The Largest Fortunes in the World are made out of the Drink Traffic.. Sixty Thousand Drunkards die every Year.. What becomes of the Drunkards Children? There are Half a Million Drunkards in Great Britain.
DRINK TRAFFIC
One Hundred and Sixty Thousand Persons convicted of drunkenness in One Year.
One Hundred and Twenty Thousand Licensed Drink Shops.
One Billion Gallons of Wine, Beer & Spirits consumed every Year in Great Britain.
Drink Bill.... £136,000,000
CHARITY
Given by Public Charities £10,500,000
Approximate Amount of Private Charity £7,000,000
Yet 10,700 children died through violence or neglect last year
There are known to be 3000 Sweaters Dens in which 5000 Children are employed
DESTITUTION
In London alone
Workhouses 51,000
Asylums 33,000
Hospitals
Homeless 300,000
Starving 222,000
Next door to Starvation 387,000
Very Poor Total 993,000
THE POOR
In Great Britain there are over 100,000 poor People without any Home at all. The Poor Law cost of Pauper Relief per Annum £10,800,000
Pauper Lunatics 78,966
One out of every 5 persons in London dies either in the Hospitals Asylums or Workhouses
43,000 poor little Children go hungry to Board Schools in London
MISERY
In Workhouses 190,000
Out Door Paupers 968,000
Out of Work in London 20,000
Gt Britain 100,000
Three Millions of People in the Ocean of Misery
SUICIDES 2297 LAST YEAR
FOUND DEAD 2157 LAST YEAR
DRUNKENNESS
FORNICATION
THEFT
ADULTERY
UNCLEANNESS
GAMBLING
LYING
UNBELIEF
DECEIT
HYPOCRISY
PRIDE
HATRED
MURDER
ENVY
COVETOUSNESS
AVARICE
WANT
PRISON
BLACK MARIA
BEGGARY
RUIN
DRUNKENNESS
OUTRAGE
BETTING
MISERY
DESPAIR
HOMELESS
UNEMPLOYED
STARVATION

'Robots run Zombies for Wealthy Parasites' 2002

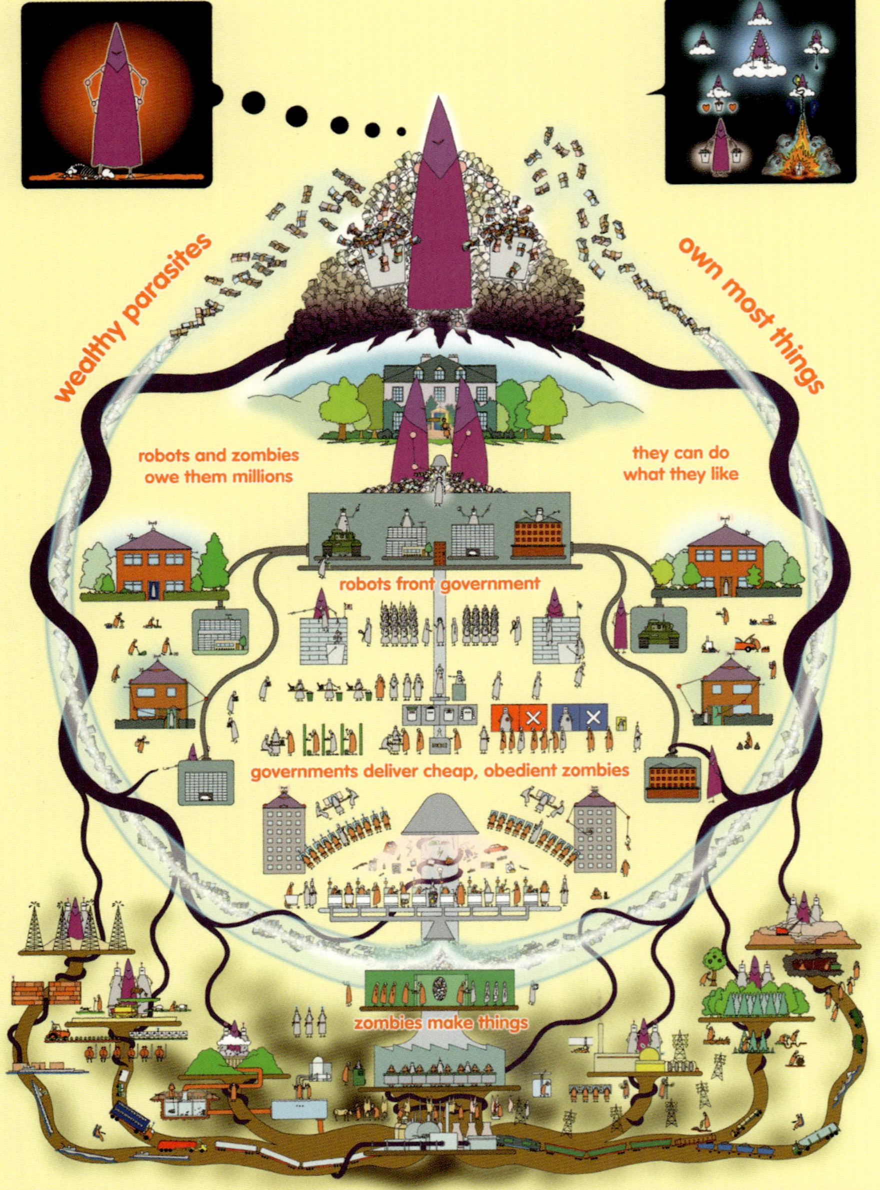

Courtesy the artist and Delaye Saltoun Gallery, London

"Power is diagrammatic."[1]
Gilles Deleuze 'The Diagram', trans. 1993

Chad McCail's work presents a schematic imagined society, which is both fantastical and eerily familiar. His work resembles Ladybird illustrations from a future society, or science-fiction cartoons from the 1950s. Despite seeming futuristic, McCail also echoes historical represents of the social structure, such as 'the great chain of being', in which every being has its place in a predetermined scheme of things. McCail's scheme here has three classes, with the higher 'parasites' "physically embodying" the social pyramid which they sit atop.
The triptych here is part of a larger sequence of 24 prints, whose colours are akin to those of medieval stained glass. The implication is that our ideas are absurd and archaic – but no less powerful for that. 'Robots run Zombies' also echoes the ideas of the earliest economists like Adam Smith and David Ricardo, who noted that there are fundamentally three classes: those who own land and property; those who manage or control production; and those who must earn a living.

1. www.ab-a.net/index.cgi?Texts/The_Diagramme

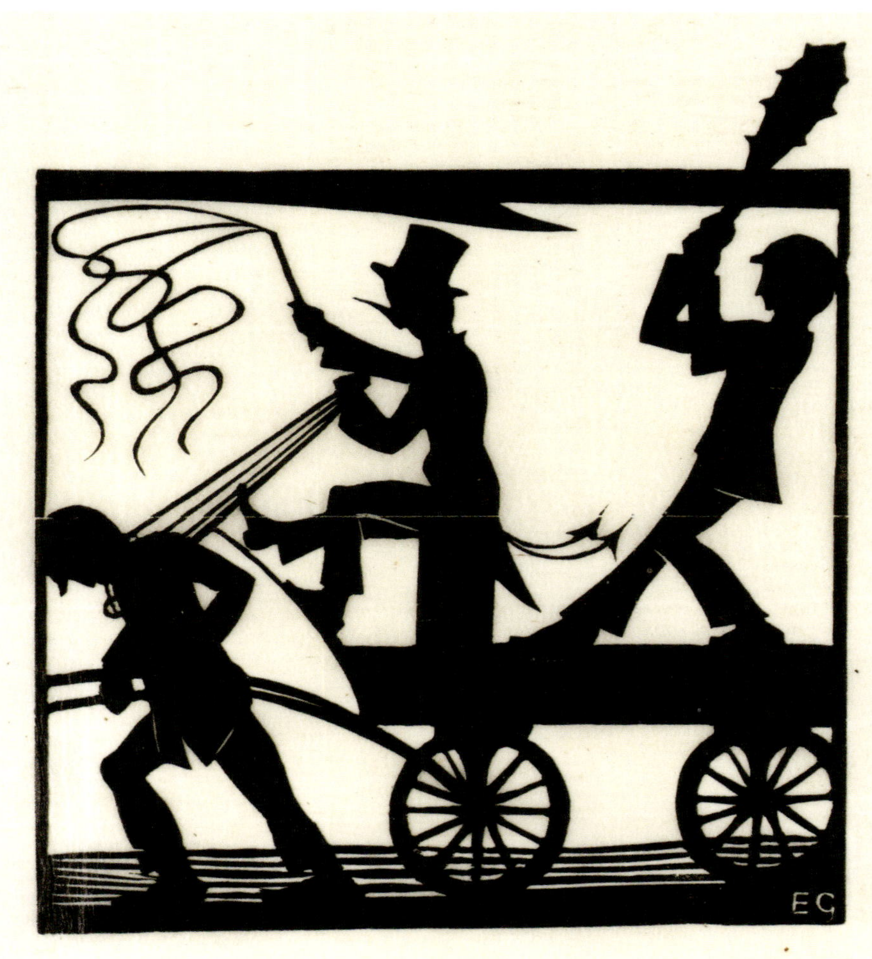

Tate, Transferred from the Library 1979

**"We have... to face the existence of a dangerous class... into which the weaker as well as the worst members of society have a continual tendency to sink.
A class which, not respecting itself, does not respect others; which has nothing to lose and all to gain by anarchy; in which the lower passion, seldom gratified, are ready to burst out and avenge themselves by frightful methods."**[1]
Charles Kingsley, 1857

At the time of Gill's print, roughly three quarters of England's population worked in manual employment or were dependent on those who did. At the same time, just 9% of the population earned half of the entire national income, with obviously little overlap. Eric Gill's print depicts the humiliation and dehumanisation of manual workers by their employers – and their revenge. Few groups in reality enacted hostilities against the social superiors. However, the metaphorical description of social groups as different animals was a commonplace. By 1915 1.5m mostly working-class men had volunteered to fight in the Great War. German troops allegedly described the relation of these heroic soldiers to their stubborn upper-class generals as that of 'lions led by donkeys'.

1. Quoted in Raban, 1974, p153

ANONYMOUS PHOTOGRAPHER

'One of Them' 1896

"The working class has been subjected to a sustained programme of social contempt and institutional erosion... the vicious circle of condescension whirls on."[1] **Ferdinand Mount, 'Mind the Gap: The New Class Divide in England', 2005**

As the historian Roy Porter has argued, "extreme distinctions in wealth were sometimes sealed by attitudes which almost denied that rich and poor came from the same species."[2] Economic and physical differences between classes in Victorian England were so pronounced that poorer groups were often described as foreign or alien. This image was made to fundraise for a church, though is scarcely sympathetic towards its imagined congregation. The accompanying text reads: "They are the poor... poor physically, mentally and spiritually – poor in strength, poor in purpose, poor in hope. It is easy to say hard things about their lack of enterprise, of forethought and of thrift... [they are] Ill-housed, ill-fed, ill-clad, void of any purpose reaching beyond the present moment – surely the sad story of their lives must blister God's book with the recording angel's bitter tears." Even aspiring social scientists like Charles Booth expressed disgust at 'the poor': "They render no useful service, they create no wealth; more often they destroy it... They degrade whatever they touch and as individuals are incapable of improvement; they may be to some extent a necessary evil in every large city."[3] The lines between 'them' and 'us' had never been more sharply defined.

1. Mount, 2005, pp273, 282
2. Porter, 1982, p50
3. Quoted in Raban, 1974, p153

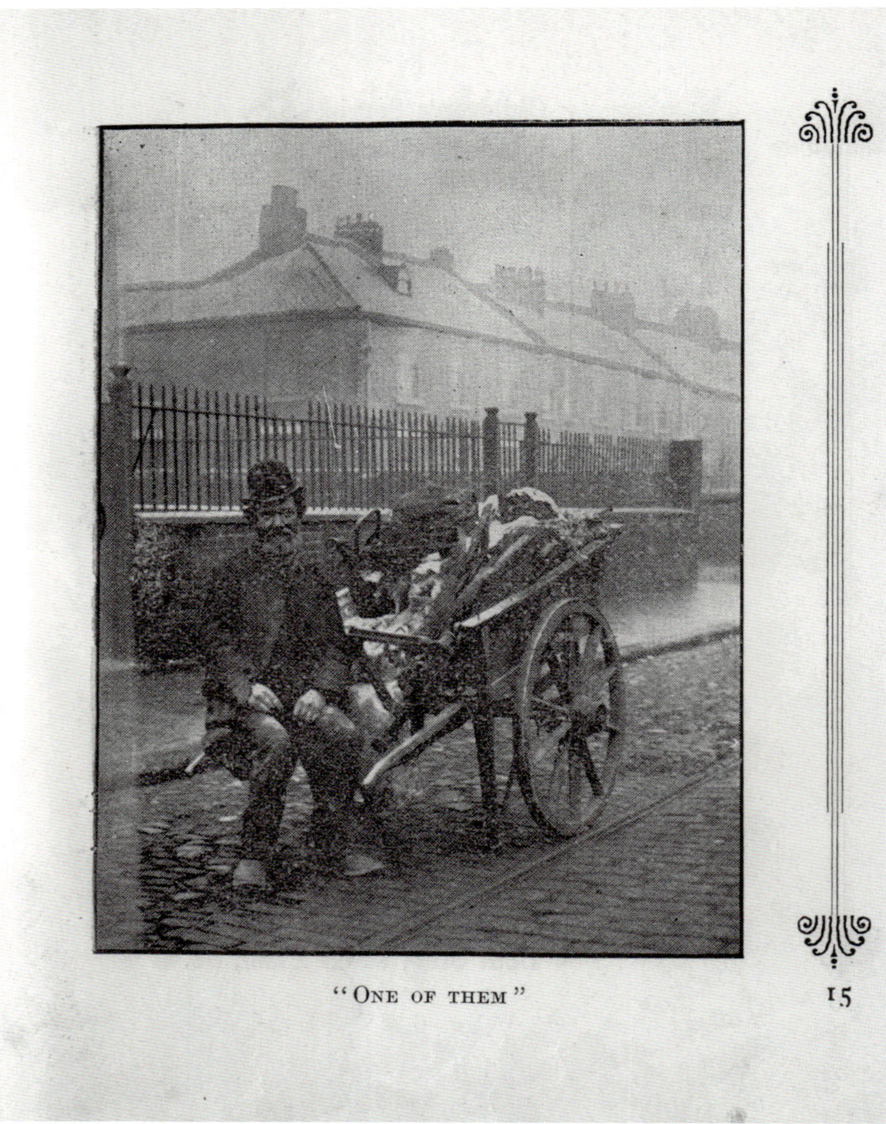

Sunderland Libraries

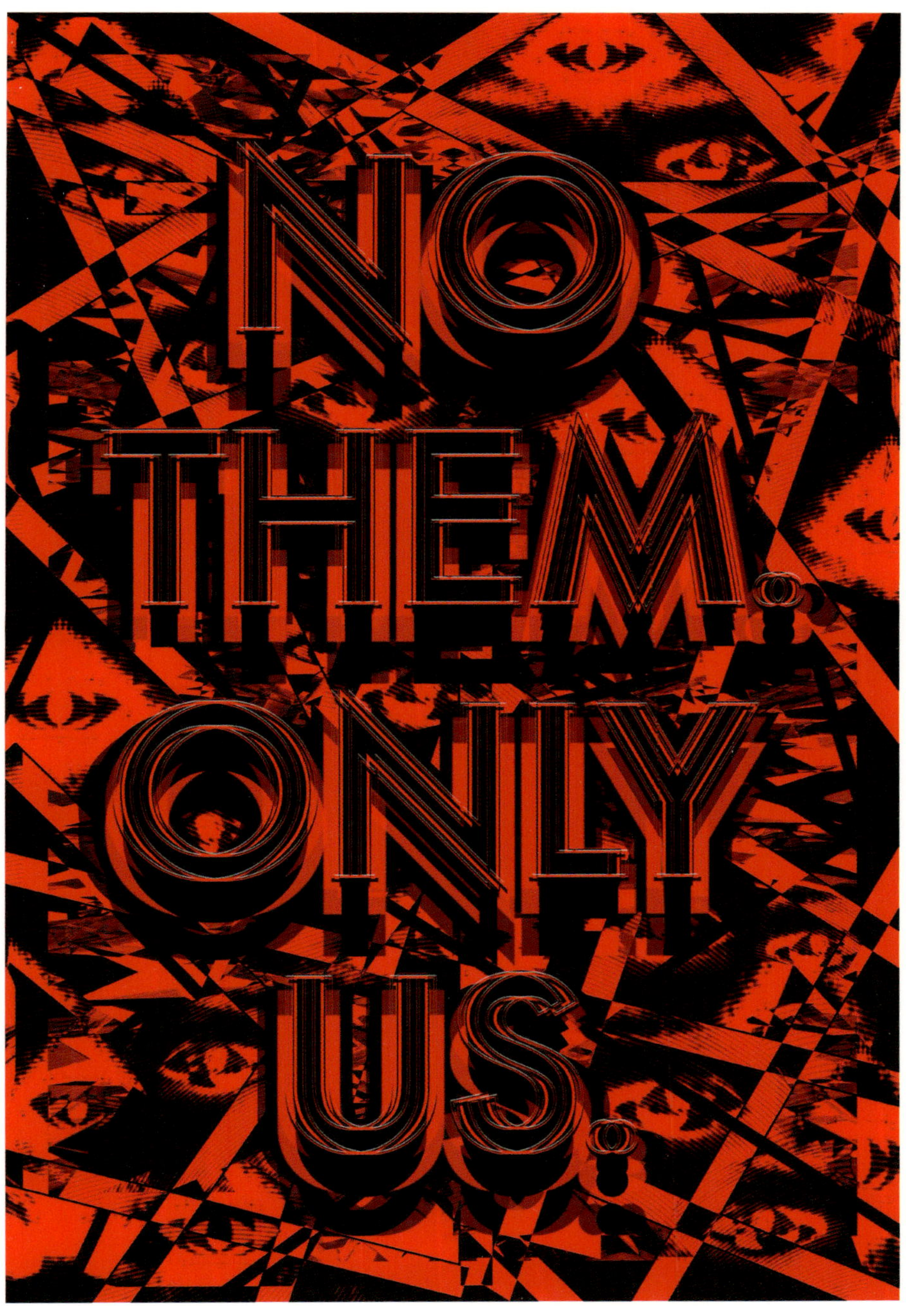

Courtesy Vilma Gold, London and Peres Projects, Berlin

"Why is difference always linked to hatred?"[1] **Samuel Taylor Coleridge**

Are we trapped in our own prejudices? Coleridge's line suggests that we are, and that social stratification results in hostility and tribalism. One of the most fundamental questions that anthropologists ask of groups is where they believe 'us' ends and 'them' begins. These terms – which have been labelled 'vague predicates' by professional philosophers – are unavoidable and essential parts of our language. Can their definitions be changed, Mark Titchner asks? The artist uses 'found' phrases from political discourse – this being from one of Bill Clinton's early speeches. For Titchner, Clinton's abnegation of progressive politics makes this an unexpected source. Secondly, the text is "empty" in his words; it can mean at least two different things, if not whatever we project onto it. Here the obvious meaning is that 'we are all co-dependent', as though extolling solidarity and fraternity. However, it might easily be a catchphrase for racist groups who would wish to exclude others from society. Titchner observes that the tipping point between one worldview and another cannot always be easily pinpointed.

1. Quoted by Sally Vickers, FT Aug 16/17 2008, Life and Arts, p14

'No Them Only Us' 2007

"Most ordinary people in England are 'rampant individualists, highly mobile both geographically and socially, market-orientated and acquisitive, [even] ego-centred'... The truth is that Britain has been an exceptionally individualistic and mobile society for generations... Britain has been a mobile society for much longer than continental Europe. What follows from that is not the absence of social distinction but, instead, a particularly finely-graded and nuanced set of patterns of living in which even the street that you live in tells a social story."[1] **David Willets, 'The Paradox of Class', 1999**

How far does our 'background' determine our chances in life? Adam Latham attempts to provide us with the tools to measure our own worldview, and is an equal opportunities offender. His provocations challenge both the preconceptions of the professionally successful and the disadvantaged, and the prejudices of both middle-class and working-class alike. Latham's position is that we can only gauge our attitudes by establishing what lie outside them. To do so, he often exaggerates myths and stereotypes to render them ridiculous or alarming, testing our credulity. He does so by recreating images distant in time, but only by two, three or four generations. His work asks us to measure our attitudes against those of our predecessors, and to ask what we imagine our own 'life-chances' are. According to Daniel Dorling social mobility has stalled in England: it is at its lowest since the 1970s. For Latham's generation, relative social positions have frozen.[2]

1. Quoting Alan MacFarlane at www.prospect-magazine.co.uk/pdfarticle.php?id=4334
2. Dorling et al, 2006

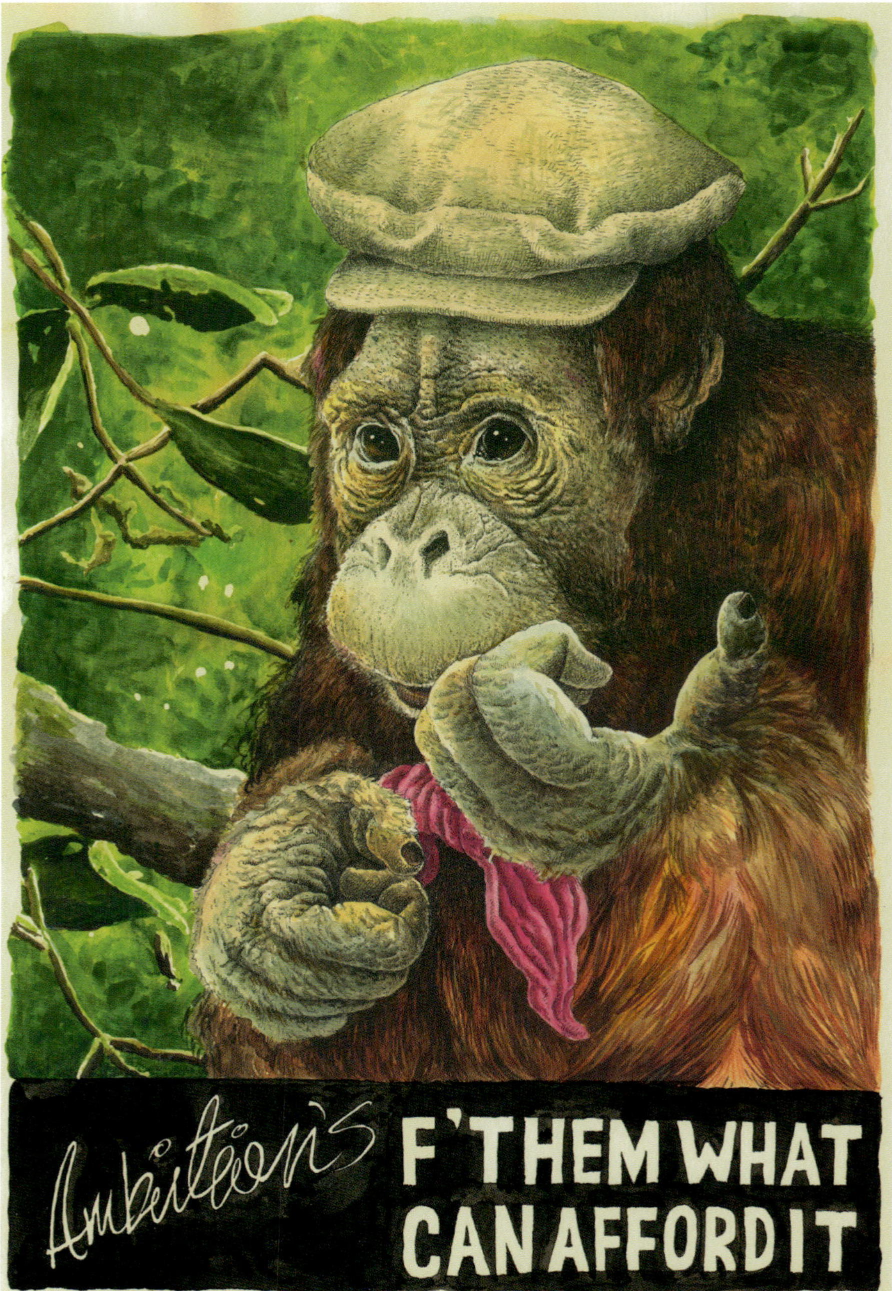

Courtesy the artist

Tate, Presented by the Patrons of New Art through the Friends of the Tate Gallery 1985

'Truisms' 1984

"We all operate to an implicit value system, an underlying belief system, a sense of what the good life entails, and an idea of how the laws and institutions of the country should be arranged." [1]
Julian Baggini, 'Welcome to Everytown', 2007

Jenny Holzer's 'Truisms' is a compendium of society's myths about itself. Almost every one of the 'truisms' can be seen to illustrate another work in 'Rank'. The work maps out the entire spectrum of political positions that we might conceivably occupy. For pessimists, or those who admire Hobbes' realpolitik, the phrase 'an elite is inevitable' might ring true. Meanwhile, Evan Holloway's 'Capital' might easily have been inspired by the truism 'disgust is the appropriate response to most situations'. Mustafa Hulusi's and Simon Bedwell's ideas are encapsulated in the phrase 'enjoy yourself because you can't change anything anyway.' Adam Latham's works proceed from the perverse position that 'low expections are good projection'. Thomas More's 'Utopia' is the ultimate expression of the sentiment that 'everyone's work is equally important'.' The International Workers of the World's capitalist pyramid articulates the principle that 'class structure is as artificial as plastic'. And Darren Cullen's work forwards the contention that 'leisure time is a gigantic smoke screen.'

1. Baggini, 2007, p3

ADAM LATHAM

'Which One Ought You Wear?' 2008

"A society must have a dominant culture. I'm in favour of hierarchical societies in which there is social mobility. We [the British] have lost the inclination for either."[1] **Norman Tebbit, 2008**

Until the late twentieth century an Englishman's social position was communicated immediately by his headwear. Headwear was a universally understood sign of both wealth and power. In the eighteenth century, the size of one's wig directly reflected one's social status and political position: indeed wigs were more expensive than paintings. In Victorian England, the height of hats signified status instantly: 'top hats' for higher groups; cloth caps for lower. Most professions also developed their own uniform including headwear. Latham's work remakes a government poster from the First World War to make us ask: how far have things changed in a century? The government's own Commission for Equality and Human Rights believes that, at the least, "disadvantages still associated with 'class' are just as deep-rooted as those associated with gender, disability and ethnicity."[2]

1. Observer Magazine, Jan 27 2008, p11
2. Richard Berthoud in 'Britain Today' (Swindon: ESRC) 2007

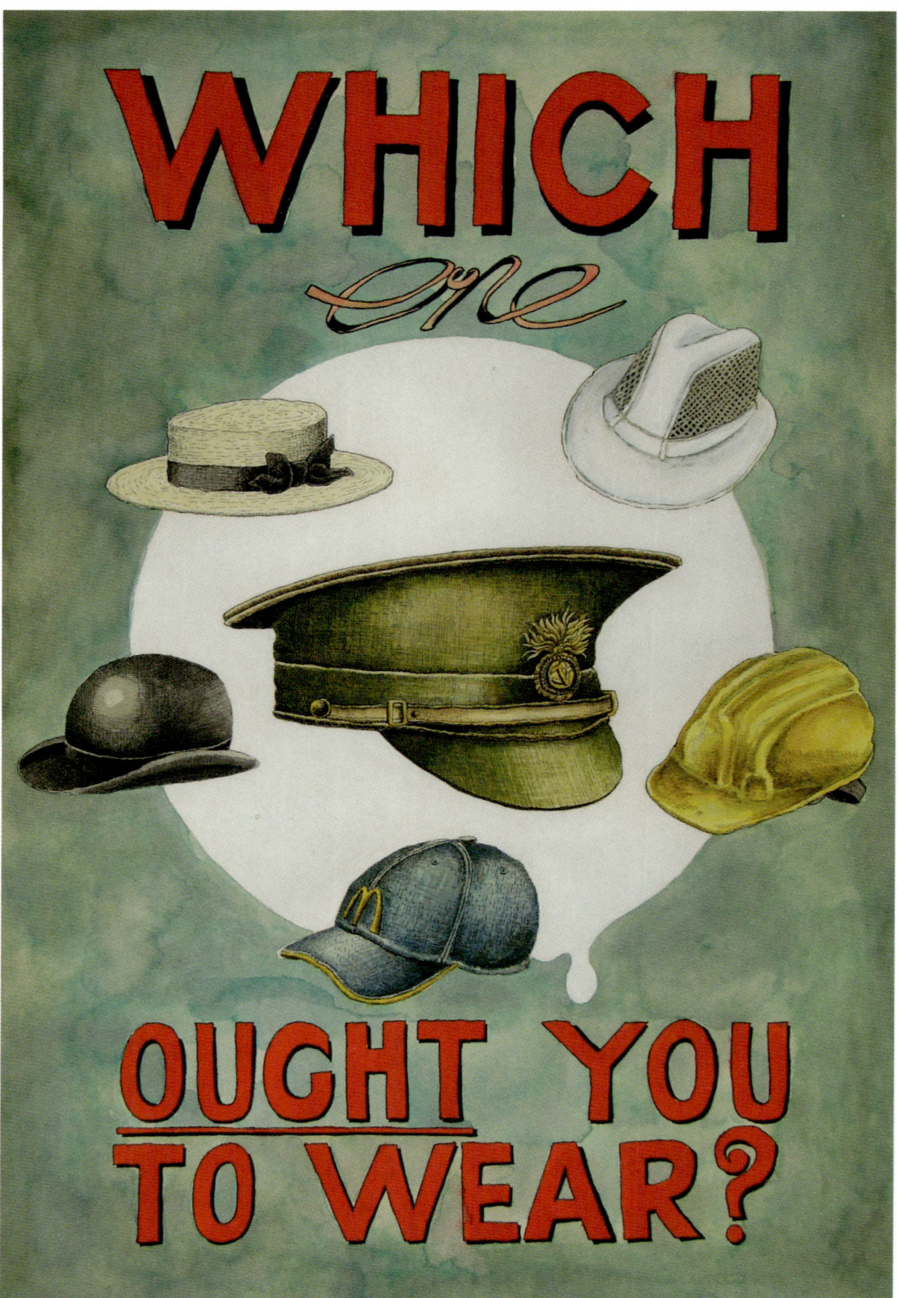

Courtesy the artist

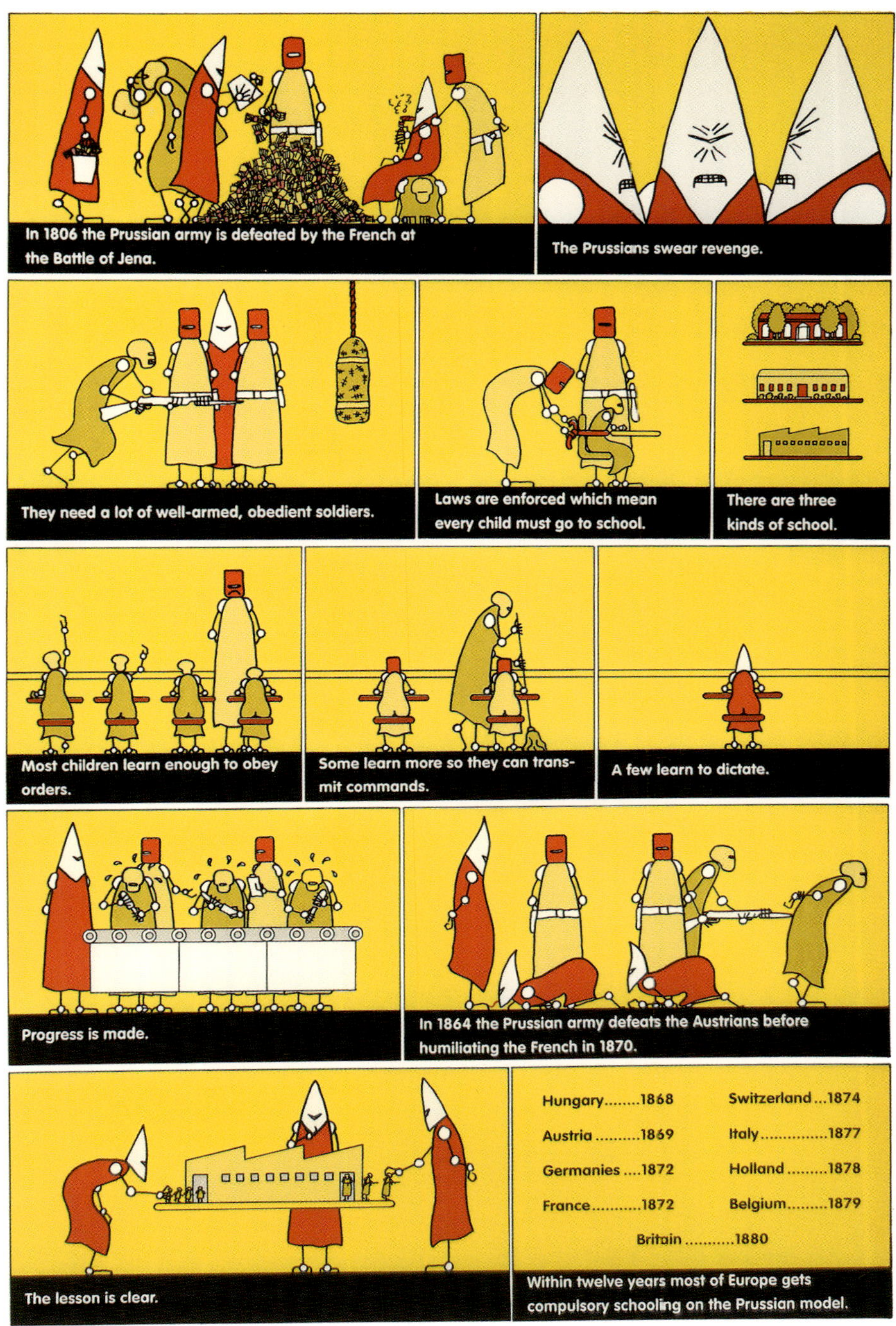

Courtesy the artist and Delaye Saltoun Gallery, London

"Society is a process. It is never static. Even its most apparently stable structures are the expression of an equilibrium between dynamic forces. For the social historian the most challenging of tasks is that of recapturing that process, while at the same time discerning long-term shifts in social organization, in social relations and in the meanings and evaluations with which social relationships are infused."[1]
Keith Wrightson, 'English Society: 1580-1680', 1982

Chad McCail's recent projects have incorporated research into the formation of the state education system across Western Europe. Several of his findings strongly suggest that the driving force behind the introduction, then extension of universal education, was to ensure military supremacy. For McCail, the role of the education system in cementing the system of three classes into being in the nineteenth century cannot be overestimated. For him, education is the means by which we acquire our position in an occupation hierarchy; the means by which we acquire the skills and social capital to participate in society at all; the way in which we are socialised – by mixing amongst our peers of similar status; and the means by which we are able to conceive of the ways in which power operates.

1. Wrightson,1982, p12

MARKUS VATER

'Spiegel lesen / Mirror Reading' 2009

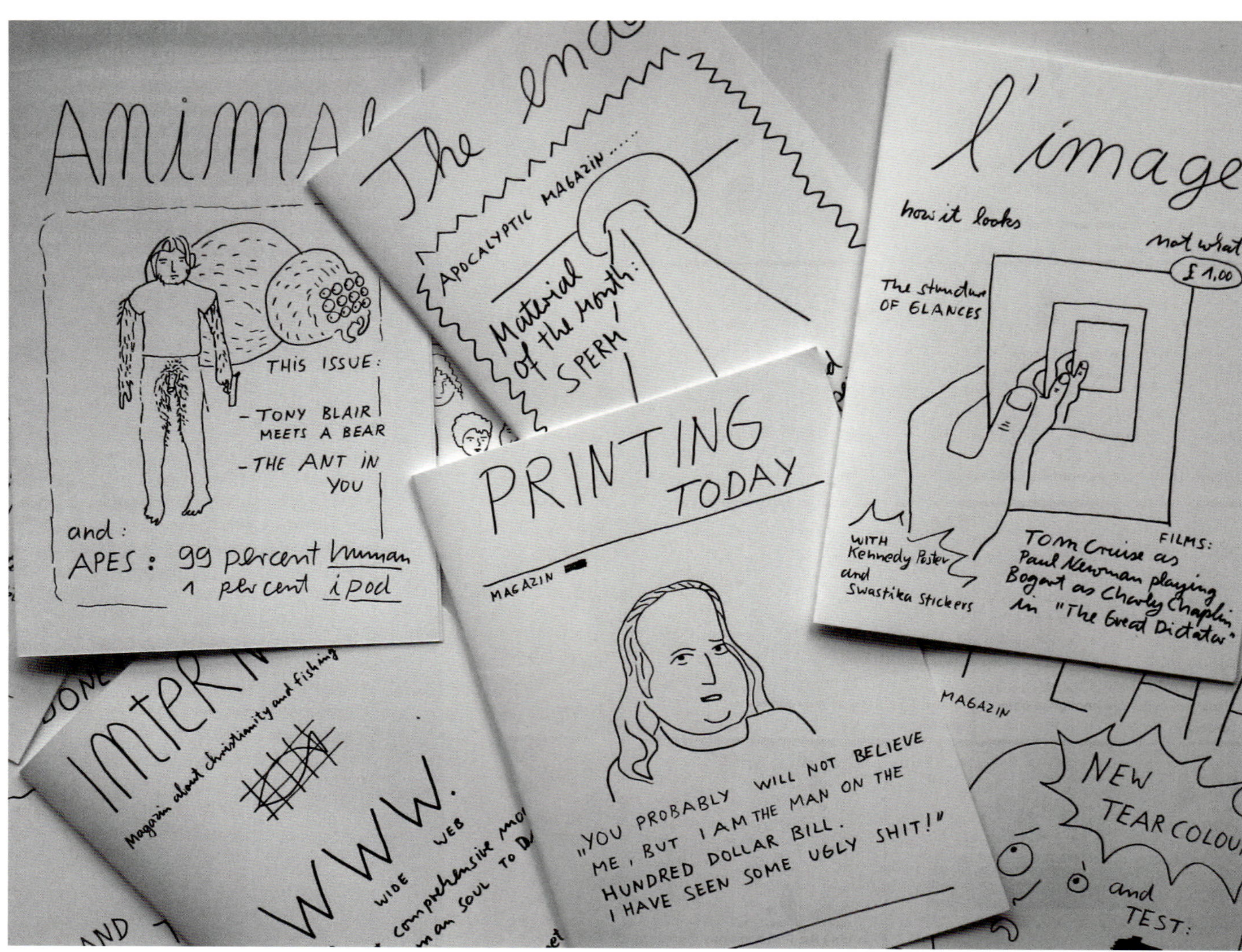

Courtesy the artist and Vilma Gold, London

"The contemporary climate favours individual aspiration rather than social solidarity or obligation."[1] Peter Wilby, The Guardian, 2006

Markus Vater has created a host of new magazines which publishers such as Emap or Condé Nast might like to consider. Vater has noted that one of the most noticeable features of the new millennium is the sea of print material that confronts us daily: ordinary newsagents stocks nearly 1000 titles, seemingly catering for every conceivable demographic group. But what if the publishing industry inadvertently had the wrong scheme of classification entirely? Vater's works propose an alternative demographic, as though a superior system of classifying society had been recently invented. His new titles also start from the recognition that most existing publications are geared towards greater 'self-realisation', than to greater knowledge of our wider society. Vater's works provide some corrective to this tendency, though do so by extrapolating individualism to a new pitch entirely.

1. Leader article, G1, June17 2006

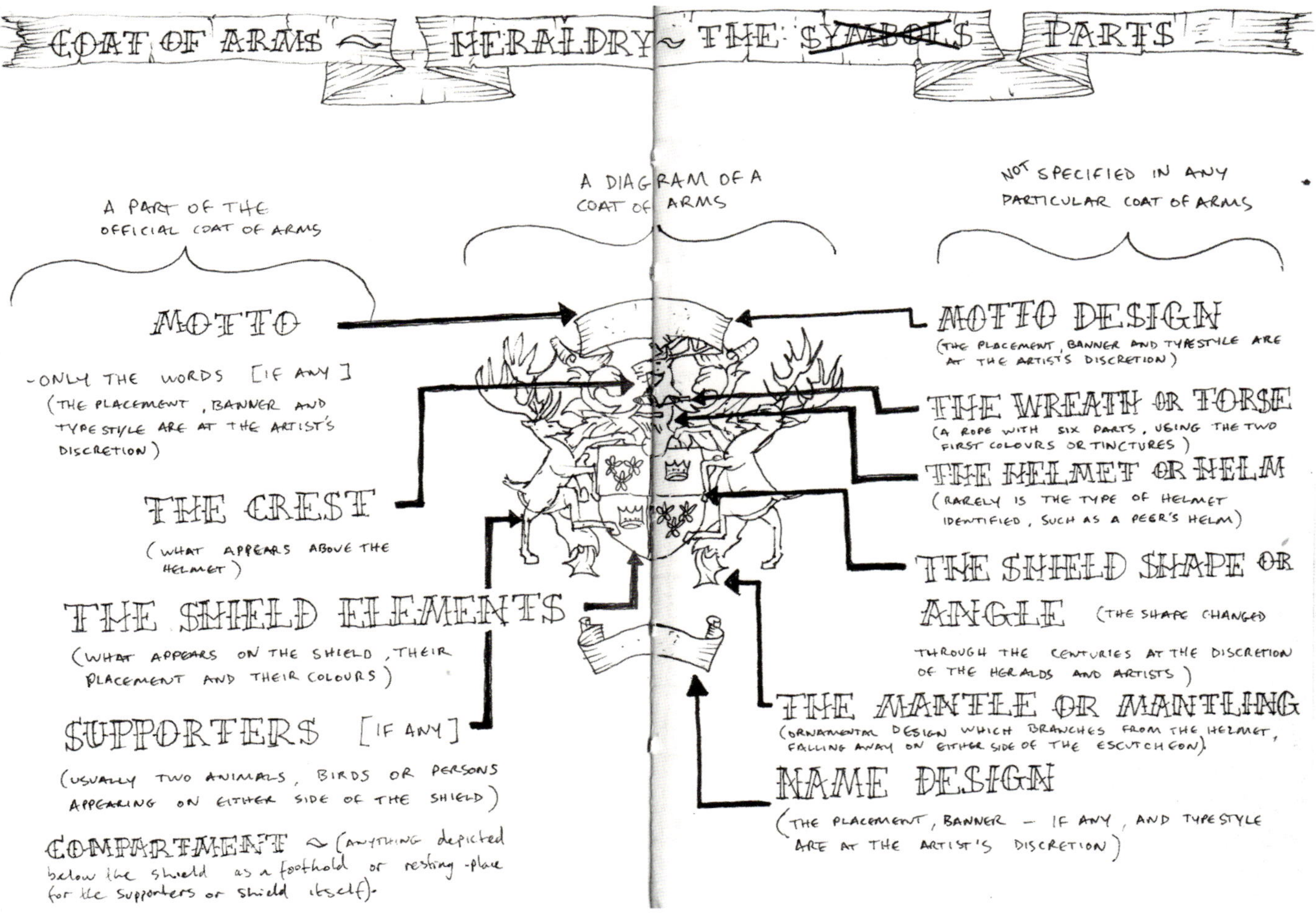

'Heraldry' 2006

Courtesy the artist and
Workplace Gallery, Gateshead

"We live under a constitutional monarchy, and under such a monarchy, an aristocracy of wealth and an aristocracy of rank are essential ingredients. It is true that aristocracies of wealth and rank exist in many other countries, but, unfortunately, there are almost impassable barriers separating them from the rest of the nation, while no such barriers exist in this country. Wealth is, to a certain extent, within the reach of all."[1]
Lord Palmerston, 1865

Ant Macari's work queries what value we accord to types of visual signs and symbols, and mixes visual languages associated with high and low status groups. Indeed he mixes visual languages from distant periods and social positions, combining medieval scrollwork with modern tattooing. Here, his work links medieval heraldry, preserved for families able to establish their 'noble' bloodline, Italian baroque scrollwork, and tattoo artists' insignia. At one time, the ability to decipher the former was restricted to higher social strata. Over time, they have become the latter: the currency of proletarian or 'vulgar' groups like sailors. Finally, such visual signs – as tattoos – became the signs of bourgeois rebellion. How, then, can we confidently ascribe status to any visual language?

1. In Illustrated London News, 8 April 1865, P235-6

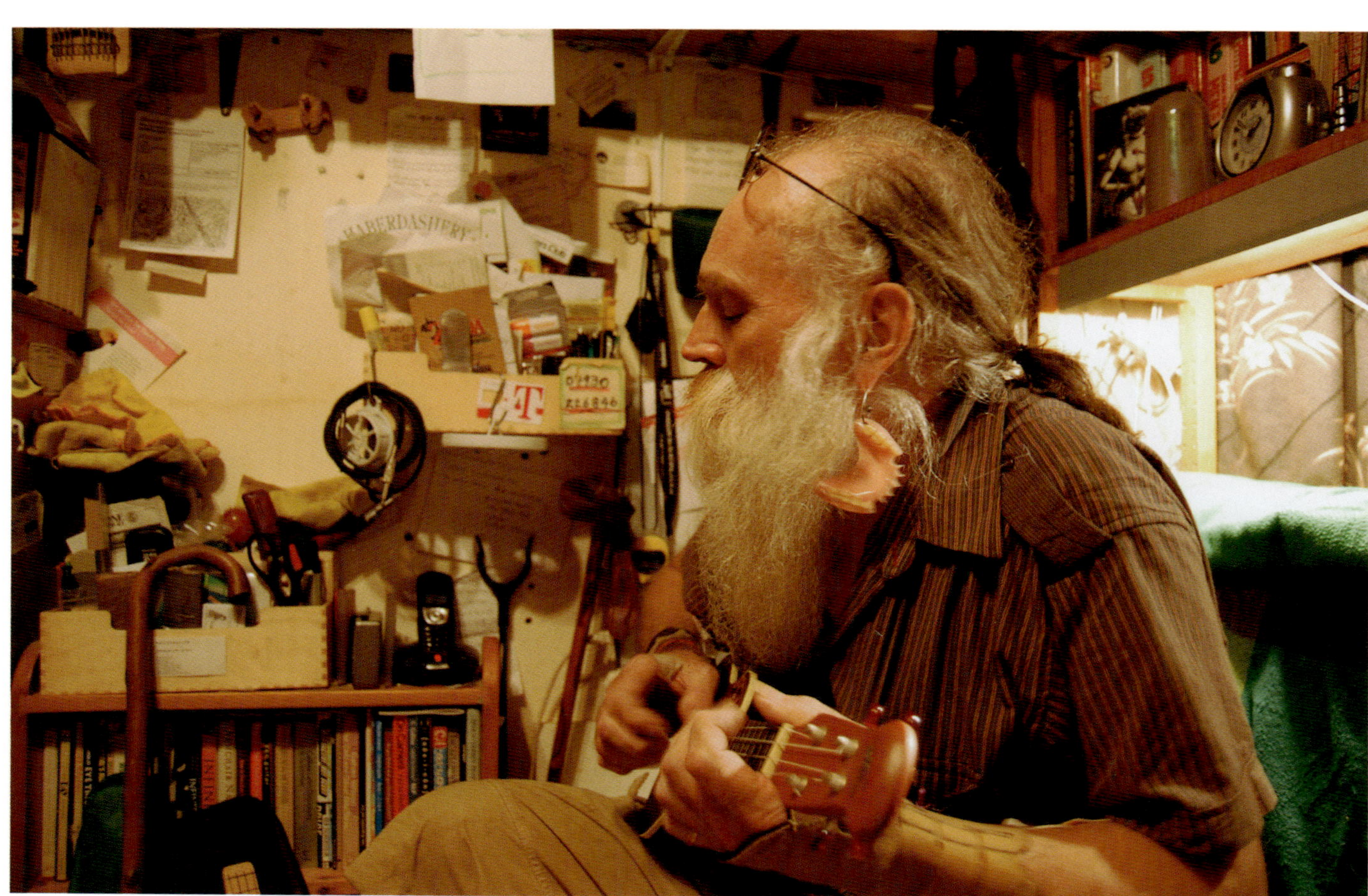

Courtesy the artist and Ancient and Modern, London

"Britain is a thoroughly modern society, with thoroughly archaic institutions, conventions, and beliefs."[1]
Stein Ringen, 'The Open Society and the Closed Mind', 1997

How could we distribute countercultural messages outside the official or dominant systems of communication? Ruth Ewan's work could be described using the title of a publication from the 1640s: 'Vox Plebis'. She re-uses the media used by subordinate social groups in the past, to bring back to life some of their alternative ideas about the social order. The video 'Six Feet of Earth' features the busker and actor known as 'Fang'. Fang plays a lullaby his father sang to him at bedtime as a child, where the lyrics are akin to those of a dark nursery rhyme. This lullaby takes the traditional 'vanitas' theme seen in the 'tree of life' elsewhere here, though adds a dark twist. The lyrics celebrate death, for its ability to level the differences between the rich and the poor. The song represents a set of political beliefs long lost to history. The artist's work is based on the fact that, whereas modern bourgeois culture is a 'literate' culture, working-class and agrarian cultures have often been oral ones, where messages are transmitted verbally through story or song. The historian Roy Porter has argued that songs were the primary means that ordinary people could create alternative pictures of what the shape of society should be: "the vox populi filtered its demands through the sympathetic magic of slogans, riddles, grattifi, effigies, songs".[2]

1. Quoted in Cannadine, 'The Rise and Fall of Class in Britain', 1999 (New York: Columbia UP), p xi
2. Porter, 1982, p103

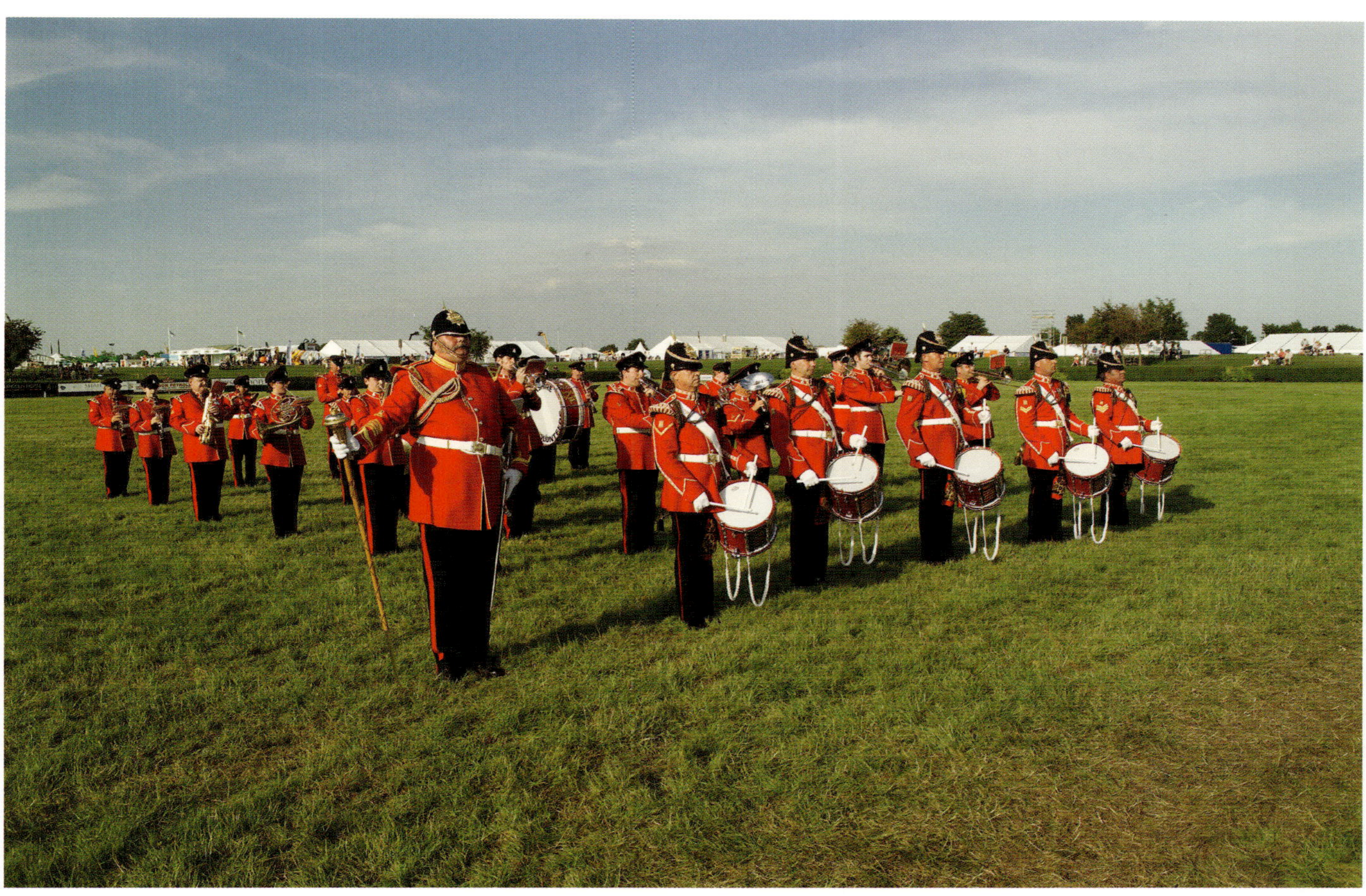

'Re-enactment #3' 2009

Courtesy the artist

"Classical rhetoricians had a catalogue of technical terms for... false starts, mistakes, repetitions, digressions and self-critical reflections... [such as] apoplanesis and aposiopesis." [1]
David Lodge, 2008

The Russian critic Mikhail Bakhtin argued that carnivals are sanctioned anarchy, clearly marked in time and space, and used by those in power as a pressure valve to forestall real revolt. Rory Macbeth's work combines symbols of the status quo and those of anarchy or carnival in unexpected ways. His work here has, in his words, "an ambivalent resonance with the way society's structure functions." Here, we encounter a marching band, who repeatedly strike up a march only for it to quickly disintegrate. The band re-assemble and start again, only for their music to disintegrate once again. In one sense Macbeth's work is an experiment in failure, or mismatched expectations. Here, he makes use of the classical rhetorical device of 'aposiopesis': where a speech is deliberately broken off in mid-flow, and left unfinished, so we have to imagine what would follow. The work is a series of 'false starts' to marching songs. Each is a kind of heroic failure, where the first few bars are played perfectly, before stopping abruptly. As Samuel Beckett said, fail again – fail better. The band genuinely do practice like this in private – though never in public. Their graft and repetition are restaged publically as a fine-tuned display. The band are, then, a microcosm of the wider society – they organise themselves and nominate their leaders, and have to perform in harmony to function at all. The brass band is, of course, a metaphor for our wider society: their structure of leadership and rank and file mirrors ours. Moreover, they create their social identities through performance, ritual and ceremony; they repeat this ad infinitum; and they announce their group identity whilst having very clearly defined individual roles.

1. Guardian Saturday Review, Nov 22 2008, P3

BENRIK LTD

'Mainstream Day' 2007

Courtesy the artists

Mainstream Day

Stop rocking the boat! Today make sure your tastes and actions don't clash with those of 95% of the population.

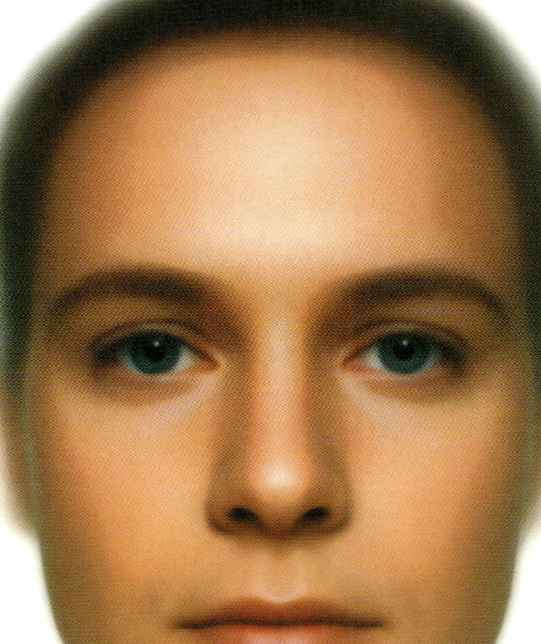

Music

Listen to Celine Dion's "The Colour of My Love" followed by "Love Doesn't Ask Why". Repeat until you know the words.

Clothes

Plain jeans and a T-shirt (nondescript) if you're under 40, chequered shirt and beige slacks if you're 40+.

Shoes

Purchase white trainers from a widely-marketed brand, from the less fancy end of the range. Size (UK): 5-7 (women) 7-10 (men).

Hobbies

Enjoy the following for half an hour each: reading, walking, listening to music, gardening.

Sex

Have sex with a partner of the opposite gender, to include: 5 minutes of foreplay, 10 minutes of missionary position, 1 orgasm (men), 1 fake orgasm (women).

Politics

Express overall agreement with the free market, but wish there was a cuddlier alternative.

Art

Buy an Impressionist post-card (Manet or Monet) and send it to a distant relative.

Sport

Support a football team, and derive much-needed emotional strength from your unspoken bond with other supporters.

Television

Yes please!

Dreams

Dream of paying off the mortgage, landing that promotion, and taking out the neighbourhood with an AK-47 machine gun.

"Despite received opinion to the contrary, England's culture remains predominantly working class. Talk of embourgeoisement is grossly exaggerated."[1]
Julian Baggini, 'Welcome to Everytown', 2007

One way to visualize the shape of society is to imagine its 'midpoint', by asking what the most commonly held ideas are. What does an 'average' Briton believe in? Benrik give voice to attitudes normally unspoken but utterly familiar, suggesting that if we were 'averaged out' these ideas would remain. The strangely ageless, genderless face is a "mathematically accurate portrait" – a composite from 225 different faces layered over one another. They ask us to think: how far away are we from this boringly median position? Carey and Delehag's work recalls that of philosopher Julian Baggini who asked where "everytown" would be – where the most typical postcode is. The research firm CACI Ltd calculated that the postcode whose population reflects the distribution of people nationally most accurately is S66, outside Sheffield and Rotherham.

1. Baggini, 2007, p64

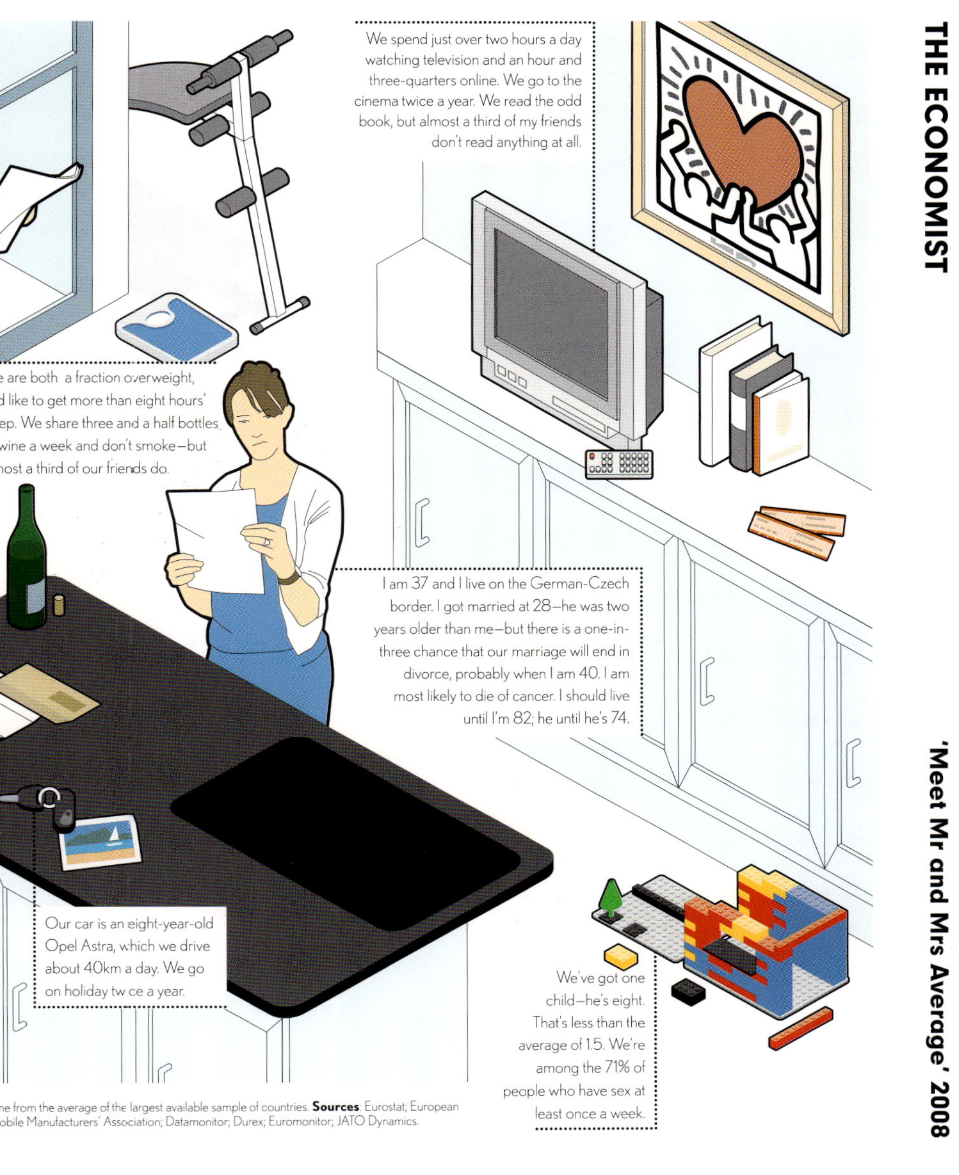

Where possible, statistics refer to the EU27 or the EU25. Otherwise they come from the average of the largest available sample of countries. **Sources**: Eurostat; European Commission; European Interactive Advertising Association; European Automobile Manufacturers' Association; Datamonitor; Durex; Euromonitor; JATO Dynamics.

artwork by Ciaran Hughes
Courtesy The Economist and the artist www.ciaranhughes.com

"Most people think they are average when asked. In most things most are not. Most say they are normal, but our atlas shows that what is normal changes rapidly as you travel across the social topography of human identity in Britain."[1]
Professor Daniel Dorling and Dr Bethan Thomas, 'Identity in Britain', 2007

As economic agents, are we Europeans or Britons first and foremost? In economic terms, we are tied to our neighbours more than we might think. The Economist and Ciaran Hughes attempted to picture a couple who embody the average demographic when looking across all 27 EU member states and some 300 million people. Through statistical comparisons they determined what incomes, occupations, hobbies and other forms of status such a couple would have. The Economist's modern 'everyman' and 'everywoman' are contented and materially prosperous, if somewhat dull.

1. Dorling et al, 2007, at www.policypress.org.uk www.policypress.org.uk

NINA BEIER / MARIE LUND

'The Way' 2007

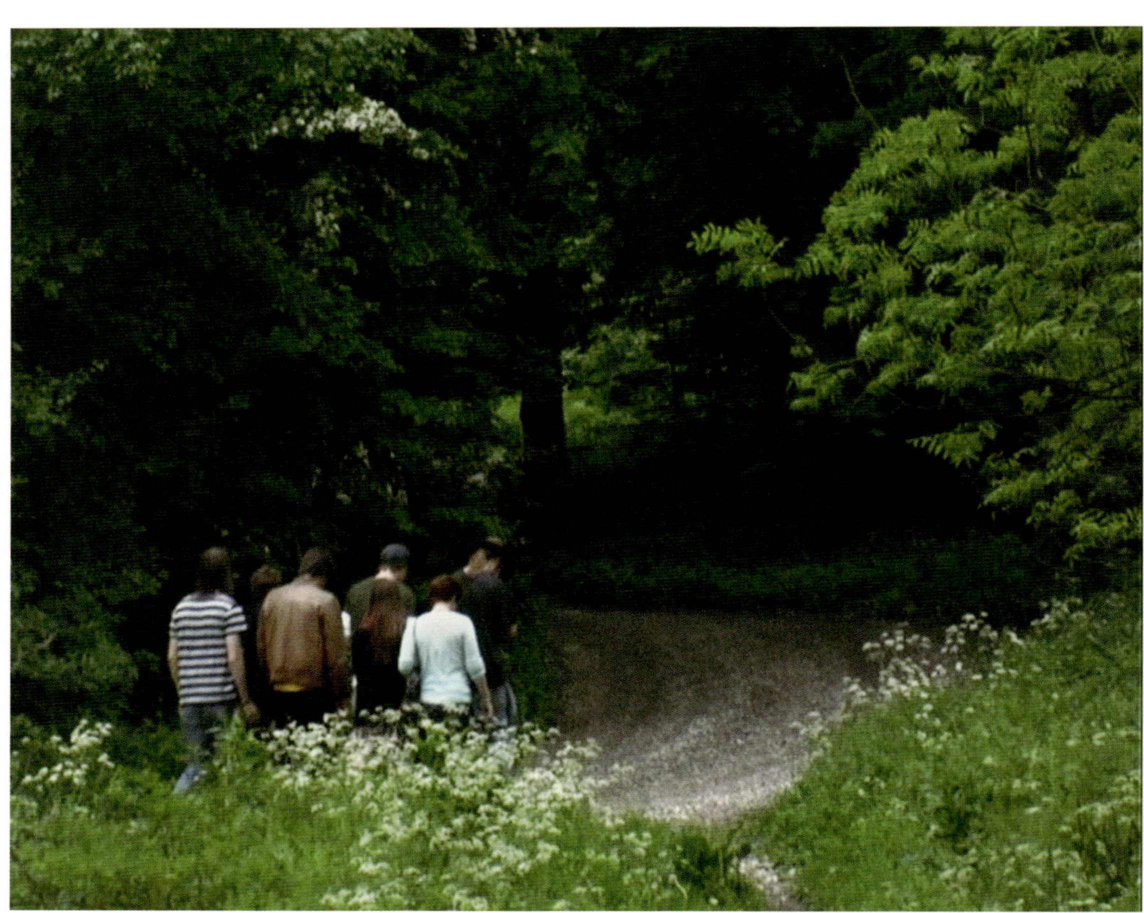

Courtesy the artists and Laura Bartlett Gallery, London

"Contemporary economists and political scientists often take if for granted that... human beings are essentially self-interested creatures... before the 20th century philosophers... did not conclude this at all... Individuals will have good reason to co-operate in most circumstances, because it is obvious that the benefits of the group for the individual depend on the contribution of the individual to the group."[1]
David Runciman, 2008

'The Way' is an experiment in seeing how groups create systems of co-operation or competition, which are often barely even visible. The video asks us to try to see how a group can make collective decisions that all members can follow. It presents a pastoral scene in which a bunch of teenagers are walking as if synchronised. They were asked to walk as a unit, at exactly the same pace, to all move in the same direction simultaneously, and to do so without speaking or looking at one another.
Taller and shorter members had to adjust their normal rhythm to create an average speed rather than following their own pace. The group is one in which fraternity and solidarity are the guiding values, and everyone ensures that they are all equal. When the path bifurcates, each member also had to anticipate which way the others would go. The work is, then, an allegory of how societies collectively decide on what political direction they should move in.

1. David Runciman, 'Why Not Eat an Éclair?' London Review of Books, Oct 9 2008, pp11-13

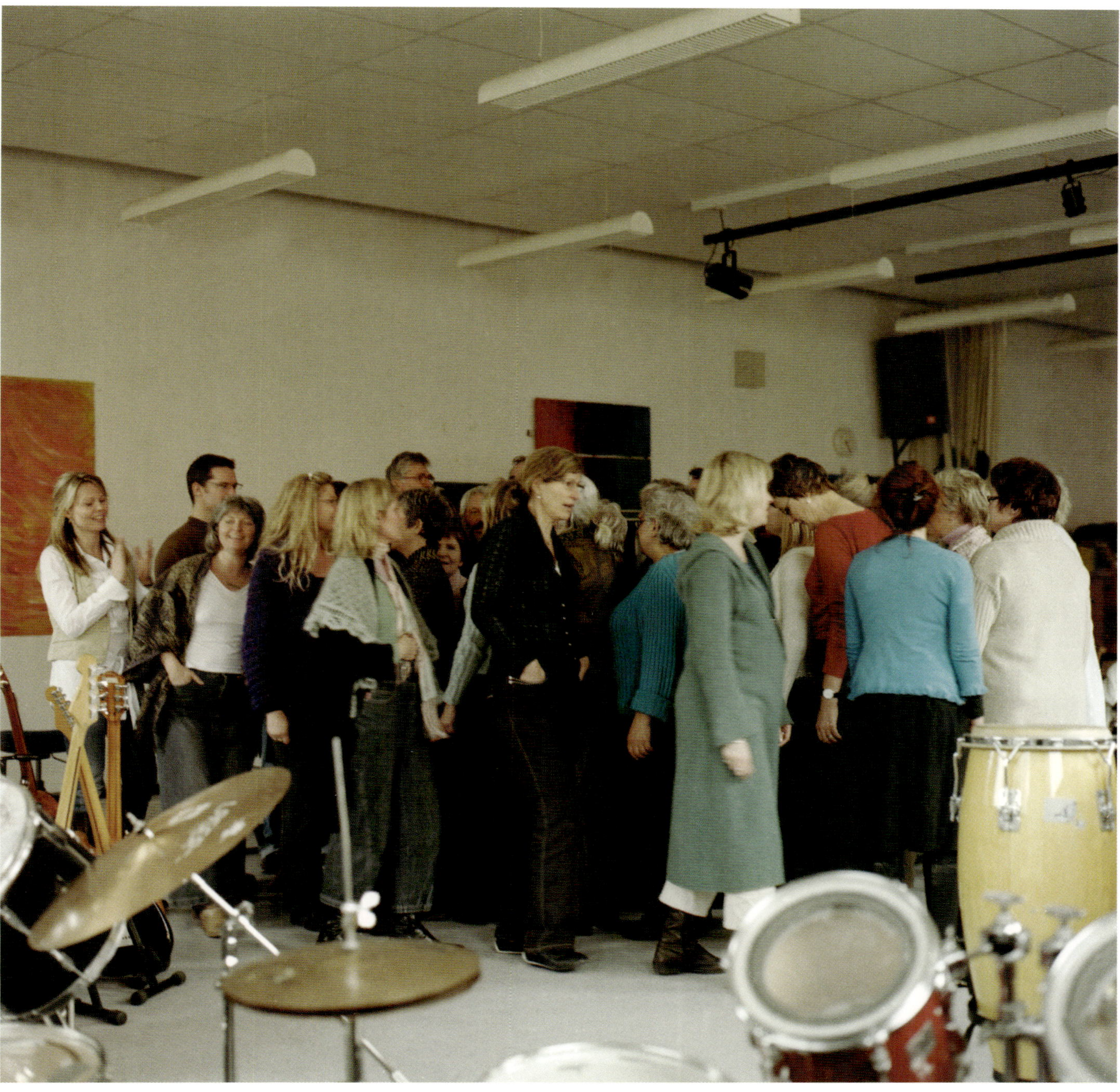

NINA BEIER / MARIE LUND

'The Most Outstanding' 2006

Courtesy the artists and Laura Bartlett Gallery, London; work here from series of 16.

"Every nation has its custom of dividing people into classes."[1]
James Nelson, 1753

Beier and Lund's works are experiments in how groups function. 'The Most Outstanding' is an allegory of how democracy functions and how sets of social relations come into being. The artists asked groups of people to order themselves hierarchically from most to least 'outstanding' to be photographed. This deliberately ambiguous term offers freedom for interpretation and manoeuvre. The bottom line is, however, that some must always be least 'outstanding' and others most, and all must subscribe to the hierarchy created. There are different ways in which outstanding is interpreted: some visible, like height; others not readily apparent. Lund and Beier's work can also be seen as a commentary on the politics and 'reward structure' both of society at large and the 'star system' of their own profession. The artists' implied question is: might there be an alternative, more equitable way of organising our patterns of cultural production?

1. Quoted in Cannadine, 1998, p102

GEORGE CRUIKSHANK

'Bank Restriction Note' 1819

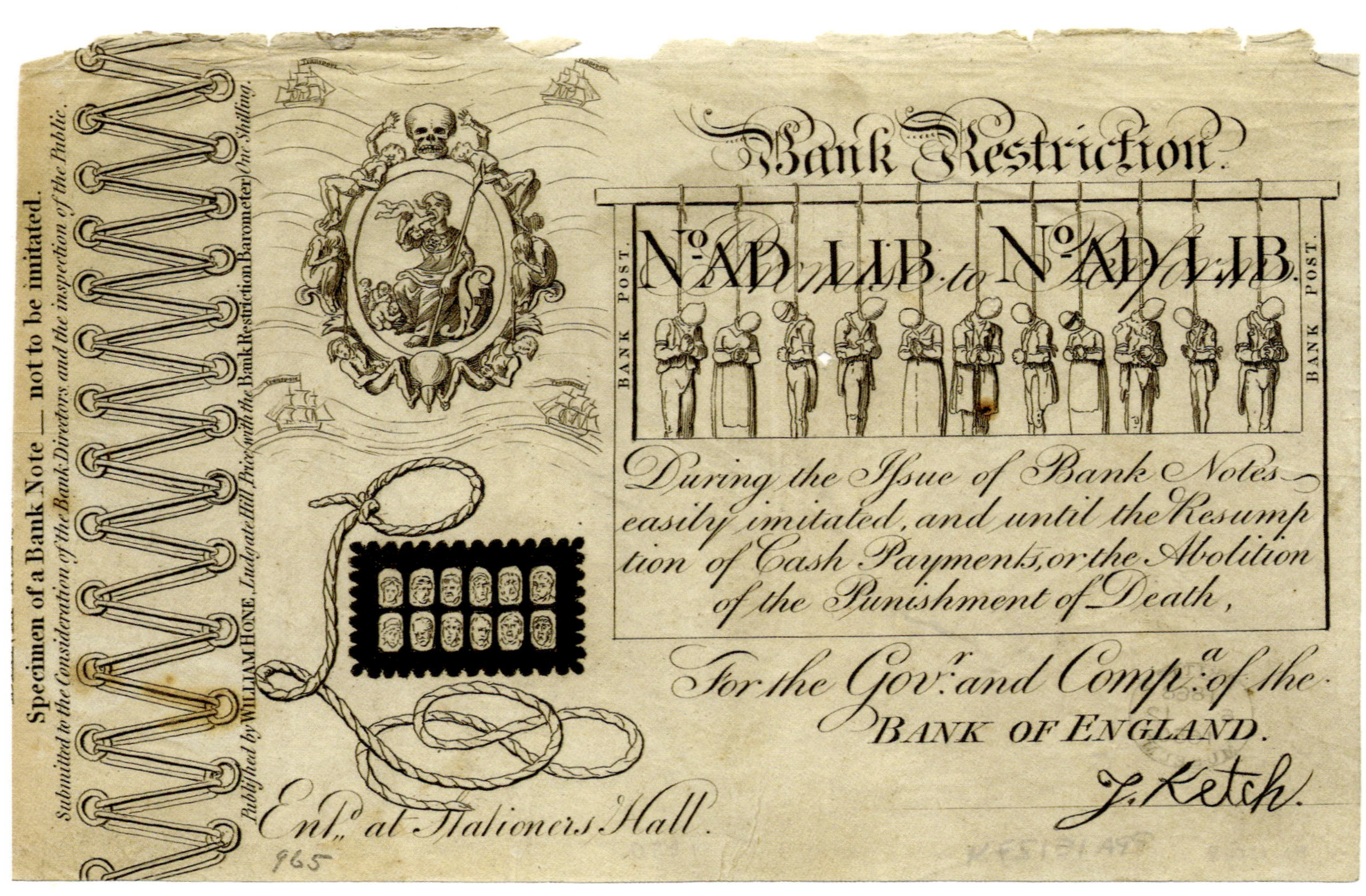

(1894 reproduction) Private collection

"Poverty is a most necessary and indispensable ingredient in society, without which nations and communities could not exist in a state of civilization." [1]
Patrick Colquhoun, founder of the Thames Police, 1798

This is one of the very few artworks to have ever helped bring about a change in the law. 'Britannia' is the oldest known symbol of the nation, and the term the Romans' used for the nation. The earliest known image of 'Britannia', as a female draped warrior is from as early as 130AD, on a coin issued by Emporer Hadrian. Britannia is normally a female warrior who represents the British State, armed with a sword and shield against hostile nations. Here, the warrior turns against her own: Cruikshank transforms Britannia into a monstrous cannibal, devouring her own children head first.

Cruikshank's image of the social structure is of the State feeding off the body of 'the people.' His work was made in protest at the cruelty of the Georgian penal code. At the time, merely handling forged banknotes was officially punishable by death. At the same time, the Bank of England, which was still a private company, could not supply enough notes for a growing population and a growing economy. Forged notes became commonplace. Cruikshank made the print in protest when a group of women were hanged for handling forged one pound notes. The print focussed popular outrage and made Cruikshank an artistic celebrity. His campaign helped reduce the penalty for forgery to imprisonment. He later described this work as "the great event of my artistic life".

1. Quoted in Porter, 1982, p133

PICTURING THE SOCIAL PANORAMA:

'OBSERVATION AND CLASSIFICATION'

"When Britons have tried to make sense of the unequal social worlds they have inhabited ... they have usually come up with versions of these same three basic and enduring models: the hierarchical view of society as a seamless web; the triadic version with upper, middle and lower collective groups; and the dichotomous, adversarial picture, where society is sundered between 'us' and 'them'."[1]

David Cannadine, 'Class in Britain', 1998

"The social diversity of the city which so delighted the 18th century citizen has during the course of the 20th, multiplied to such an extent that no overview is possible."[2]

Jonathan Raban, 'Soft City', 1974

How do we visualise the different constituent groups of our society and their relations? This section of the exhibition brings together those who have attempted to picture their entire society, or take a cross-section through it. How many groups should we subdivide the nation into to make sense of it? Any attempt to make a 'panoramic' picture of society will have to go beyond the binary or tripartite models David Cannadine outlines above. As the social anthropologist Kate Fox has written, "the real-life ways in which the English think about social class and determine a person's position ... bear little relation either to simplistic three-tier models, or to the rather abstract alphabetical systems based entirely on occupation."[3]

The earliest scheme here is Gregory King's 1688 account of England's wealth and social groups: King divided English society in 26 ranks and degrees, which is more subtle than memorable. Shortly after, Daniel Defoe proposed a seven-tier classification from "the great" at the top to "the miserable" at the bottom. The two most fully developed systems, the one used by government for censuses called NS-SEC, and the 'A' to 'E' scheme developed by the marketing industry, have some overlaps. Indeed in recent years researchers have attempted to map one onto the other.

Part of this section profiles several eminent Victorians' attempts to make sense of their new world, of innumerable new professions and social groups. It includes both single images and monumental series or cycles of prints which seen together create a typology. Depicting such scenes required powers of observation and novel schemes of classification. In such pictures, it is though all the world is a stage, and the cityscape a spectacle in which we all take part. Picture-makers also had to make imaginative use of contemporary locations where different classes might plausibly meet. Artists such as George Bernard O'Neill represented the public spaces of museums and art galleries when they were brand new to most cities. The short texts that follow draw upon brand new research into who attends these institutions today, and what 'the public' might be now.

1. Cannadine, 1998 pp19-20
2. Raban, 1974, p129
3. Fox, 2004, p93

'MATTERS OF RANK'

'Rank' assembles things which might not otherwise enter the same room or keep each other company. The exhibits, representing categories such as frontispieces, hand-coloured prints, cartoons, diagrams, statistical diagrams, magazine illustrations, maps, advertisements, paintings, photographs, computer printouts and graffiti have arrived from other times and spaces. Some are on loan from archives and museums, some come from the hands of contemporary artists, others from the periodical press (present and past) and there are some whose original context is a textbook, an atlas or a university lecture. The exhibition cuts across received categories which keep things apart in our everyday consciousness: high versus low, art versus commerce, universal versus ephemeral, academic versus practical, serious versus frivolous and private versus public. The invites questions about social ranking because it brings together so many different ways of imagining, depicting, endorsing and challenging social hierarchies, past and present.

It is sometimes said that English people are adept at placing and classifying each other, but they are far from unique in that respect. Social inequality is universal; it characterizes all known human societies and all societies must, if they are to endure, provide answers to the question: why are power and privilege distributed as they are within the social order? Answers have taken various historical forms which have given rise to different ways of ranking people and imagining the social order. The theme of this exhibition is that visual depictions mediate the relationship between self and society: as art works, cartoons, illustrations and as diagrams, they are a means by which the social structure is internalized and incorporated as a person's frame of reference, whether it be feudal or capitalist, aristocratic or meritocratic, conservative or socialist.

Feudal lords, entrepreneurs and bankers do not exercise the same kinds of power. Their identities arise from differing patterns of human association and social ranking. The earliest images shown here imagine a world of estates, of people whose lives are lived through the medium of their rank and where power is incarnate in lords, rulers and their families. The 'Rhetorica Christiana' of 1579 and John Goddard's 'The Tree of Man's Life' of 1638 both depict enclosed estates where rank is sanctioned according to a 'great chain of being' and where individual social mobility, whilst not unknown, is not celebrated as the basis for a social order. Because the bonds of a feudal society are quite different to those of a capitalist one they are linked to different ways of imagining the social order. They are also tied to different ways of 'pulling' rank, of asserting one's own social position or cultural capital over others. Goddard's depiction of men as "the like, and unlike" pictures a world in which people improve themselves within their ascribed rank and according to particular criteria, whereas our world is predicated on the idea that improvement can occur in relation to 'universal' criteria such as measured IQ and educational performance.

The master narrative of 'Rank' is of an historical transition from an estate society to a market society, from a pre-modern world of personalized power in which the reproduction of privilege is visible, to a modernity in which the reproduction of privilege has become relatively opaque and impersonal.
The compulsion to rank others often arises from the uncertainties of modernity. Modernization, understood as a long-term process of historical change in which the fixed hierarchies of traditional dissolved, transformed work by turning it into paid employment and stigmatizing those who could not or would not work. Dignity, which is never far from rank, changed its currency. The sociologist Zygmunt Bauman observes:

"Ranks were 'lower' or 'higher' well before the advent of modernity. So were their ways of life. Yet they were seen as separate entities, to be prevented rather than encouraged to come into direct contact with each other – each being viable in its own right and dependent but on itself for its own reproduction. 'Superiority' of one rank over another... was hence a category of comparison, and not a concept standing for a specific task the 'superior' rank bore in relation to other ways of life. Such a task, on the other hand, is the essence of the thoroughly modern idea of 'hegemony': the role of the 'superior' way of life and its carriers as the moral mentor, missionary and pattern to be followed by all the others... "[1]

A pivotal image in the exhibition is Abraham Bosse's seventeenth century frontispiece to Thomas Hobbes 'Leviathan'. Hobbes has long been an important point of departure for thinking about social order because social scientists have taken 'society' to be a functional solution to the problem of his 'state of nature'.
Bosse's image is significant because of the reciprocity it establishes between the gaze of the Leviathan and that of the people. The commanding presence of the central figure is 'traditional' in its iconography, and in its demonstration of power-incarnate in the individual ruler's gaze. Conversely, there is the impersonal power that is gathered in the return gaze of the people, whose security is grounded in the Leviathan.[2]

This print, depicting the intersection of two gazes, is also a signpost towards a future of modern, impersonal and anonymous patterns of domination.

The possibility that a society might be organized through impersonal modes of domination, through factories, bureaucracies and police forces, was not self-evident to our ancestors. Nor was it certain that the metropolitan spaces of the poor and the dispossessed were governable. Thus, some images here exhibit anxiety about a world whose solidity was melting into air, as Marx and Engels expressed it in one of their Shakespearian moments. The spectre of the crowd – its fluidity, movement and subversion of order – haunted the nineteenth-century imagination but fired the creativity of social critics, writers and painters like WP Frith. The rookeries of London's East End, of Shoreditch and the Jago spawned visions of otherness and touristic venture into the unknown, like Doré's. The crowd now appeared as an aggregate, as a population that had to be not only understood but classified so that people could be scientifically ranked. The struggle to understand a population in aggregate is, moreover, one aspect of the emergence of the modern state, whose need to survey its populous runs from the development of censuses in the early nineteenth-century to the development of DNA databases, and the widespread use of CCTV cameras.

It may well be that "the rich are always with us" as Simon Bedwell argues – but today they have changed their spots, disappearing into the wallpaper of impersonal power. In a society where power is increasingly bureaucratic and corporate, it becomes difficult to 'see' the powerful let alone to represent them artistically or scientifically. One nineteenth-century strand of visual depiction filters modernity through the lens of the Old Order; George Cruikshank's 'British Bee Hive' represents an 'organic' division of labour through the language of estates. Another strand reads this image against the grain, challenging the idea that ranks are warranted by the collective good with the charge of hypocrisy. Both RJ Hamerton's 'Capital and Labour' and the International Workers of the World's pyramid present those 'on top' as undeserving. However, as the chains of social and economic interdependence become longer, the humanities and the social sciences must find new and persuasive depictions of the circuits of power in which individuals are enmeshed. Evan Holloway's 'Capital' is one such example.

Who determines a person's rank? Where is the script? Marie Lund and Nina Beier raise the intriguing possibility of a formal group-photograph in which the order of precedence is collectively discovered at the moment of depiction. Are these people applying existing rules, ones that are perhaps implicit in their association, or are they creating them ex nihilo? Such a system of ranking would contrast markedly with the culture of mid-Victorian 'Good Society', centred on the strong classifications of the London Season, on its prescribed rituals of presentation at Court and visiting cards, of 'cutting' those beneath one's own station to assert one's separate position. This was a mode of ranking which maintained the coherence of the upper class, in the face of modernity's disruptive outsiders. George du Maurier's well known cartoons for Punch anatomized Victorian society's fashionable foibles, satirizing the failure of the wealthy newcomers, who had been thrown upwards by their industrial wealth, to master the established rules of etiquette.[3]

In the nineteenth and twentieth centuries the principles of rank were progressively nationalized and rationalized according to the lights of tradition and expertise.
In Britain the collective imaginations of the nation-state were galvanized by 'invented traditions' such as a 'popular' monarchy. How people, faced with the great divisions of modernity like class, age, gender and ethnicity, came to think of their commonality is one of the central puzzles of social science. How were the 'imagined communities' of nations conjured out of the complexity, impersonality and opacity of modern social life? By the mid-twentieth century, universalism was a largely unchallenged principle of social and cultural provision. The state, partly through schooling, progressively monopolized the definition of ranking and self-worth. The consequence was the creation of a quite modern pattern of ranking, in which the poorest and least powerful were stigmatized and humbled.
The peasant who overstepped the mark might, of course, be humbled by a master who returns them to their 'place'. But as Richard Sennett has argued, contemporary universalistic ways of 'sorting' people mean that humiliation is readily converted into self-blame by those who fail to 'make it'.[4]

This exhibition is an appreciation of how the impersonalization of power spurs the imagination to picture our social world, across both the visual arts and the social sciences. Contemporary Britain is awash with examples of how rank is measured and social mobility calculated. Yet there is one wider question that is a key feature of current political discourse: how far we have moved from a society of collective ascription to one of individual achievement. Measuring rank is now the province of distinctively modern forms of expertise, which capture complexity through visual methods of mapping and graphing. One problem is how to tabulate, map, visualize and imagine a given distribution of wealth when the results may well be at odds with the immediate experiences of individuals and their common sense. The SASI team's maps of levels of poverty, for example, show us both where most of us live, and just how unequal we are, precisely because poverty is measured relative to average income. Just as artists may break the conventions of representation so too may cartographers and social scientists devise new ways of seeing, as their Worldmapper project has also proven. In that respect, the sociological imagination has a visual dimension.

Finally, I want to draw attention to the link between the graphic arts, rank and social criticism, however muted or radical be the latter. Almost all the images shown here are prints of one kind or another. This is important because in the past the printed image, perhaps as satire or as political commentary had the potential to unsettle, to disturb any given system of ranking. As the print 'Staunch Reformers' from the British Museum testifies, the relations between groups in the dominant hierarchy – how they have identified or dis-identified with one another – is seldom straightforward. Moreover, prints had until very recently a powerful influence as shared representations of the social order and of the state of the nation, and like John Tenniel's 'Telescopic Philanthropy', solidified ideas or debates. Yet printmaking was often also seen as an inferior art, and its practice and purchasers often those outside the élite. The satirical tradition of William Hogarth and James Gillray reminds us that the bite of the print is more than a matter of etching or cutting the block. The graphic arts and political commentary have a long connection for several reasons, and the phenomenon that I want to draw attention to is of the politically radical engraver. In the nineteenth century, engravers such as William Blake, Henry Vizetelly, Abraham Rambaich, James Linton and others were voices of radicalism and dissent. These people are interesting in matters of rank for they were professional hybrids, part artist and part craftsman. It is no accident that their gaze penetrated the issue of rank, for they themselves were difficult to place within the hierarchy of the arts. Their occupation connected them to the world of commerce, and it committed them to technical changes within the means of representation that revolutionized image-making. They were amongst those who queried the order of things.

Gordon Fyfe is a fellow of Keele University where he was previously senior lecturer. His publications include 'Picturing Power: Visual Depiction and Social Relations' (Routledge); 'Art, Power and Modernity: English Art Institutions 1750-1950' (Continuum)

1. Zygmunt Bauman, 'Intimations of Modernity', 1992, (London: Routledge) p7
2. The work of Bredekamp is indispensable for an appreciation of this image: H. Bredekamp 'Thomas Hobbes's Visual Strategies' in P. Springborg (ed) 'The Cambridge Companion to Hobbes's Leviathan', 2007, (Cambridge: CUP) pp. 29-60
3. Leonore Davidoff, 'The Best Circles: Social Etiquette and the Season', 1986, (London: Hutchinson)
4. Richard Sennett and Jonathan Cobb, 'The Hidden Injuries of Class', 1972, (Cambridge: CUP)

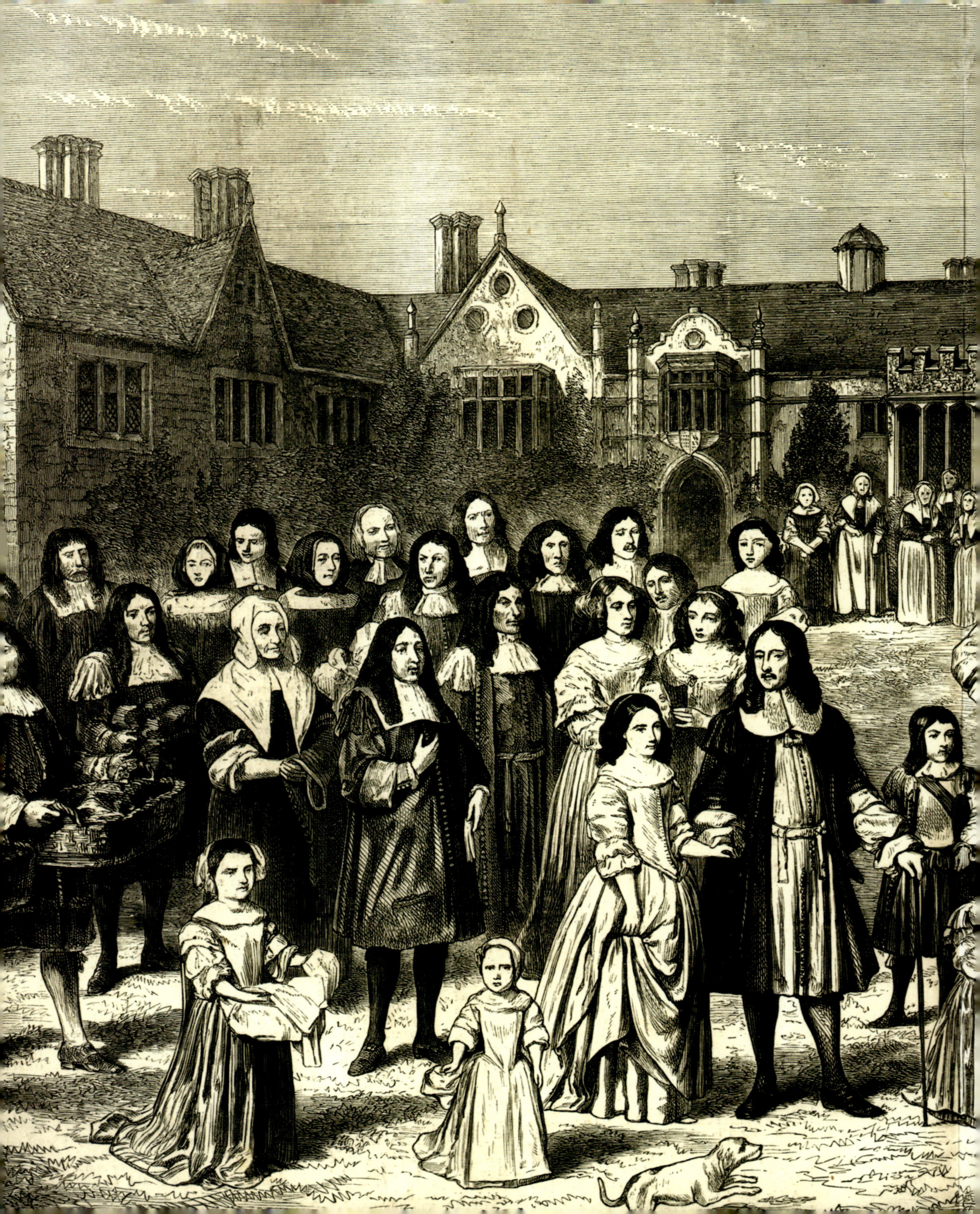

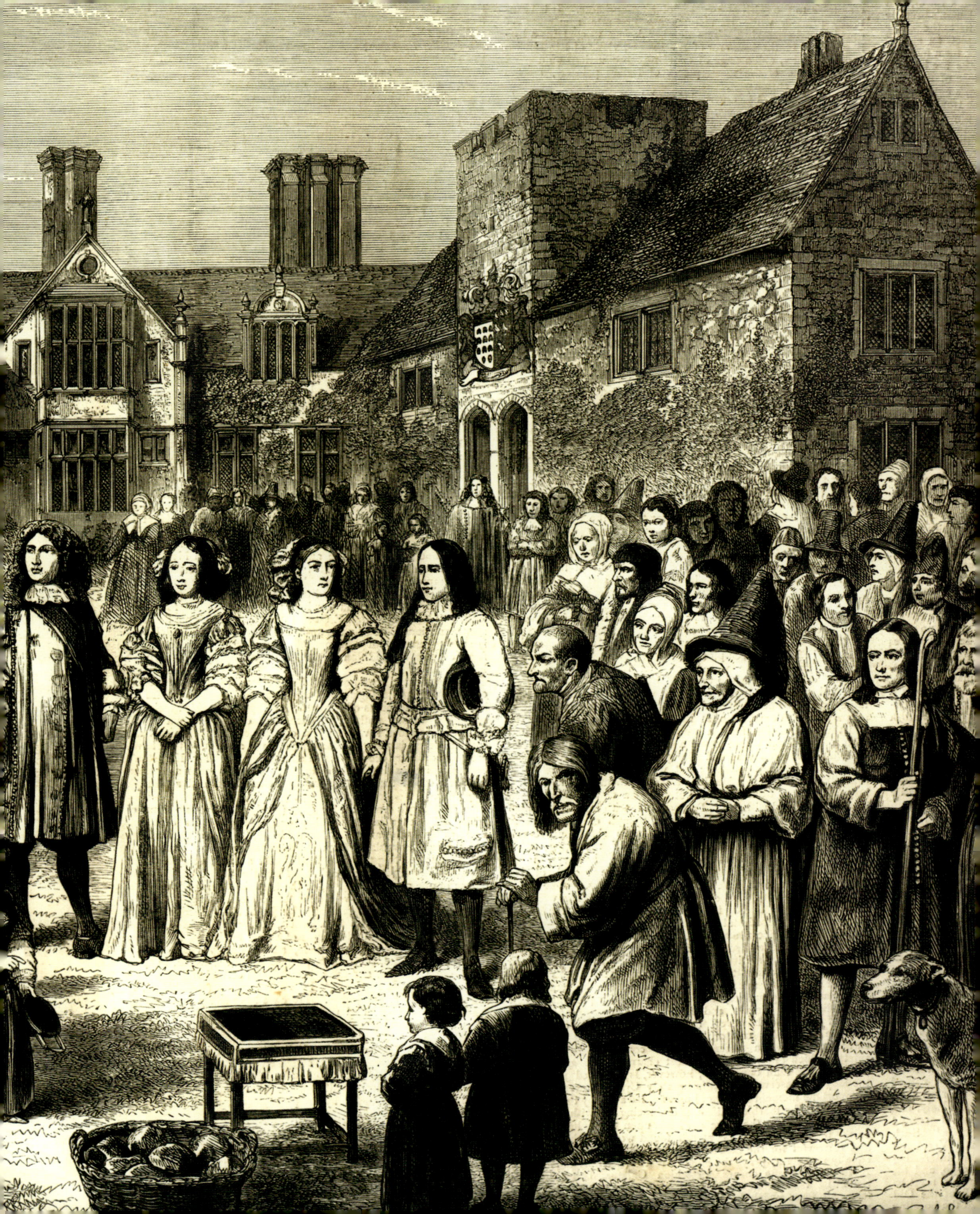

AFTER GILLIS VAN TILBORCH

'The Tichborne Dole' 1871

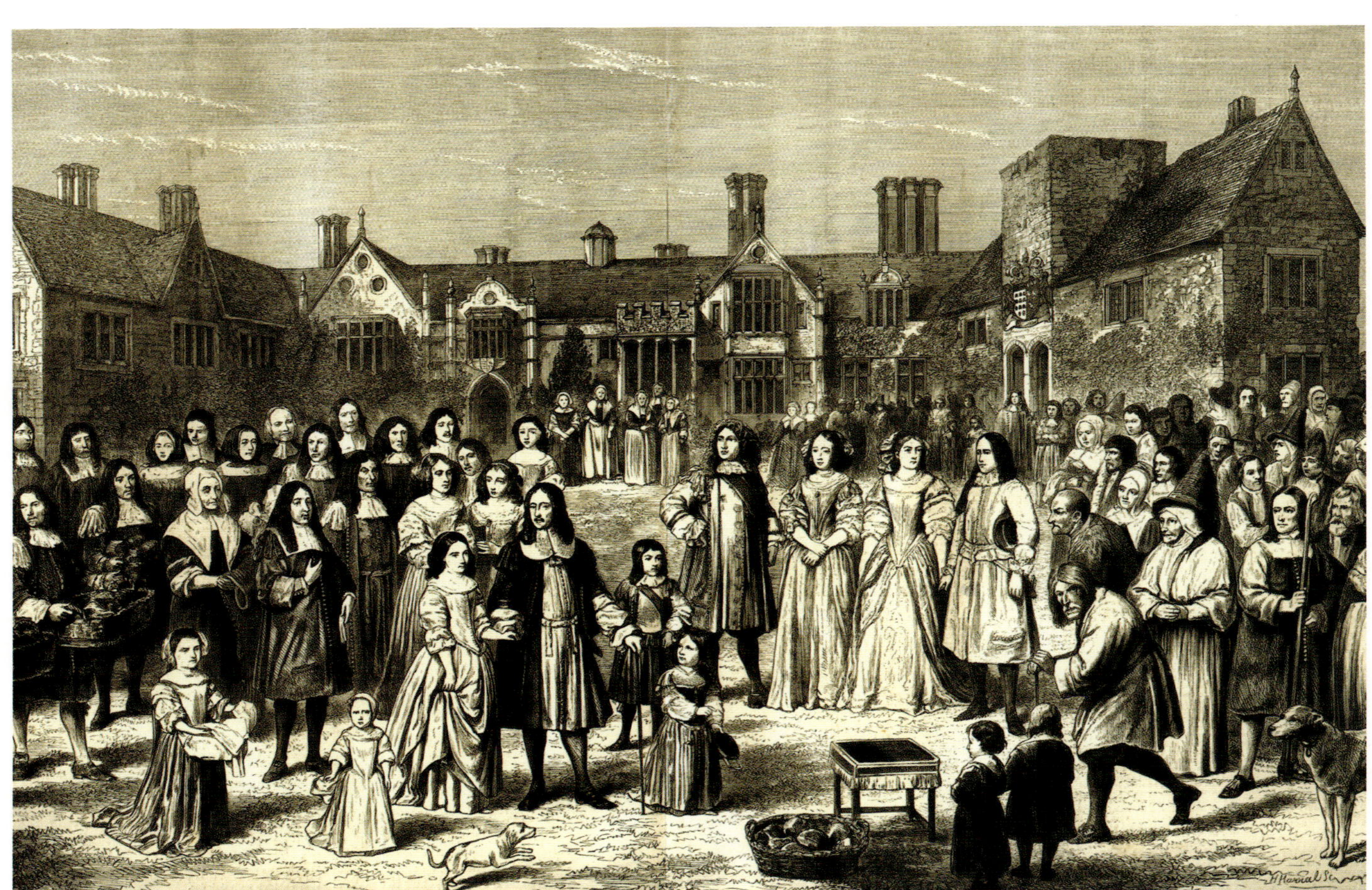

Sunderland Libraries

"Until the 1950s social differences were based on factors which were not relative to occupational status or money, but on characteristics associated with at least two or three generations of family privilege."[1] **Peter Bromhead, 'Life in Modern Britain'**

This is one of the very few images from pre-modern times which depicts a whole village: it is a social panorama of parish life, and hence a microcosm of the nation.
The story of the image is bizarre and politically charged. Shortly after the English civil war, the landowner Sir Henry Tichborne commissioned a record of the annual ceremony he administered of distributing gifts of bread to members of his parish.
This has been seen as a manoeuvre to restore medieval social ties of patronage and deference – of ''noblesse oblige' – between rich and poor, after the turmoil of war. This 'dole' was allegedly established as the dying wish of the lady of the house in 12th century, though have been reinvented in the seventeenth.

Her husband agreed to give the 'dole to tenants within a fixed area, the perimeter of which was detemined by how far his dying wife could crawl to. Reputedly, Lady Mabella struggled round a 23-acre field still called The Crawls. Nine centuries and thirty generations later, the dole is still distributed: the land is owned by the same family and estimated to be worth £20m. The current owner Anthony Loudon remarks "we give a gallon of flour to each adult in the parish of Cheriton and Tichborne. About 900 are entitled to it."[2]

1. Bromhead, 1971, p8
2. http://property.timesonline.co.uk/tol/life_and_style/property/buying_and_selling/article550430.ece

GREGORY KING

Estimates of the wealth and population of England and Wales in 1688

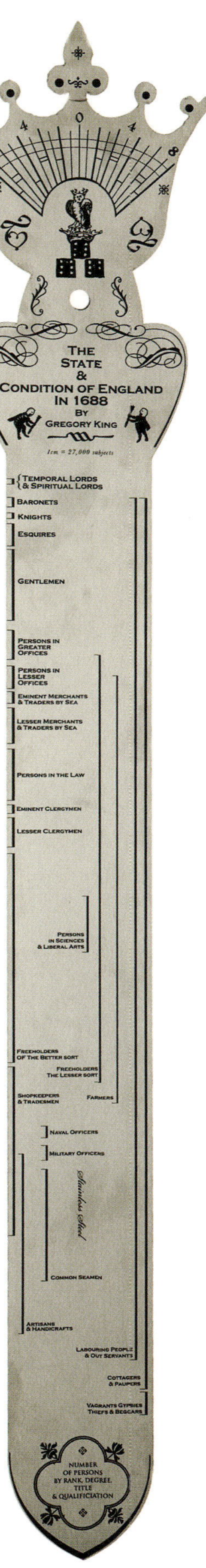

image by Ben Branagan & Gareth Holt

"[An] Englishman acquired his sense of public identity in relation to his birth, his property, his occupation and his social rank... Distinctions in wealth between top and bottom were vast [but] the English social ladder was indeed precisely graded... [in] a social order whose gross inequalities were landscaped in gentle gradients rather than in giant steps."[1]
Roy Porter, 'English Society in the Eighteenth Century', 1991

How do we imagine that the shape of society has changed, generation upon generation, from pre-industrial times? Prior to the first census in 1801, there were few attempts to undertake comprehensive 'social surveys', and most, like Gregory King's, were based on guesswork or outmoded data. King based his typology of the nation on tax returns, classifying society into 26 groups, and estimating the size and wealth of each. The historian Roy Porter has simplified the 26 types into the eight overall categories: 12.4% landowners; 24% farmers and freeholders; 3% professionals including clergy; 4% merchants and shopkeepers; 4% artisans and handicraftsmen; 27% labouring people and out-servants; 29% cottagers and paupers; 7% the armed forces. King underestimated the size of retail and manufacturing: by 1700 England had a substantial "fat middle" in one historian's words.

1. Porter, 1982, pp48-9

OFFICE FOR NATIONAL STATISTICS

Distribution of Real Disposable Household Income in the UK, 1974–2004

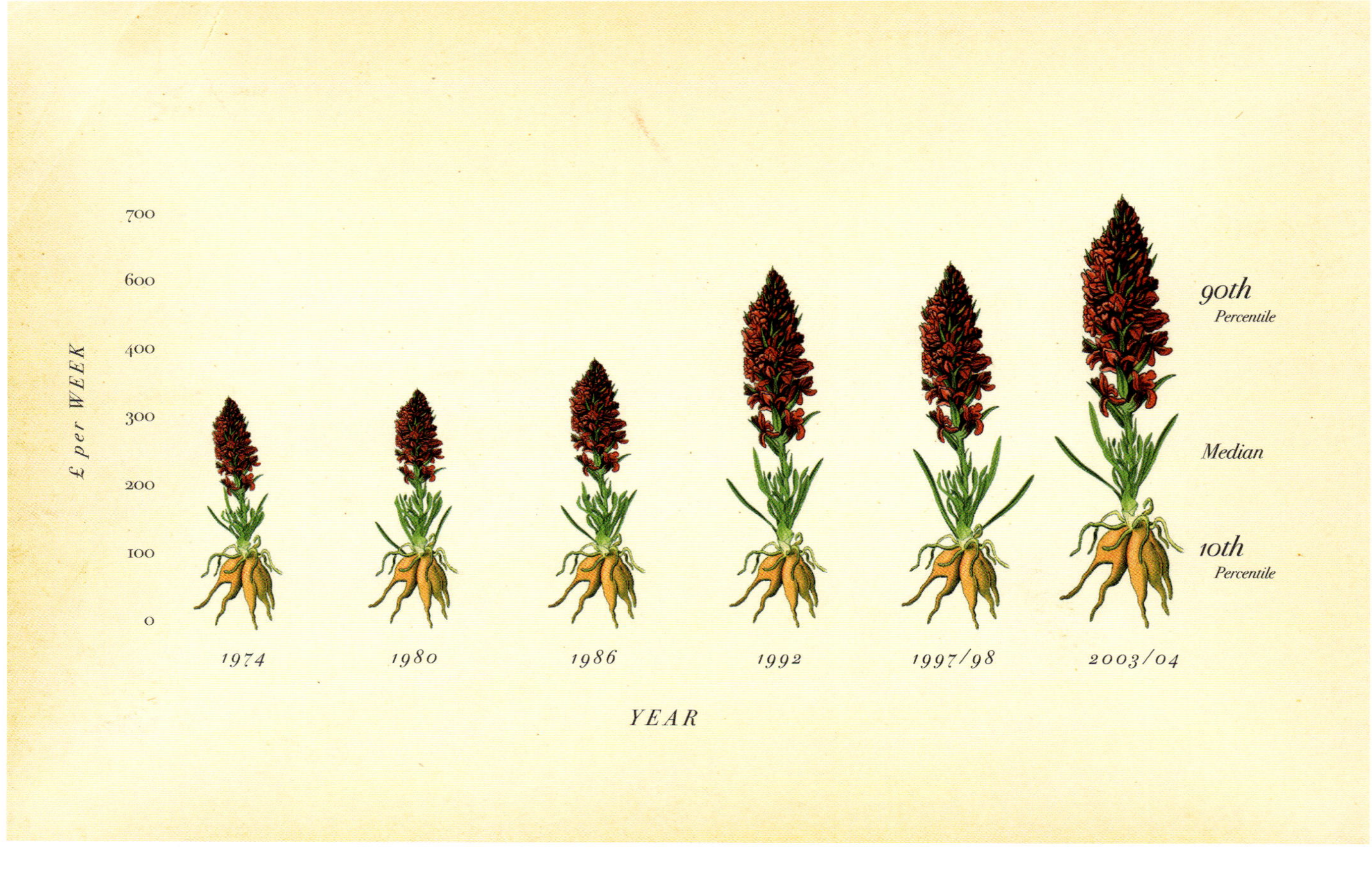

"Don't cut down the tall poppies. Let them rather grow tall. I would say, let our children grow tall and some taller than others if they have the ability in them to do so...What are the lessons then that we've learned from the last thirty years? First, that the pursuit of equality itself is a mirage. What's more desirable and more practicable than the pursuit of equality is the pursuit of equality of opportunity."[1] **Margaret Thatcher, speech, 'Let our children grow tall', 1975**

"In the 1980s and 90s... the spread of wages... opened out like a fan – the gaps between each wage bracket grew equally. A different pattern has emerged in recent years. Thanks in no small part to the minimum wage, the lowest-paid have kept pace with – and even closed in on – workers in the middle... the highest 10% have kept running away from the middle. [There is] a widening wage gap at the expense of the middle, rather than the poor"[2] **'The Rich and the Rest', The Guardian October 11 2008**

Who has benefited most in the UK from economic growth over a generation? How have the poorest, middling and richest groups fared over time? The Office for National Statistics have reported that the country's highest earners have gained disproportionately since the '70s: their incomes have tripled. However, even the bottom 10% have nearly doubled their purchasing power. Surprisingly, the groups who have been experienced the smallest rise in incomes are those in the middle of the economic spectrum.

1. www.margaretthatcher.org
2. 'The Rich and the Rest', leader, Guardian G1, Oct11 2008, p32

image by Ben Branagan & Gareth Holt

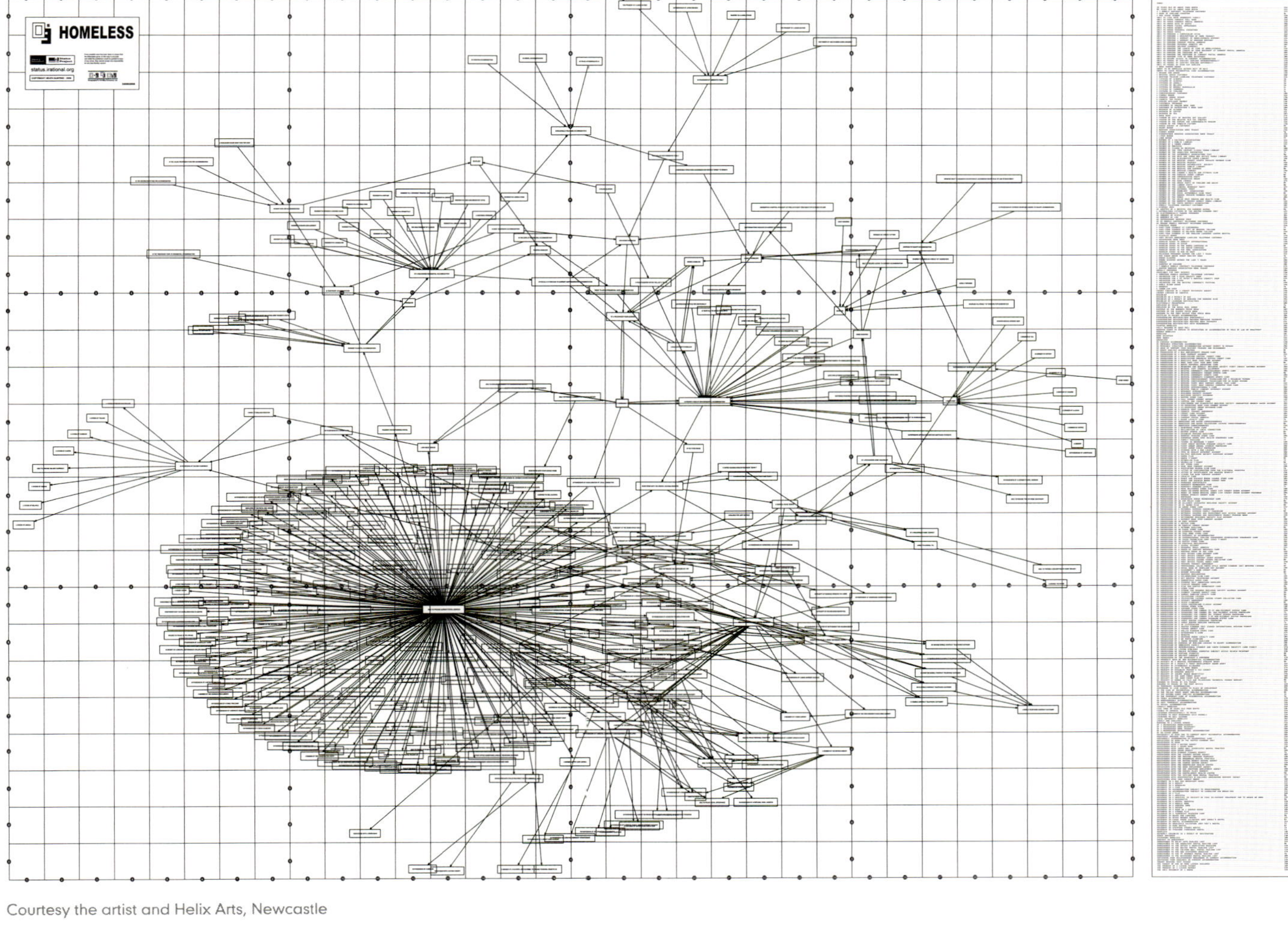

Courtesy the artist and Helix Arts, Newcastle

"Power and advantage are convertible... Together they define the character of strata and the relations between them in a stratification system."[1] **AH Halsey, 'Social Change in Britain', 1986**

What forms of 'status' – both in terms of hierarchical position and legal status – do each of us occupy? Heath Bunting's work investigates what networks we participate in as members of a society. 'The Status Project' is the result of six-year enquiry into all the ways in which we can possess different types of formal or legal status, from possession of a passport to that of a supermarket reward card. The project looks at how the construction of our public identity lies in sets of data, held by both businesses and government agencies. It maps out how comprehensively we are monitored and our activities mapped out. Through our consumption, our access to essential services or residency, we can be easily tracked and the patterns of our behaviour monitored. And yet, Bunting finds, there are innumerable ways to defeat or frustrate such systems should we be inclined. The artist has described the project as "an expert system for identity mutation": it is available as an online database documenting more than 5000 entries. One of Bunting's more startling findings is that it only requires a couple of 'steps' to obtaining a passport from scratch, and indeed a vote.

1. Halsey, 1986, p27

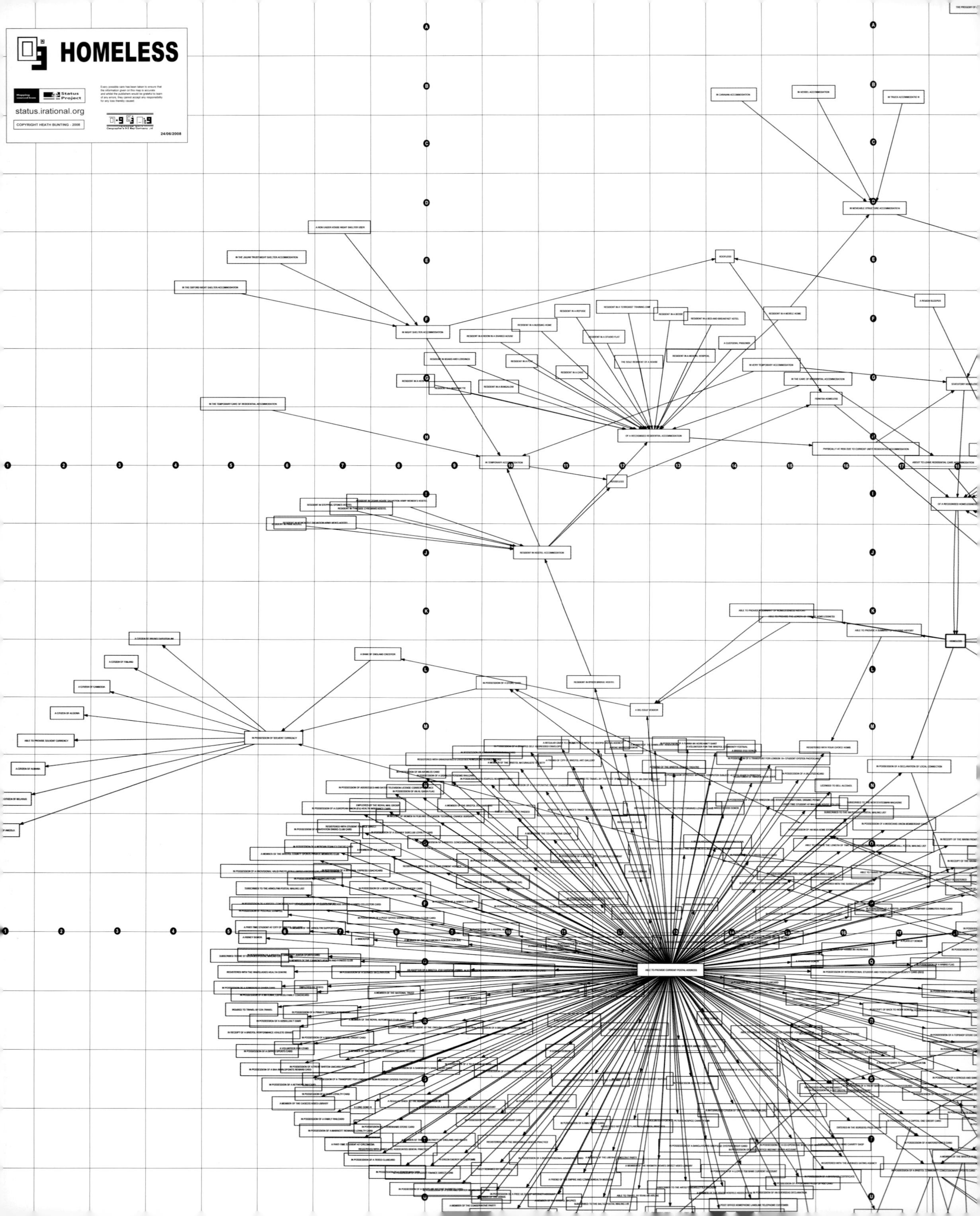
HOMELESS
Mapping sourced from
Status Project
status.irational.org
COPYRIGHT HEATH BUNTING - 2008
Every possible care has been taken to ensure that the information given on this map is accurate and whilst the publishers would be grateful to learn of any errors, they cannot accept any responsibility for any loss thereby caused.
24/06/2008
A NON EAGER HOUSE NIGHT SHELTER USER
IN THE JULIAN TRUST NIGHT SHELTER ACCOMMODATION
IN THE OXFORD NIGHT SHELTER ACCOMMODATION
IN NIGHT SHELTER ACCOMMODATION
RESIDENT IN A ROOM IN A SHARED HOUSE
RESIDENT IN BOARD AND LODGINGS
RESIDENT IN A BUNGALOW
IN THE TEMPORARY CARE OF RESIDENTIAL ACCOMMODATION
IN TEMPORARY ACCOMMODATION
IN CARAVAN ACCOMMODATION
IN VESSEL ACCOMMODATION
IN TRUCK ACCOMMODATIO N
IN MOVEABLE STRUCTURE ACCOMMODATION
ROOFLESS
A ROUGH SLEEPER
RESIDENT IN A REFUGE
RESIDENT IN A TERRORIST TRAINING CAMP
RESIDENT IN A BED AND BREAKFAST HOTEL
RESIDENT IN A MOBILE HOME
RESIDENT IN A NURSING HOME
RESIDENT IN A STUDIO FLAT
A CUSTODIAL PRISONER
RESIDENT IN A MENTAL HOSPITAL
THE SOLE RESIDENT OF A HOUSE
RESIDENT IN A CAVE
IN VERY TEMPORARY ACCOMMODATION
IN THE CARE OF RESIDENTIAL ACCOMMODATION
STATUTORY HOMELESS
FERATSA HOMELESS
OF A RECOGNISED RESIDENTIAL ACCOMMODATION
PHYSICALLY AT RISK DUE TO CURRENT UNFIT RESIDENTIAL ACCOMMODATION
ABOUT TO LEAVE RESIDENTIAL CARE ACCOMMODATION
HOUSELESS
OF A RECOGNISED HOMELESSNESS
RESIDENT IN HOSTEL ACCOMMODATION
RESIDENT IN STEPPING STONES HOSTEL
RESIDENT IN BYRON BRIDGE HOSTEL
ABLE TO PROVIDE A SUMMARY OF HOMELESSNESS HISTORY
ABLE TO PROVIDE A SUMMARY OF HOUSING HISTORY
HOMELESS
A CITIZEN OF BRUNEI DARUSSALAM
A CITIZEN OF FINLAND
A CITIZEN OF CAMBODIA
A CITIZEN OF ALGERIA
ABLE TO PROVIDE SOLVENT CURRENCY
A CITIZEN OF ALBANIA
A BANK OF ENGLAND CREDITOR
IN POSSESSION OF SOLVENT CURRENCY
A BIG ISSUE VENDOR
REGISTERED WITH YOUR CHOICE HOMS
IN POSSESSION OF A DECLARATION OF LOCAL CONNECTION
LICENSED TO SELL ALCOHOL
ABLE TO PROVIDE CURRENT POSTAL ADDRESS

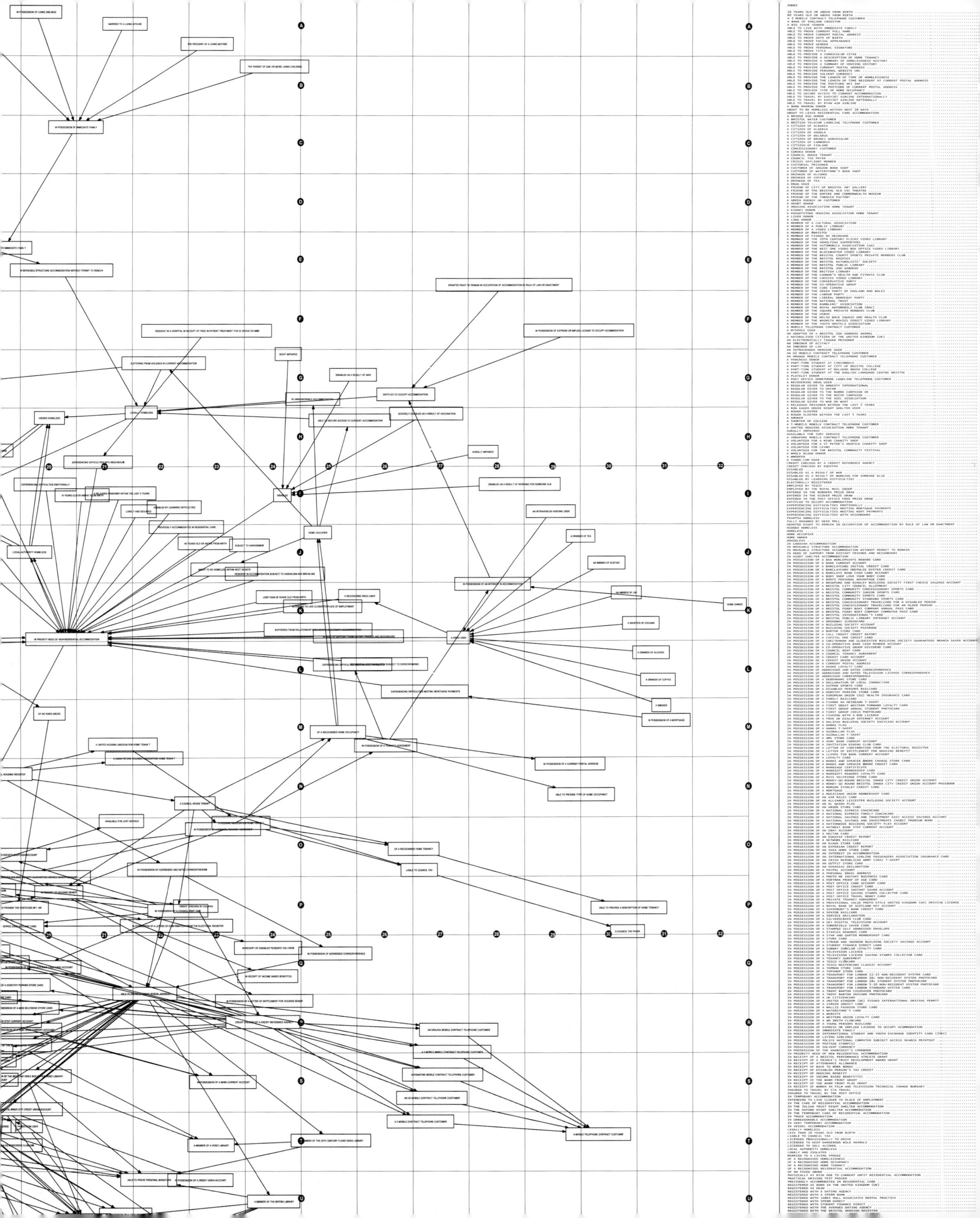

CHARLES JAMESON GRANT

'The Whig and Tory Union, or the devil turned miner' 1833–35

"We have shown the example of a nation in which every class of society accepts with cheerfulness the lot which providence has assigned to it; while at the same time each individual of each class is constantly trying to raise himself in the social scale, not by violence and illegality, but by preserving good conduct and by the steady and energetic exertion of the moral and intellectual faculties with which his creator has endowed him."[1] **Lord Palmerston, speech on 25 June1850**

In the 1830s Grant created an extraordinary series of 131 political cartoons for 'penny papers' which left no position unspared. 'Penny papers' were the main way working men received the news, and these woodcuts were meant as barbed journalism rather than art. Their rugged crudeness, though, reflects their grotesque subjects perfectly. Political and religious leaders are shown as animals – mostly reptiles and vermin – in a rogues' gallery meant to disgust. For Grant, even other radicals were part of the problem rather than the solution. 'The Whig and Tory Union' is self-mocking: Grant portrays working men as the 'devil' ready to pull the floor from under the feet of a corrupt, self-congratulatory parliament.

1. http://en.wikisource.org/wiki/Don_Pacifico_Speech

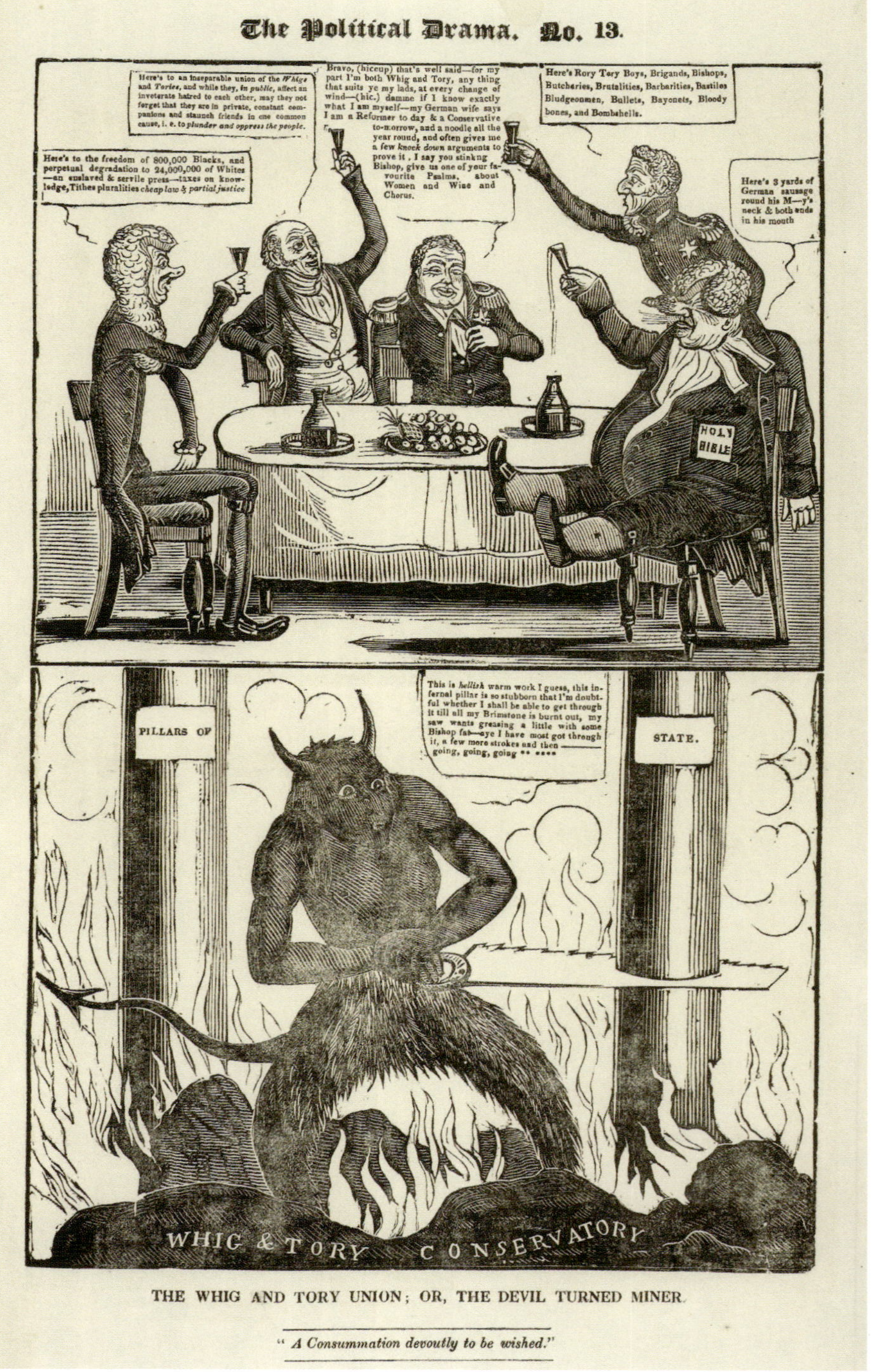

from the series 'The Political Drama'
Working Class Movement Library, Salford

'London: A Pilgrimage' 1872

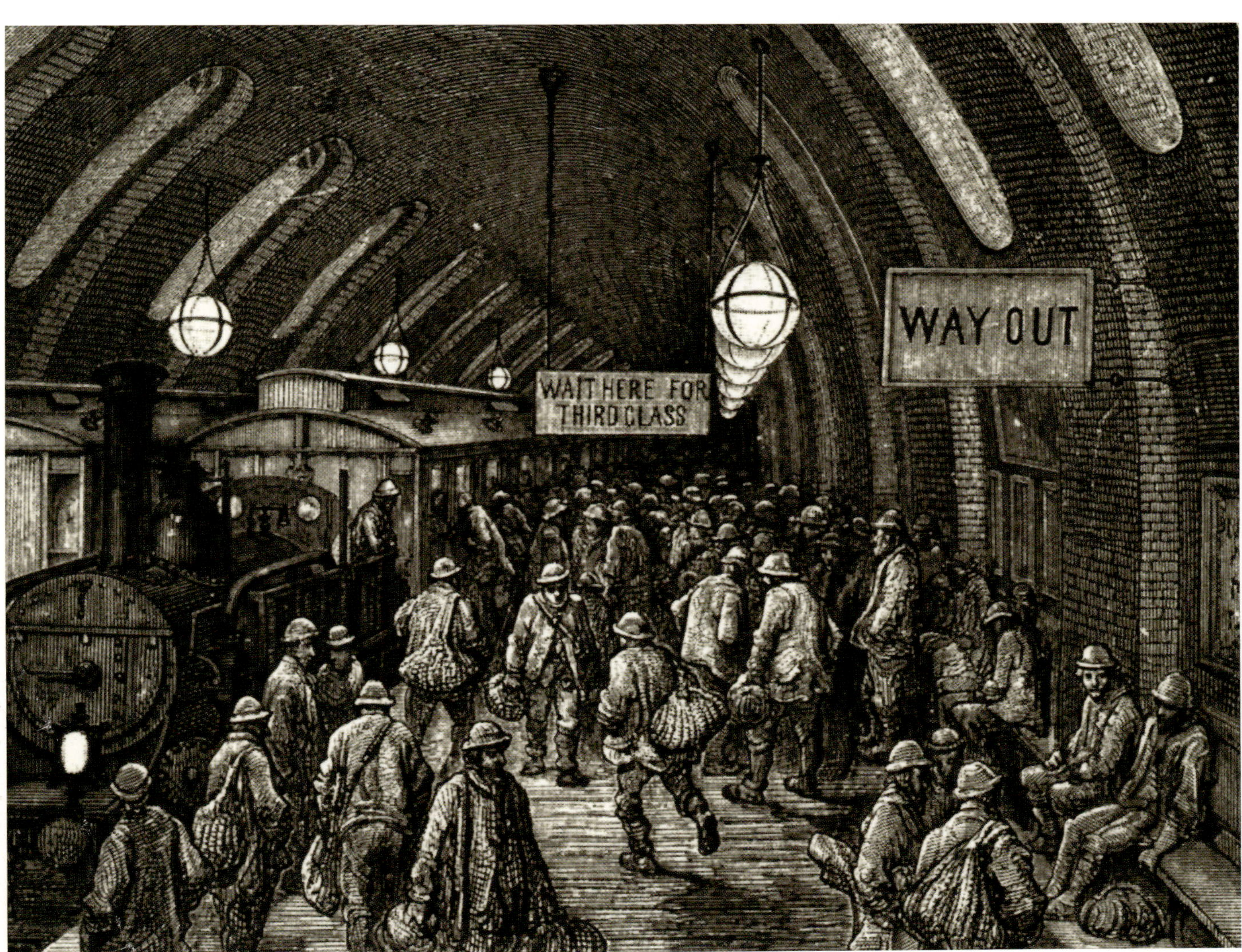

Private collection

"Life in London is, by definition, a game which only a few can win..."[1]
Peter Ackroyd, 'London: The Biography', 2000

Doré was the most famous printmaker in Britain by 1870, and paid the equivalent of over £1m to produce this epic panorama of London life. It is one of the greatest of all Victorian 'social panoramas' and an attempt to picture what historian Asa Briggs has called "London: the wonder and horror of the age."[2] Doré's work is close to Dickens' novels: squalor and riches sit side by side in the biggest city the world had ever seen. The overall tone is echoed by analyses like Friedrich Engels': "A town, such as London, where a man may wander for hours together without reaching the beginning of the end, without meeting the slightest hint which could lead to the inference that there is open country within reach, is a strange thing. This colossal centralisation, this heaping together of two and a half millions of human beings at one point, has multiplied the power of this two and a half millions a hundredfold; has raised London to the commercial capital of the world... But the sacrifices which all this has cost become apparent later."[3]

1. Ackroyd, 2000 (London: Chatto and Windus) p340
2. Briggs, 1983 p194
3. www.marxists.org/archive/marx/works/1845/condition-working-class/index.htm

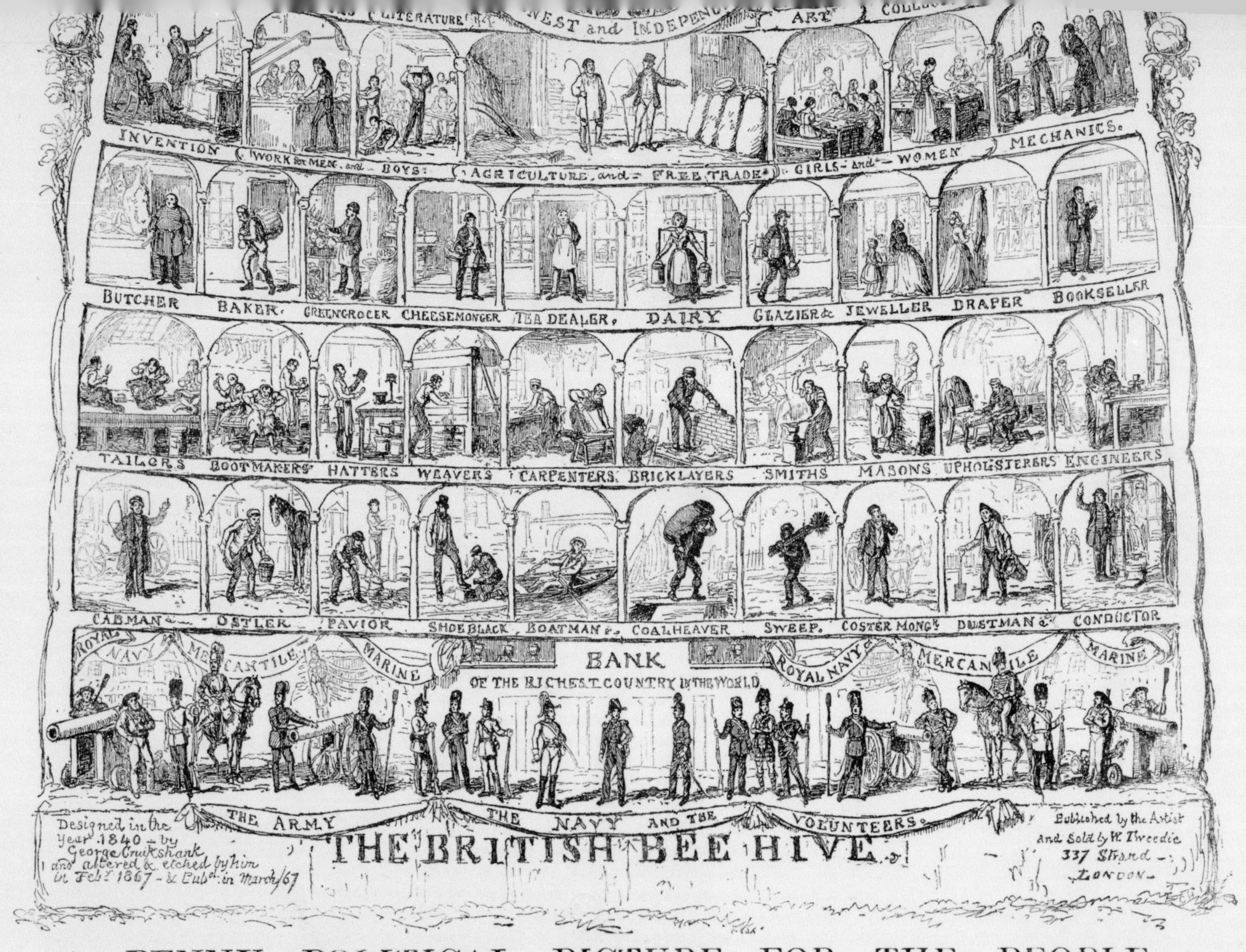

A PENNY POLITICAL PICTURE FOR THE PEOPLE,

WITH A FEW WORDS UPON PARLIAMENTARY REFORM.

BY THEIR OLD FRIEND, GEORGE CRUIKSHANK

Published by W. Tweedie, 337, Strand.

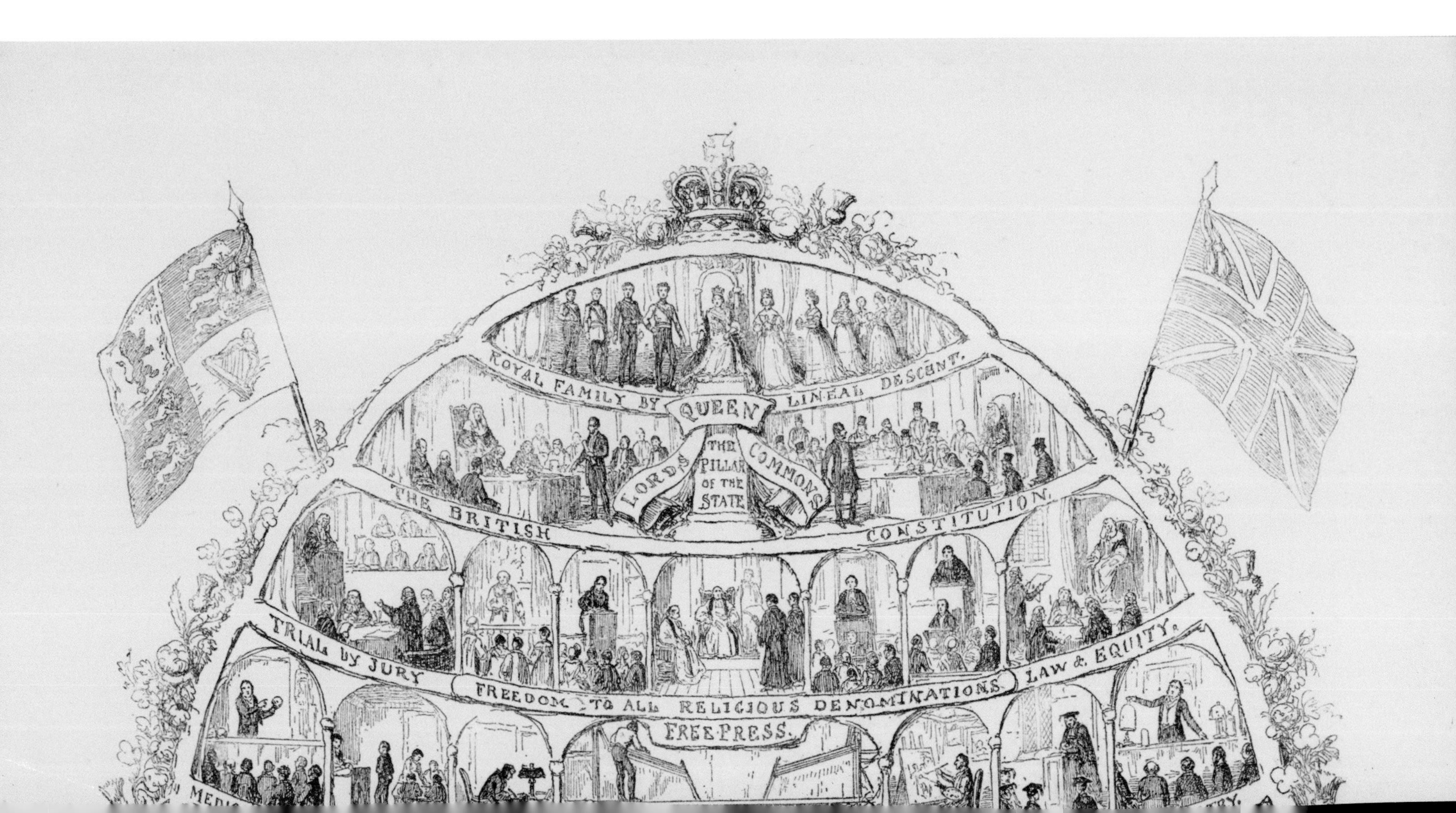
ROYAL FAMILY BY LINEAL DESCENT.
QUEEN
LORDS
THE PILLAR OF THE STATE
COMMONS
THE BRITISH CONSTITUTION.
TRIAL BY JURY
LAW & EQUITY.
FREEDOM TO ALL RELIGIOUS DENOMINATIONS
FREE PRESS.

'The British Bee Hive: A Penny Political Picture for the People' 1840 / 1867

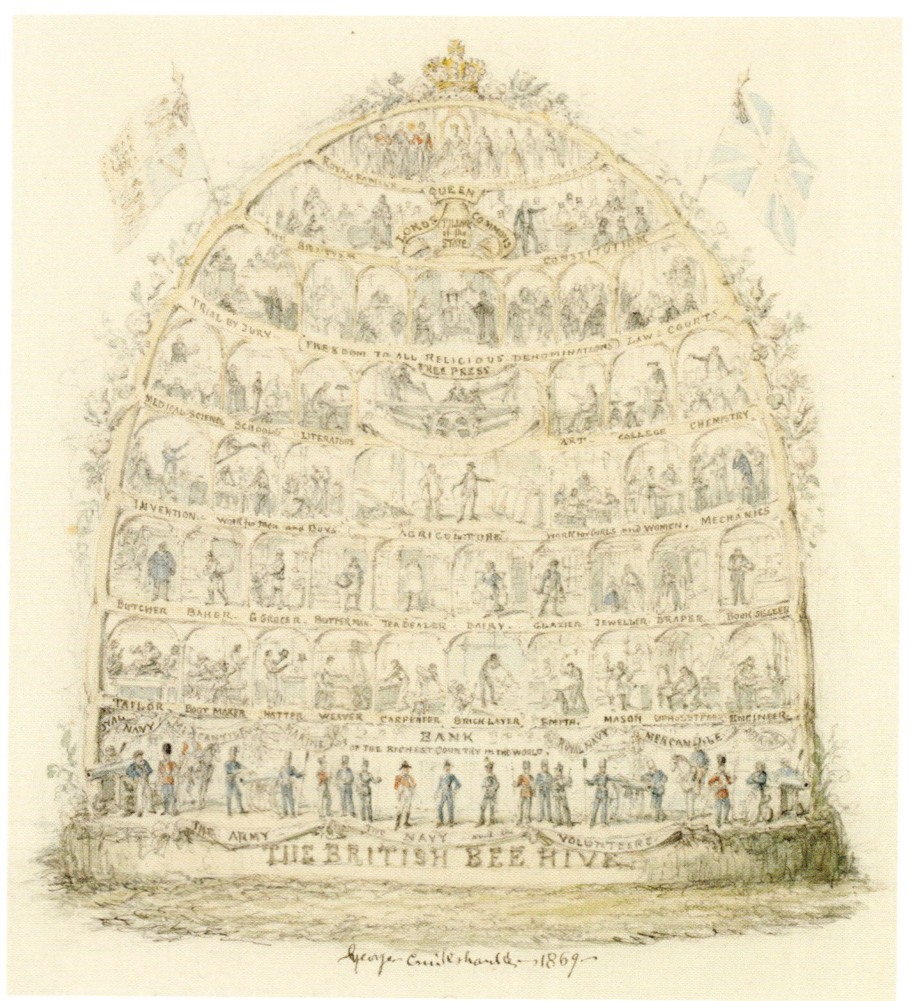

Victoria and Albert Museum.
Given by Mrs George Cruikshank

"I therefore publish this "Bee Hive" and add a few words to show and explain – not only the form of the governing power, but also the structure of society which has been formed, and which has prospered so well, so wonderfully well, under this current system... God preserve our gracious queen, our glorious constitution and our beautiful bee hive."
From 'The British Bee Hive'

Cruikshank's work echoes what the sociologist AH Halsey has called "the extraordinary combination of solidarity and hierarchy in British society.'[1] The social order is arranged according to each profession's imagined importance in a pyramid. 'Work' is the glue that binds us together and which defines our identities. Bees, as a singularly industrious species with a clear division of labour, have provided a metaphor for human social structures since Roman times.

However, the sex of 'queen' bees was only discovered in the seventeenth century: until then it was thought 'king' bees ruled each hive, reflecting patriarchal ideas. What is of note here, though, is how Cruikshank has an entirely different conception of society to his grandparents' generation. As historian David Cannadine has noted, it was only in the 1770s that Adam Smith first "advance[d] the proposition that social status and social identity were primarily determined not by honour or prestige ranking, and still less by religion and politics... but by occupation and relation to the means of production."[2] By the time of Victoria's reign, as the labour force was increasingly differentiated and new professions emerged, the criteria determining social worth were substantially rethought.

1. Halsey, 1986, p21
2. Cannadine, 1998, p47

DEXTER DALWOOD

'After Gustave Doré Over London by Rail' 2007

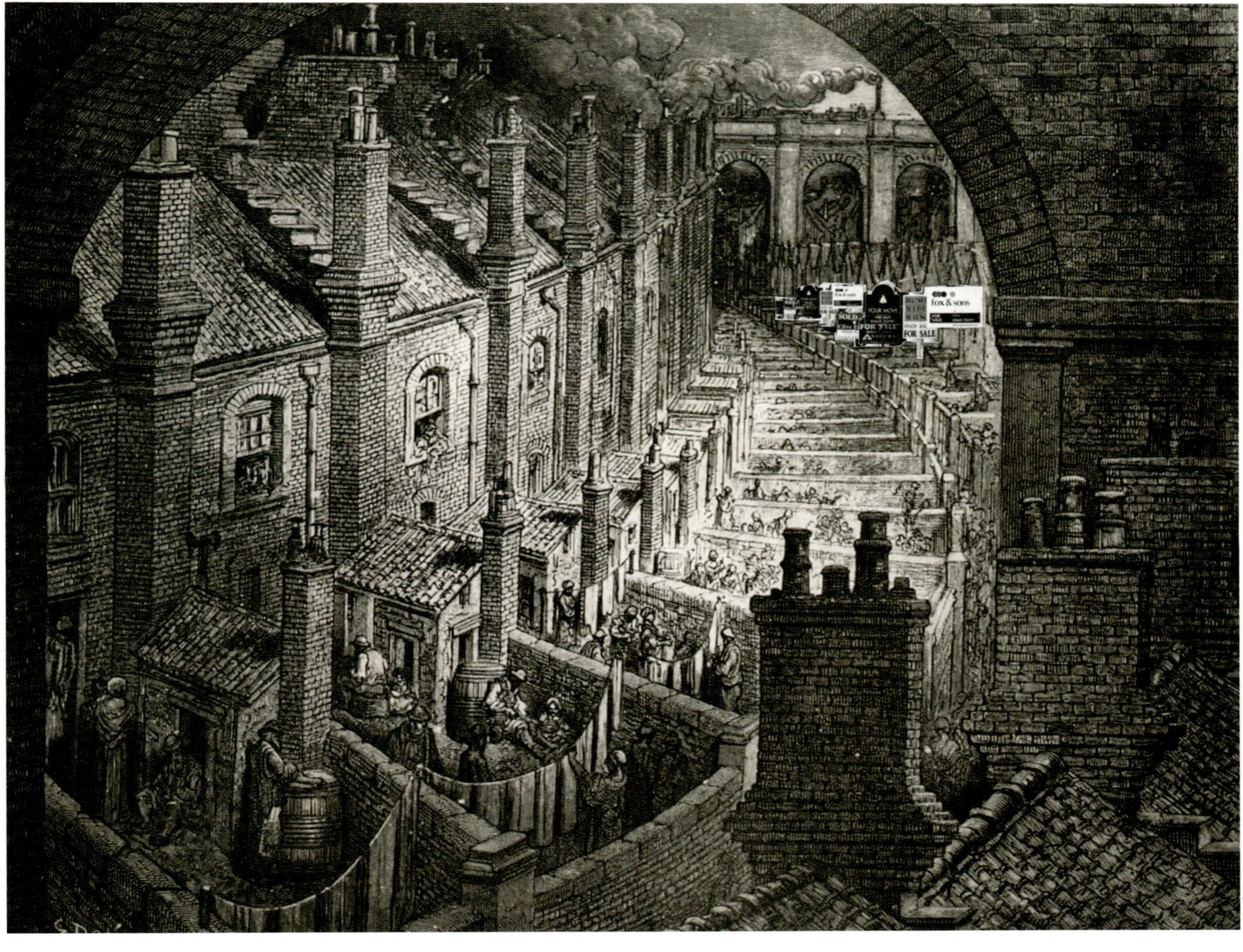

Courtesy the artist and Gagosian Gallery, London

"Terraced houses were astonishingly cheap to build – originally within the budget of City clerks, if now only within the budget of City bankers…"[1]
Harry Mount, 'Mortar the Point', 2008

One recent Prime Minister argued that Britons were "all middle class now".[2] Dexter Dalwood's work might seem to reverse this claim and suggest that market forces have made us all working class.
His reworking of one of Gustave Doré's prints implicitly compares what our incomes can buy us over time: as we have become ever richer what we can buy has diminished.
His image echoes the writer Iain Sinclair's description of London as characterised by "boutique squalor". These houses, once squalid but now seen as gentrified, were believed to be near Waterloo. They were clearly built for those at the bottom of the pile. Any similar house in this location would fetch £500,000-£700,000 today – between 24-28 times the average annual salary of £24,000 in 2006. Our great-great grandparents would have thought these houses for the poor. Today fewer than 5% of earners could afford them on their salaries alone. This is the result, in part, of an unevenly distributed economy.
The academic AH Halsey has remarked that some markets, like the housing market, are "a zero-sum game – if you win I lose – or even a negative sum game, in the people consume resources in mutually cancelling efforts to gain market advantage".[3]

1. Harry Mount, 'Mortar the Point', Time Out Oct 16-22 2008, p66
2. http://www.guardian.co.uk/uk/2007/oct/20/britishidentity.socialexclusion1
3. Halsey, 1986, p21

"All society would appear to arrange itself into four different classes: I) Those that Will Work; II) Those that Cannot Work; III) Those that Will Not Work; IV) Those that Need Not Work... My earnest hope is that the book may serve to give the rich a more intimate knowledge of the sufferings, and the frequent heroism under those sufferings, of the poor... whose misery, ignorance, and vice, amidst all the immense wealth and great knowledge of 'the first city in the world' is, to say the very least, a national disgrace to us."[1] from Volume IV, 1862

The journalist Henry Mayhew created what is often seen as the first private survey of city life – the first attempt to look at one's fellow citizens with an anthropologist's eye. He subtitled it a "cyclopaedia" of social types. The problem of how to create a new typology preoccupied him: "Those who obtain their living in the streets... are so multifarious that the mind is long baffled in its attempts to reduce them to scientific order or classification." The scheme he finally invented judged people firstly by their type of occupation then by the type of goods they dealt with. His was an attempt to create a 'catalogue' of new social types in the biggest city in the world – a means to map out the social co-ordinates of the new city and make it intelligible. Mayhew realised that, as whole hosts of new occupations were being developed, the existing schemes of classification on offer were insufficient to his needs. Or as Jonathan Raban remarks, "We had better heed Mayhew's method and recognise that we need some outlandish scheme of classification, as conventional hierarchies fail to apply to the modern city... Mayhew discovered a honeycomb of caste groups, each one circumscribed by the commodities in which it dealt."[2] By contrast, contemporaries often simply reduced the vast majority of the urban population to a single 'mass' or 'crowd'; Matthew Arnold describing the poor simply as "those vast, miserable, unmanageable masses of sunken people."[3]

1. Preface to Volume IV, 1862
2. Raban, 1974, p97
3. arnold.classicauthors.net/culture/culture7.html

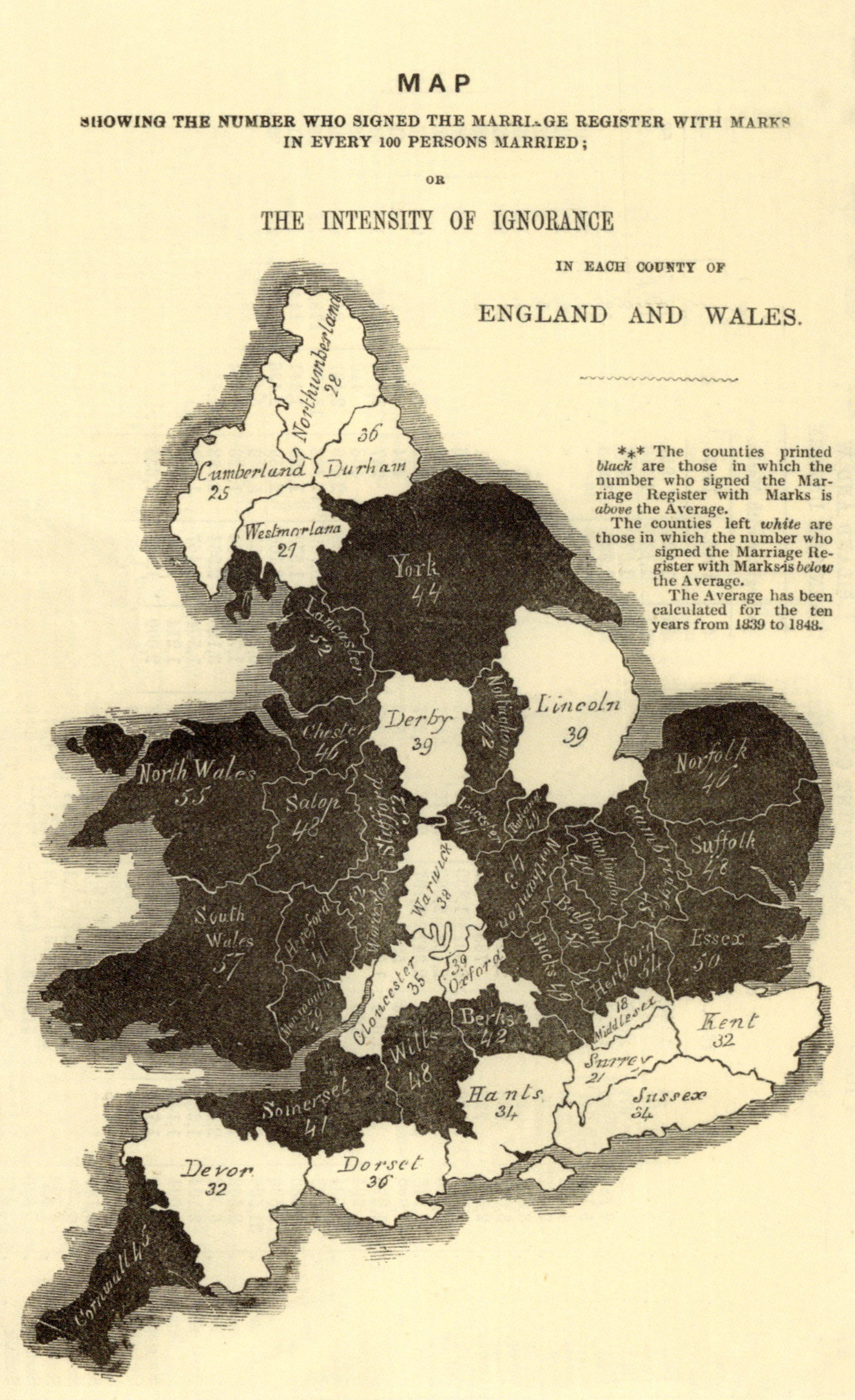

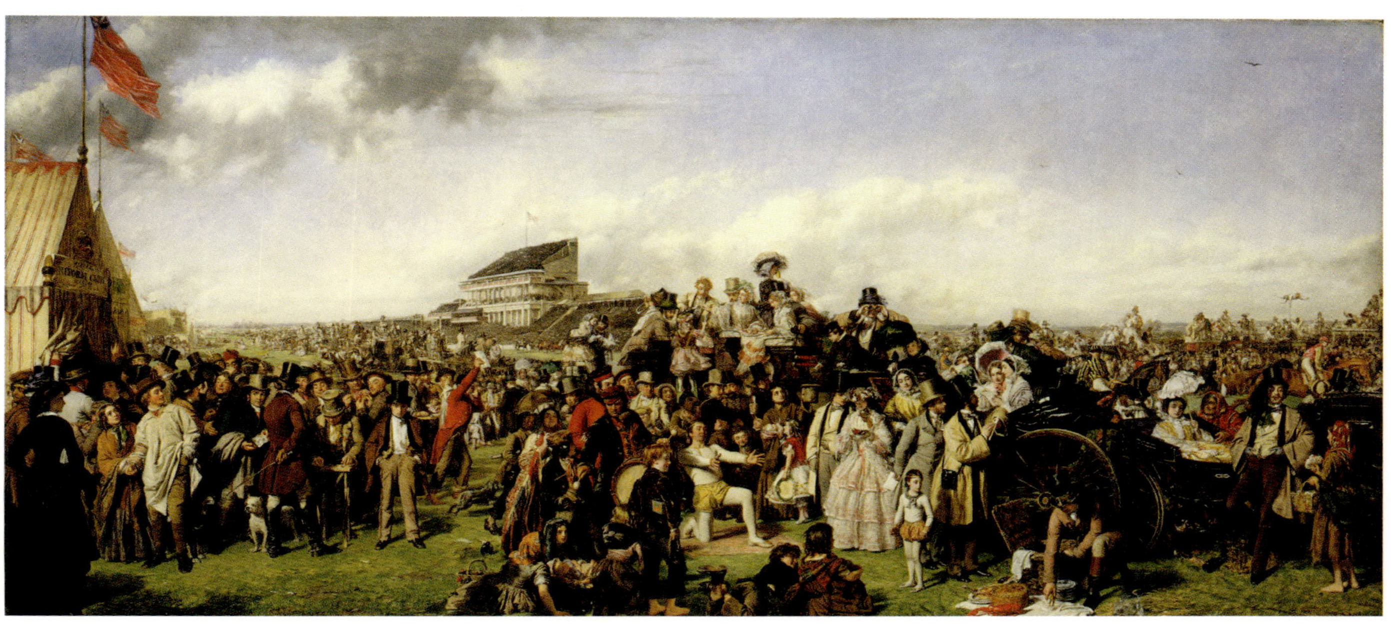

Tate, Bequeathed by Jacob Bell 1859

WILLIAM POWELL FRITH

'Derby Day' 1856–58

"The essentially hierarchical plan of English society is the great and ever-present fact (to the mind of a stranger); there is hardly a detail of life that does not in some degree betray it."[1]
Henry James, 'London at Midsummer', 1875

Frith was the undisputed master of the mid-Victorian painted 'social panorama' in which a spectrum of social types are represented. London's population rose from 1.1m to around 3m in the fifty years before Frith painted Derby Day to become the world's largest ever city. Moving around the city and encountering so many social types was often described as a 'parade' to be observed and classified. The Derby specifically was described by the London News as "the great leveller… a most revolutionary gathering clearly subversive of the proper distinctions which should always in a well-governed country exist between class and class."[2] This unique situation in which all classes could mingle freely provided an ideal opportunity to create a complete panorama of society. Frith's cast of characters are differentiated not merely by their clothes, bodily types, and headwear, but by their physiognomies. The idea that people were innately superior or inferior was becoming widely accepted, and was reinforced by the fact that amongst poorer groups average height dropped between 1750 and 1850, due to poor diet, poor housing and overwork. City life made physical distinctions between groups greater. Seventy five years later, Walter Benjamin parodied Victorian artists' drive to represent emergent social types: "what a wonderful workshop the… middle-class was for sculpture of the most varied kind. What unexpected types, what richness of invention in the character of the faces."[3]

1.From 'English Hours', 1875 (London: Penguin 1960 edition) p99
2. Quoted by Mary Cowling in 'The Artist as Anthropologist', 1989 (Cambridge: CUP), p126
3. Benjamin, trans. 2000, p92

OFFICE FOR NATIONAL STATISTICS

Socio-economic classification of the working population, Spring 2002

"What the latest census showed was increased and in some places, accelerating social polarisation... Although the social polarisation that the 2001 Census reveals is extraordinary by British standards, British standards of social polarisation may well still be low in international terms and the polarisation does little to alter the geographical hierarchy of places ordered from rich to poor."[1]
Phil Rees and Daniel Dorling, 'A nation still dividing', 2003

Do we agree with the economist JK Galbraith, who argues that in the US and to a lesser extent in the UK, the majority occupy a "culture of contentment", in which a prosperous majority – roughly 2/3 of the population – let the remainder "go to hell?"[2] Censuses are the primary official portrait of the nation. They are the principal way in which the State knows its citizenry and how it is organised. The official system for classifying social groups has the acronym 'NS-SEC': the National Statistics Socio-Economic Classification. At the top level it has eight groups of occupations though maps out a total of 3800 professions across the population. Despite its complexity, the scheme resembles that developed for the 1911 census, which has five principal groups roughly corresponding to the modern 'A-E' scheme. The 1911 categories were: Class I: 'Professional (wholly non-manual); Class II: 'Intermediate Income Groups'; Class III: 'Skilled Occupations'; Class IV: 'Partly Skilled Occupations'; Class V: 'Unskilled Occupations' (wholly manual). The first full census was in 1801; Victorian censuses literally record an individual's "rank or occupation": this is the principal way in which individuals were classified after age and gender.

Source: Labour Force Survey, Office for National Statistics.

1. www.sasi.group.shef.ac.uk/publications/2004/dorling_and_rees_nation_dividing.pdf
2. Quoted in Andrew Marr, 'Ruling Britannia', 1995 (London: Michael Joseph) p328

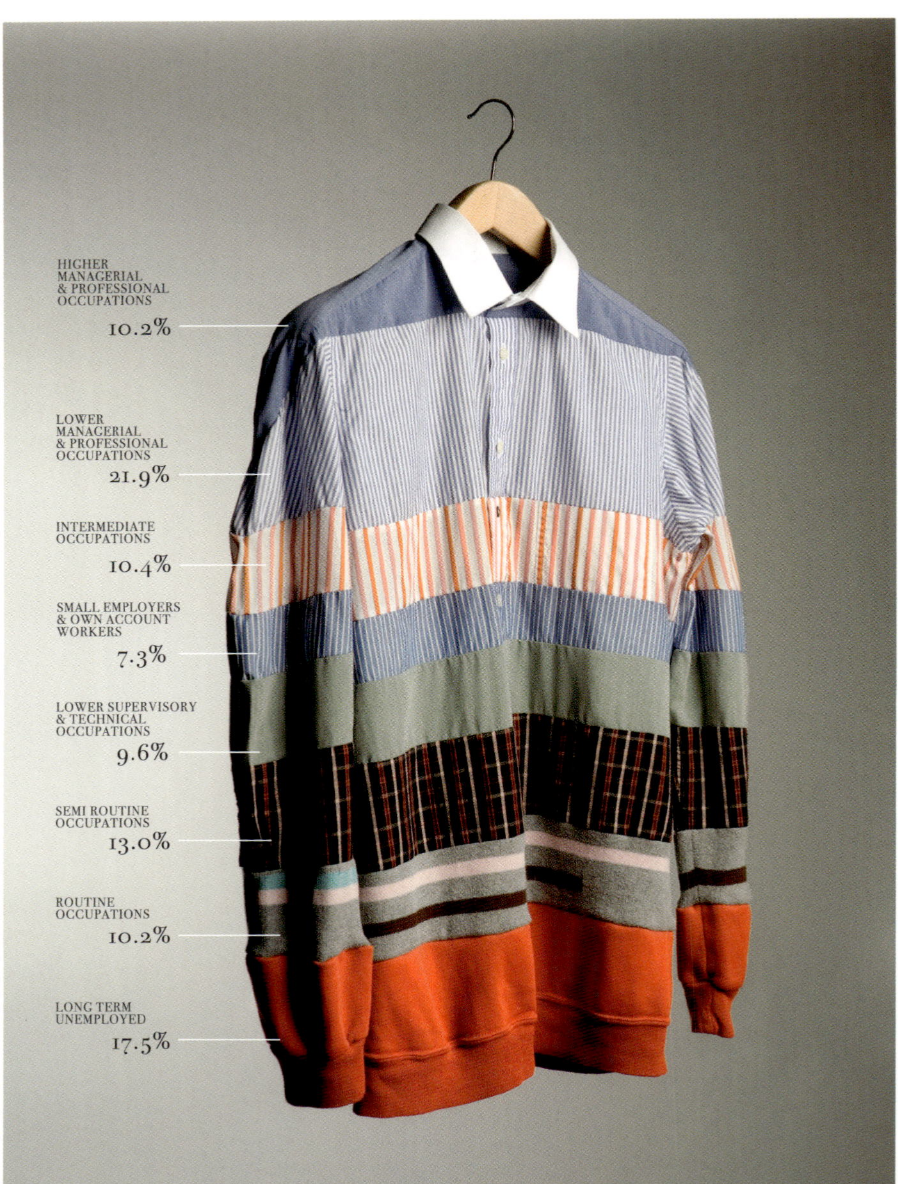

image by Ben Branagan & Gareth Holt

NATIONAL READERSHIP SURVEY / IPSOS MORI

Alphabetical socio-professional classification, updated 2008

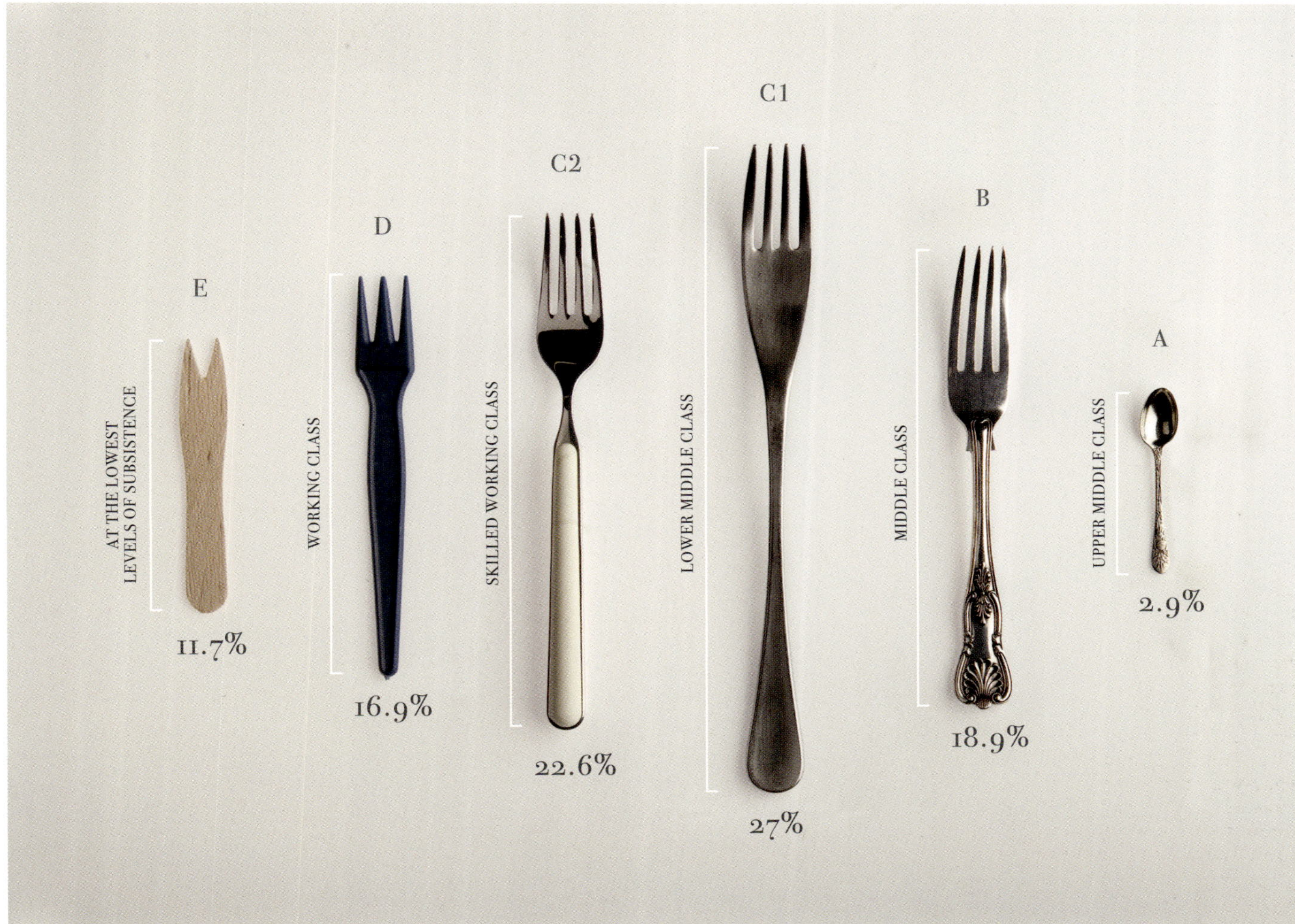

Social class	Professional function	Typical occupations
A Upper-middle class	Higher managerial / professional	Doctor, director
B Middle-class	Intermediate managerial	Teacher, engineer
C1 Lower middle-class	Supervisor, clerical or junior	Salesman, artist
C2 Skilled working-class	Skilled manual worker	Bricklayer, electrician
D Working class	Semi-skilled and unskilled manual	Operative, machinist
E Subsistence levels	State pensioners / no other income	Casual labourer

"Consider the arbitrariness of current values... The lowest paid occupations in 2002 were cleaners, caterers, carers, classroom assistants, launderers, dry-cleaners and check-out operators. The top-ten highest-paid occupations were: company financial managers, insurance brokers, solicitors, pilots, management consultants, data-processing managers, doctors, top-rank police officers and marketing and sales managers."[1] Polly Toynbee, 'Hard Work': Life in Low Pay Britain, 2003

This scheme for dividing society into income groups was originally developed by the National Readership Survey over 50 years ago but is now the standard system for market research. Social grades are determined by the occupation of the 'Chief Income Earner' in each household. The size of the organisation worked for, and number of people managed are also considered. Every single major occupation is graded.

image by Ben Branagan & Gareth Holt

1. Toynbee, 2003, p9

ERNEST WALCOUSINS

'He who serves best' 1922

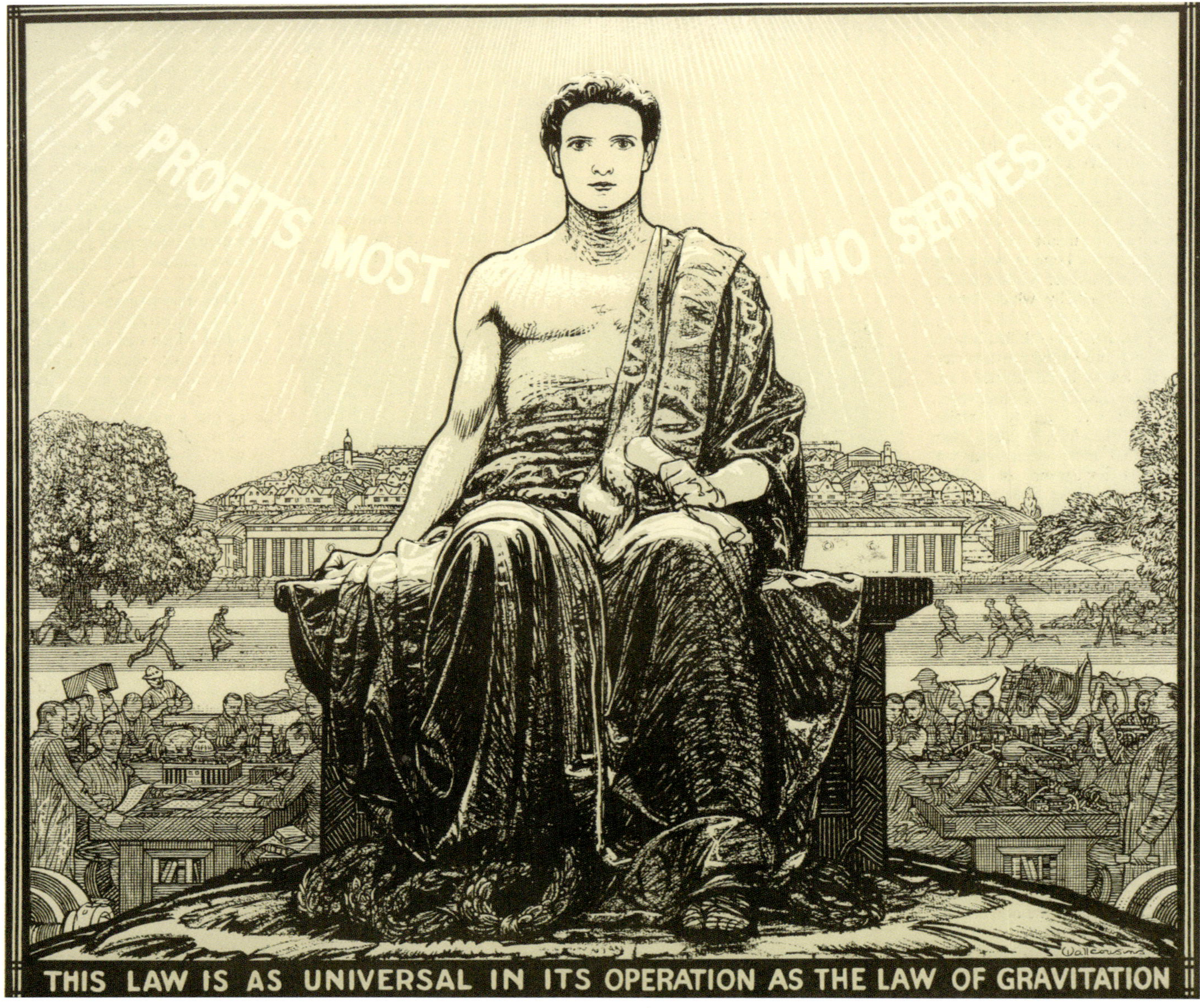

Wallcousins' image for 'Bibby's Annual' of 1922 resembles Thomas Hobbes' motif of a giant, heroic figure symbolising the whole of society. However, Wallcousins' hero is an everyman rather than an individual ruler, representing 'the marketplace' in which everyone gains by participating. Hobbes' vision of society was of all individuals being thrown into perpetual competition, and required to defend their property or be enslaved by others. Wallcousins' image is based on an almost utopian optimism about the fairness of commerce by contrast. In Wallcousins' vision, exactly as in those of later Soviet realism, the heroic exertions of workers create a harmonious, prosperous society.

PICTURING ECONOMICS:

'VISUALISING CAPITAL'

"Men and women live their productive relations."[1]

Thomspon, 'The Making of the English Working Class' 1963

What do we imagine to be the distribution of wealth and income across our society, or across the globe? How can we identify the key thresholds are between one group and the next? The images in this section range from those which state bald economic facts, to protests about the nature of wealth distribution, to representations of forms of currency. To caricature the differences between political left and right, we might say that for the latter, the dominant image of society is of a march, with those behind reaching the point occupied by 'leaders' after an interval of time. For the left, it has been a pyramid, representing the domination of resources by a minority.

More pessimistic thinkers from both sides of the spectrum, from Thomas Hobbes to Friedrich Engels, have seen society as a permanent struggle between all. For both Hobbes and Engels, survival is only possible by accumulating enough power over others to avoid being crushed by them. In one critic's description of Hobbes' ideas, the dynamo driving modern societies is that "every individual is necessarily pulled into a constant competitive struggle for power over others".[2] In Hobbes' own words, "I put for a generall inclination of all mankind, a perpetuall and restlesse desire of Power after power, that ceaseth onely in Death... the Value or worth of a man, is as of all other things, his Price."[3] Does modern commerce involve us all in a struggle for supremacy fought to the death?

Many of the early images here represent different 'classes' as points on a line, on a single vertical axis. This is patently insufficient to create a rounded, three-dimensional picture of our entire set of social relations. How we estimate each other in terms of their social ranking involves factors ranging across 'birth', gender, occupation, and education, as well as wealth. Nevertheless, economic differences are inseparable from other forms of differentiation or stratification. The problem at stake here is how wealth, power, and status are interrelated in society's organization.

1.EP Thomspon, 'The Making of the English Working Class', 1963, (London: Gollancz), p11
2. CB Macpherson, 'Leviathan' 1986 edition (London: Penguin), p36
3. Hobbes in, ibid, p37

'INEQUALITY KILLS'

Does inequality really matter? The poor have what their grandparents would think unimaginable luxuries – TVs, telephones and washing machines. Why should it matter to them if in some unseen stratosphere the gated kleptocrats on company boards award themselves staggering sums of money? Does anyone really mind the gap?

That is a reasonable question and it niggles away at those on the left, too. Equality has gone out of fashion. Social justice now means heaving the poorest over the poverty threshold and lifting the life chances of children from lower social classes. Tony Blair said early on that he was not bothered about wealth, only about abolishing poverty. Talk of inequality sounds like the old politics of envy. Equality of opportunity, yes, but equality for its own sake, why?

Here is the answer. There is a mountain of irrefutable evidence from all over the world showing the damage done by extreme inequality. However rich a country is, it will still be more dysfunctional, violent, sick and sad if the gap between social classes grows too wide. Poorer countries with fairer wealth distribution are healthier and happier than richer, more unequal nations.

Life expectancy in rich nations correlates precisely with levels of equality. So Greece, with half the GDP per head, has longer life expectancy than the US, the richest and most unequal country with the lowest life expectancy in the developed world. The people of Harlem live shorter lives than the people of Bangladesh. When you take out the violence and drugs, two-thirds of the reason is heart disease. Is that bad diet? No, it is mainly stress, the stress of living at the bottom of the pecking order, on the lowest rung, the stress of disrespect and lack of esteem. Bad nutrition does less harm than depression.

Tests have found that subordinate, low-status monkeys had high levels of the stress hormone, cortisol, which leads to arteriosclerosis. When the high-status monkeys were all put together and low-status monkeys put in another enclosure, all the pecking orders changed. When some previous high-rankers became subordinate they developed all the same physical symptoms, including a five-fold increase in arteriosclerosis within less than two years. Meanwhile, some of the low-ranks who suddenly found themselves dominant, had sharply dropped levels of stress hormone.

Social status and respect matter beyond anything, and the psychological damage done by being at the bottom is crippling. A survey of Whitehall civil servants found junior ranks were three times more likely to die in a year than seniors, with a fine sliding gradation from top to bottom according to status.

Homicide rates (and other crimes) track a country's level of inequality, not its overall wealth. The fairest countries have the highest levels of trust and social capital. The American states that have the more equal income distribution also have most social trust: New Hampshire, the most equal, is least likely to agree that "most people would try to take advantage of you if they got the chance."

Social environment can be more toxic than any pollutant. Low status and lack of control over one's life is a destroyer of human health and happiness. The wealth gap causes few to vote or participate in anything in a world of fear, conflict and hostility.

It is not primarily five-a-day fruit and veg or obesity that need targeting, but social injustice itself. Infant mortality is mainly a result of low-birth weight babies, something the government has tried hard to improve. These days small premature babies are not caused by bad diet: even poor nutrition by British standards will rarely harm a foetus. It is stress in pregnancy that does. High cortisol levels which affect the foetus for life – and poorer mothers are more depressed, with less social support. Psyche matters more than vitamins, all through life. An orphanage in hungry post-war Germany found children on the same diet were found to have grown most under the kindest matron and least under the unkindest matron.

Poverty in rich nations is not a number of the absence of a particular necessity. A poor vicar may bring up his children well on lentils and respect. But for most people respect is measured in money. Low pay tells people that their labour and they themselves are worth little. Poverty is not, as the government imagines, a line to pull people over but it is a position on a line. If it tilts too sharply upwards, the pain of those at the bottom can be measured in hard statistics. Inequality is the real enemy.

EVAN HOLLOWAY

'Capital' 2005

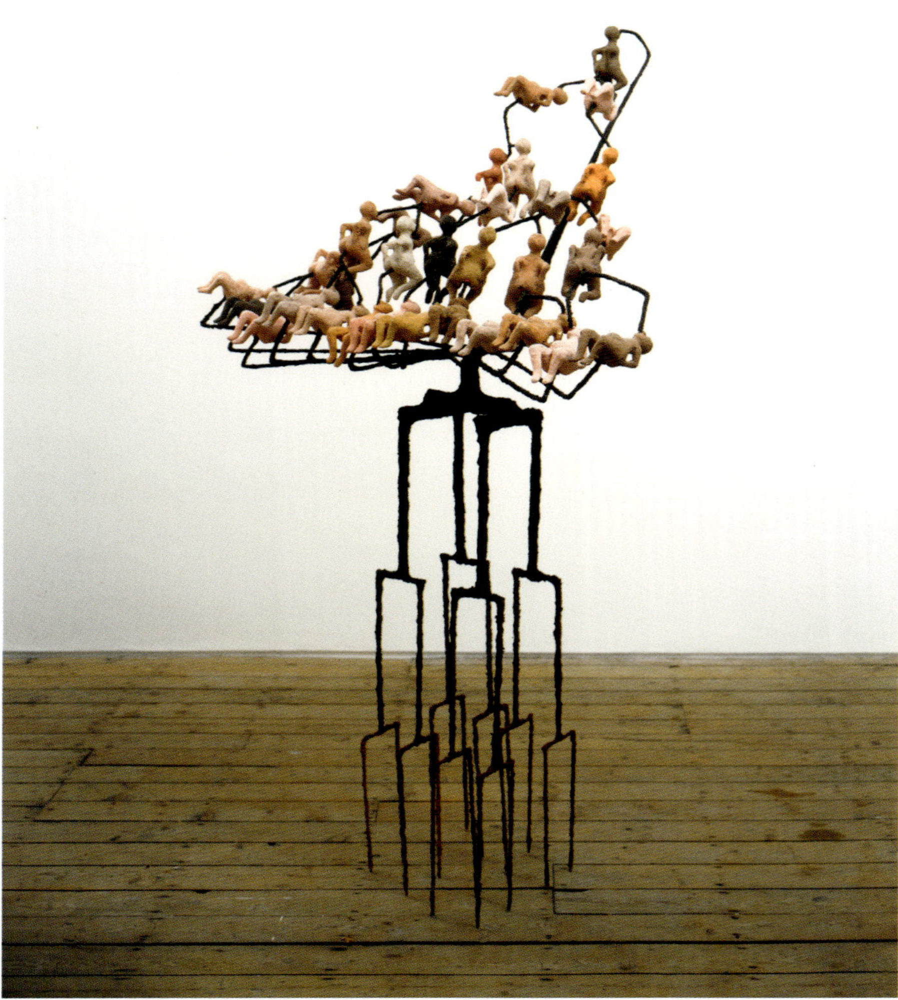

Courtesy Frank Cohen Collection
Image courtesy The Approach, London

"Trickledown theory – the less then elegant metaphor that if one feeds the horse enough oats, some will pass through to the road for the sparrows."[1]
JK Galbraith, undated

The US constitution is based upon the founding idea expressed in the Declaration of Independence that "all men are created equal."[2] But Evan Holloway's work echoes Friedrich Engels' description of modern commerce as "reciprocal plundering under the protection of the law, so shameless, so openly avowed that one shrinks before the consequences of our social state."[3] The USA is the world's richest country by a long measure; but it is also one of the world's most unequal countries: 1% of the population command 15% of the country's income.
The scatological subject and crude form of Evan Holloway's sculpture are intended to repulse and disgust, to make us feel what he feels about American politics during the 2000s. At one level his work can be read as a ribald pun on the term 'gross domestic product', the most common measurement of national income. At another, it is an illustration of the dominant image of how society and the economy functions in right-wing America. Broadly speaking, 'trickledown theory' argues that lowering taxes for the rich make the economy more dynamic. The image underpinning the idea of 'trickledown' is that the economy is like a fountain where 'liquid' capital only flows from the top to the bottom.

1. Quoted by Dorling at www.worldmapper.org
2. http://www.nps.gov/revwar/unfinished_revolution/01_all_men_are_created_equal.html
3. www.marxists.org/archive/marx/works/1845/condition-working-class/index.htm

INDUSTRIAL WORKERS OF THE WORLD

'Pyramid of Capitalist System' 1911

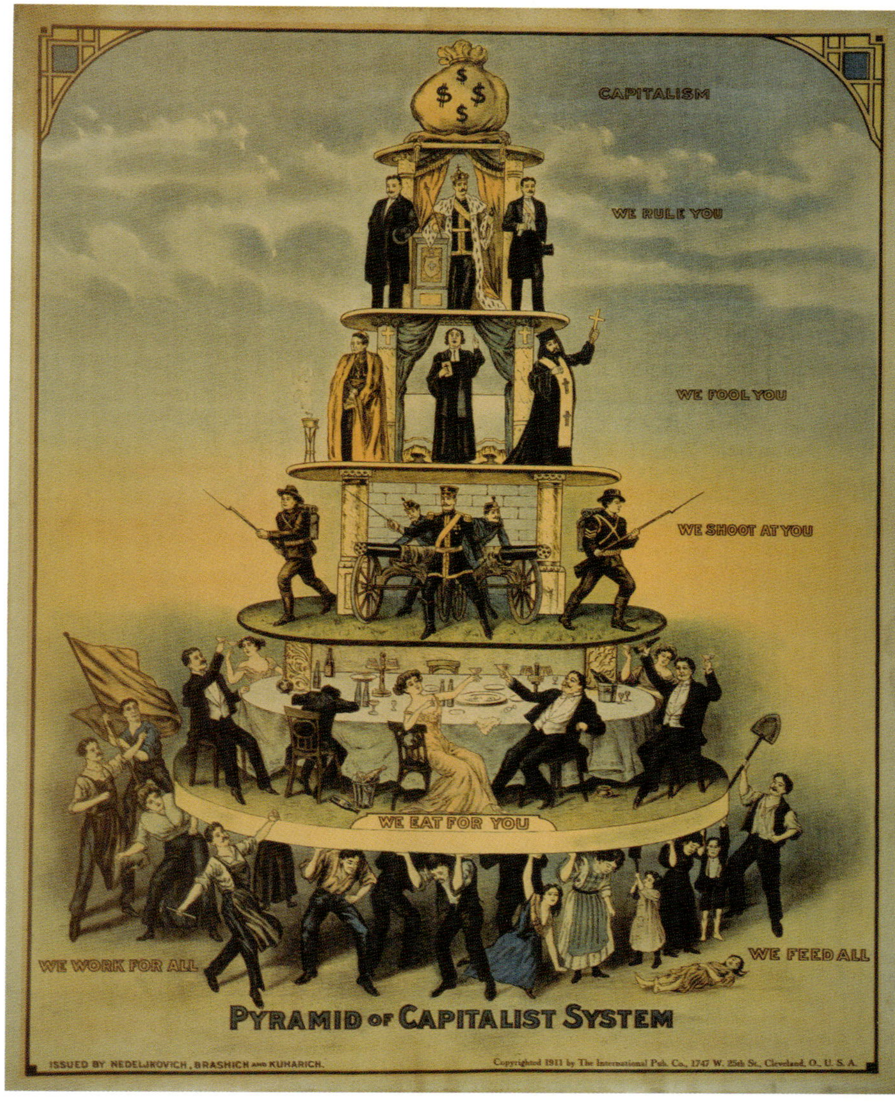

Courtesy Industrial Workers of the World

"That appointed chain / Which when in cohesion it unites / Order to order, rank to rank / In mutual benefit / So binding heart to heart."[1] **Robert Southey, 1830**

That the shapes of industrial societies are 'pyramids' has long seemed indisputable. The IWW's poster was so simple and potent that it was recreated by left-leaning groups in almost every industrialised nation at the time of the First World War. More recently, the academic AH Halsey has argued that post-industrial nations' occupational structures have changed "from the shape of a pyramid to that of an electric light bulb."[2] Fewer and fewer Britons are employed in manual labour. When this picture was made, three quarters of the population were in or dependent on manual labour. By mid-century it was roughly half. Today, it is under a sixth of us. However, peoples' perceptions of their status do not appear to correlate to this. A 1990s MORI poll which recreated a poll 50 years earlier revealed that over two-thirds of people would call themselves "working class" now even though only 40% of people described themselves in this way in the 1940s.[3]

1. Quoted in Cannadine,1998, p36
2. Halsey, 1986, p32
3. Greg Hadfield and Mark Skidforth 'Class',1994 (London: Bloomsbury) p8,

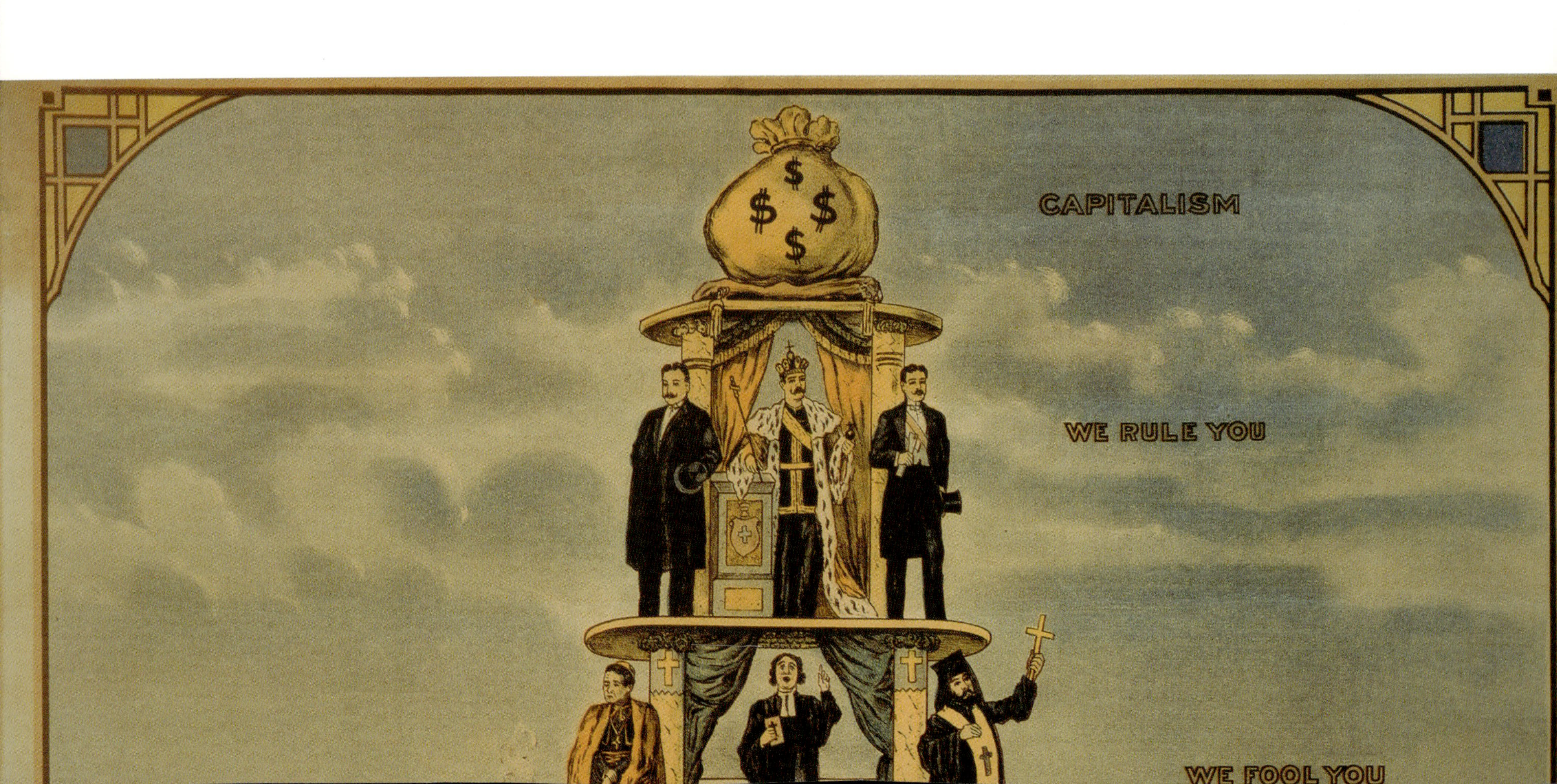
CAPITALISM
WE RULE YOU
WE FOOL YOU

WE SHOOT AT YOU

WE EAT FOR YOU

WE WORK FOR ALL

WE FEED ALL

PYRAMID OF CAPITALIST SYSTEM

ISSUED BY NEDELJKOVICH, BRASHICH AND KUHARICH.

DR FRANK A. COWELL

'Income distribution in the United States 1913–1997' 2007

image by Ben Branagan & Gareth Holt

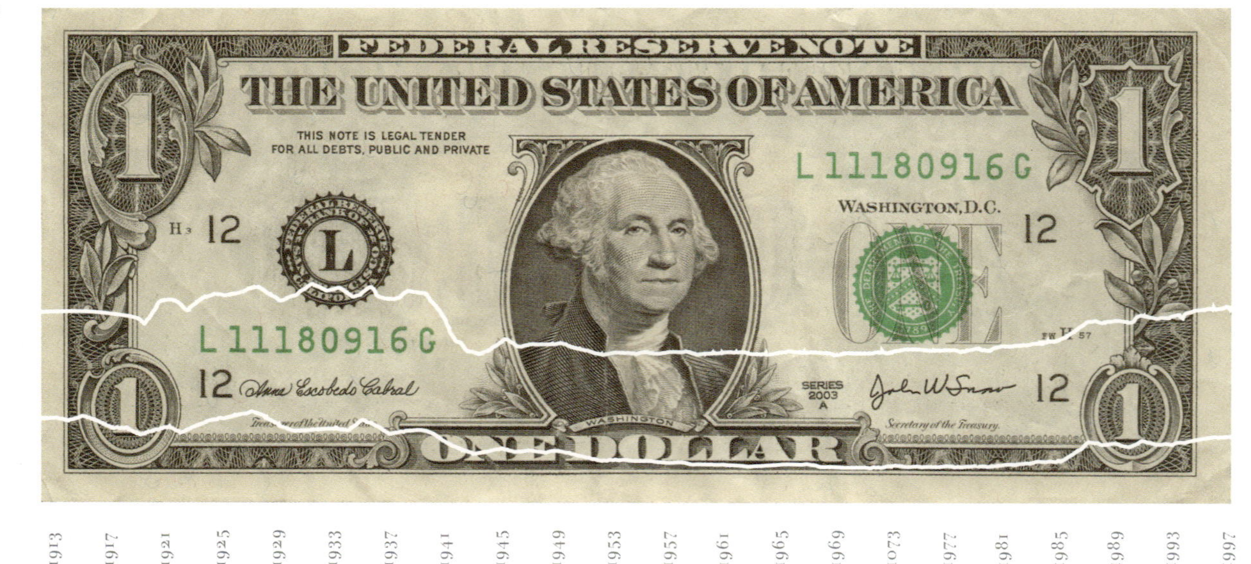

"Few things are more evident in modern social history than the decline of interest in equality as an economic issue... This has been particularly true in the USA."[1]
JK Galbraith, "The Affluent Society", 1958

How much inequality should we tolerate? Today, the richest 300,000 Americans earn as much as the poorest 150 million, and enjoy an average incomes 440 times greater.[2] When America was at its most equal in the 1960s and 1970s, the top 1% earned only 10% of the nation's income. Before WWII, it had been up to a quarter of all income; it is more than one seventh now. Yet the myth of the US as classless is longstanding. George Washington, in 1788, optimistically wrote that the founding of an independent America would give birth to a new social order, and a new conception of social relations: "the distinction of classes begins to disappear..." The journalist Polly Toynbee has argued that this founding story has actually helped sustain inequalities, as it sustains the myth that everyone begins with the same life chances and is as likely to prosper: "gross inequality is morally comfortable so long as there is a plausible story of the rise of the fittest. Everyone needs a justification for the way we live."[3] Frank Cowell has investigated different ways in which levels and types of inequality can be understood. His graph reveals the contours of the financial landscape which Americans have occupied over the post-war period.

1. Quoted by Cannadine, 1998, p37
2. Financial Times Weekend Nov 29-30 2008, Life and Arts, p17.
3. Toynbee, 2003, p1

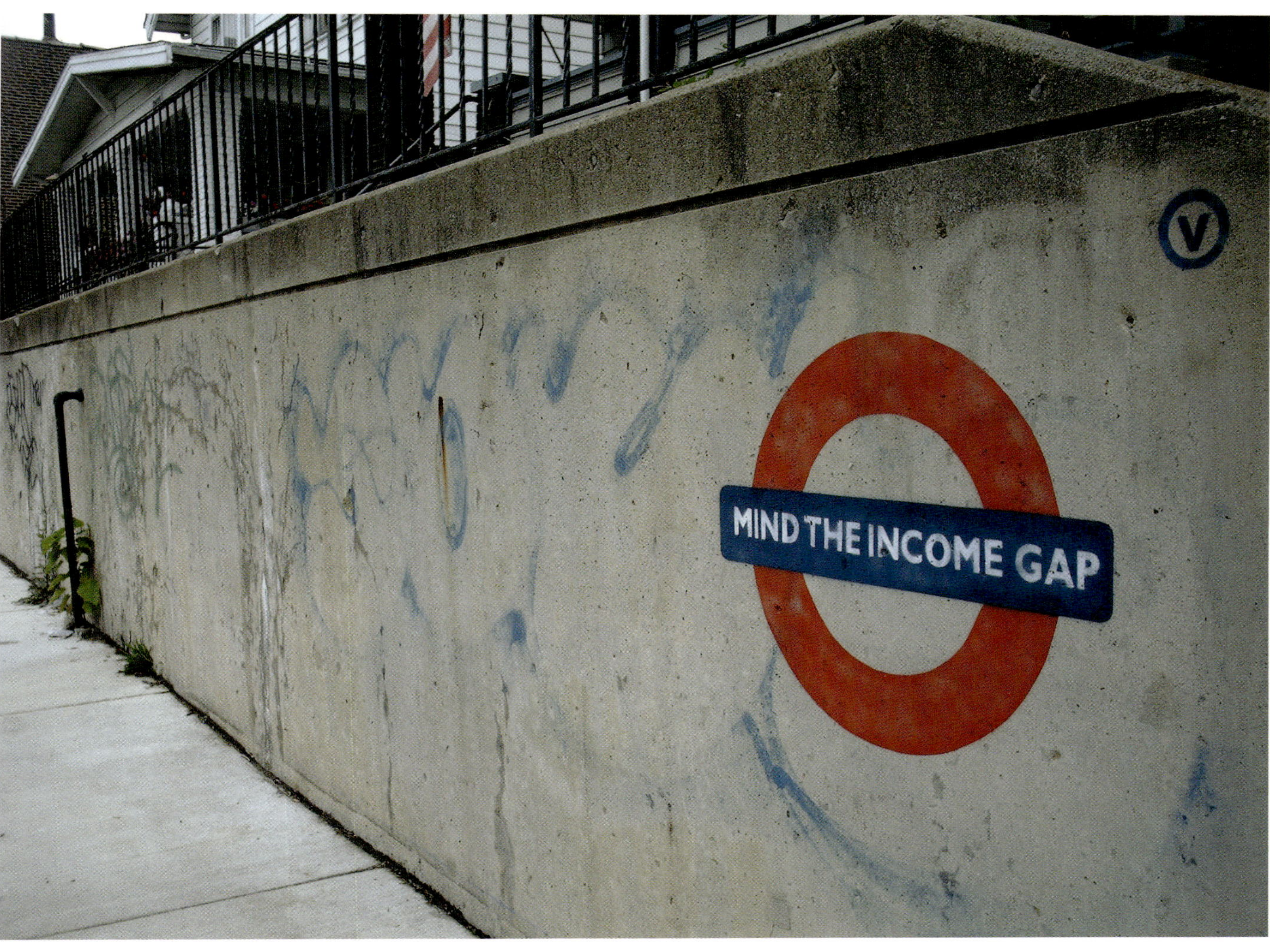

'Mind the Income Gap' 2007

"Normally speaking, it may be said that the forces of a capitalist society, if left unchecked, tend to make the rich richer and the poor poorer and thus increase the gap between them."[1]
Jawaharlal Nehru, 1960

The assumption that every individual has the opportunity to 'improve' their economic position and social standing might reasonably be said to underpin America's social structure. The founding story of the nation is based in part on ideas observed by visitors in the 1760s: that Americans "have no notion of rank or distinction" and that "all mortifying distinctions of rank are lost in common equality."[2] This work pays homage to Thomas Jefferson, the main author of the American Declaration of Independence, who argued that "a little rebellion, now and again, is a good thing."[3] As Professor Daniel Dorling has written, "income differences are closely correlated to social mobility, with countries like Britain and the USA (the 'land of opportunity') enjoying significantly less social mobility than, for example, Norway and Sweden… levels of poor health and extreme violence are consistently worse in more unequal societies. High levels of inequality play a crucial part in corroding social relations."[4] Dorling has asked the question: does the uninhibited pursuit of wealth actually make people worse off in terms of their own well-being, or in terms of their 'social capital' – their bonds with others?

1. Quoted in Felipe Fernandez-Armesto, 'Ideas that changed the world', 2003, (London: DK) p37
2. Henry Hulton and anonymous British official quoted by Cannadine, 1998, p37
3. www.law.georgetown.edu/faculty/forman/Documents/Rebellion.pdf
4. http://sasi.group.shef.ac.uk/publications/commentary/red_pepper_inequality_kills..pdf

'They Rule' 2004

Image: screenshot from www.theyrule.net

"Capital cheats...you must admire the absolute initiative capital enjoys... Ownership of money burns your fingers, like power. We need people to take this risk for us and we should be eternally grateful to them."[1] **Jean Baudrillard, 'America', 1986**

'They Rule' is an online project which makes the hidden structures of power in society visible. In On's words it "aims to provide a glimpse of some of the relationships of the US ruling class." The work allows users to browse through directories of names of the board members of each of the US's top 500 companies in 2004. We are able to create maps of connections between them as several sit on up to six or seven different companies. For Josh On, "this ruling class" should be seen as intimately intertwined – as "a 'band of hostile brothers." Some surprises await: the same individuals sit on the boards of both Pepsi and Coca Cola for example, which as competitors should be mutually exclusive positions. Josh On's intention is to create a visual metaphor for the 'web' of connections that bind corporate America together. 'They Rule' is a playful research tool with serious intent. Though the data was collected from publicly available files, it is ordinarily out of sight and out of mind.

1. Jean Baudrillard, 'America', 1986, (London: Verso) pp80, 61

THE ATLANTIC MONTHLY AFTER JAN PEN

American earned incomes by human scale, 2007

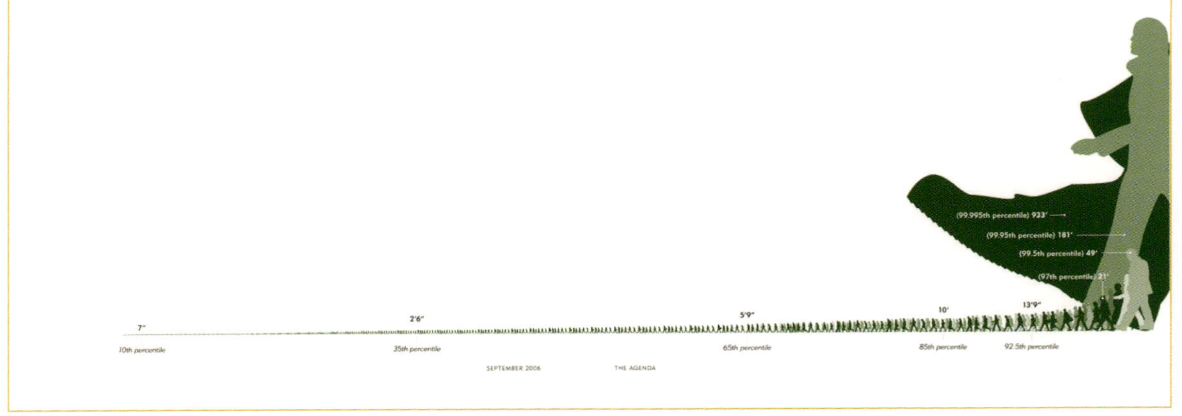

Strangely, this statistical image is scarcely different to that from Hobbes' 'Leviathan' some 350 years earlier. Does this reflect something fundamental about our mindset? Do Anglophone societies, who have long placed a premium on 'liberty' or 'freedom', simply raise certain individuals into symbolic positions of power, or into hero figures? The Economist Jan Pen was the first to visualise society as a parade of people in which different incomes could be represented by different scales. Here, a handful of giants tower over the rest of the population, like Hobbes' sovereign monarch surveying his land. The 'median' average income is here 6' tall here. One third earn more than this – and two-thirds less. This much alone tells us something about the structure of American society. However, it is the shape of the 'curve' that is revealed here. The wealthiest 1/20,000 of the population command incomes 155 times greater than the average Joe. Moreover, as Atlantic Monthly have reported, "the highest earners are now capturing most of the gain in national income caused by economy-wide productivity growth… The top 1% captured far more of the real national gain in salary income than the bottom 50%". What is it in our collective mentality that makes such inequalities tolerable?

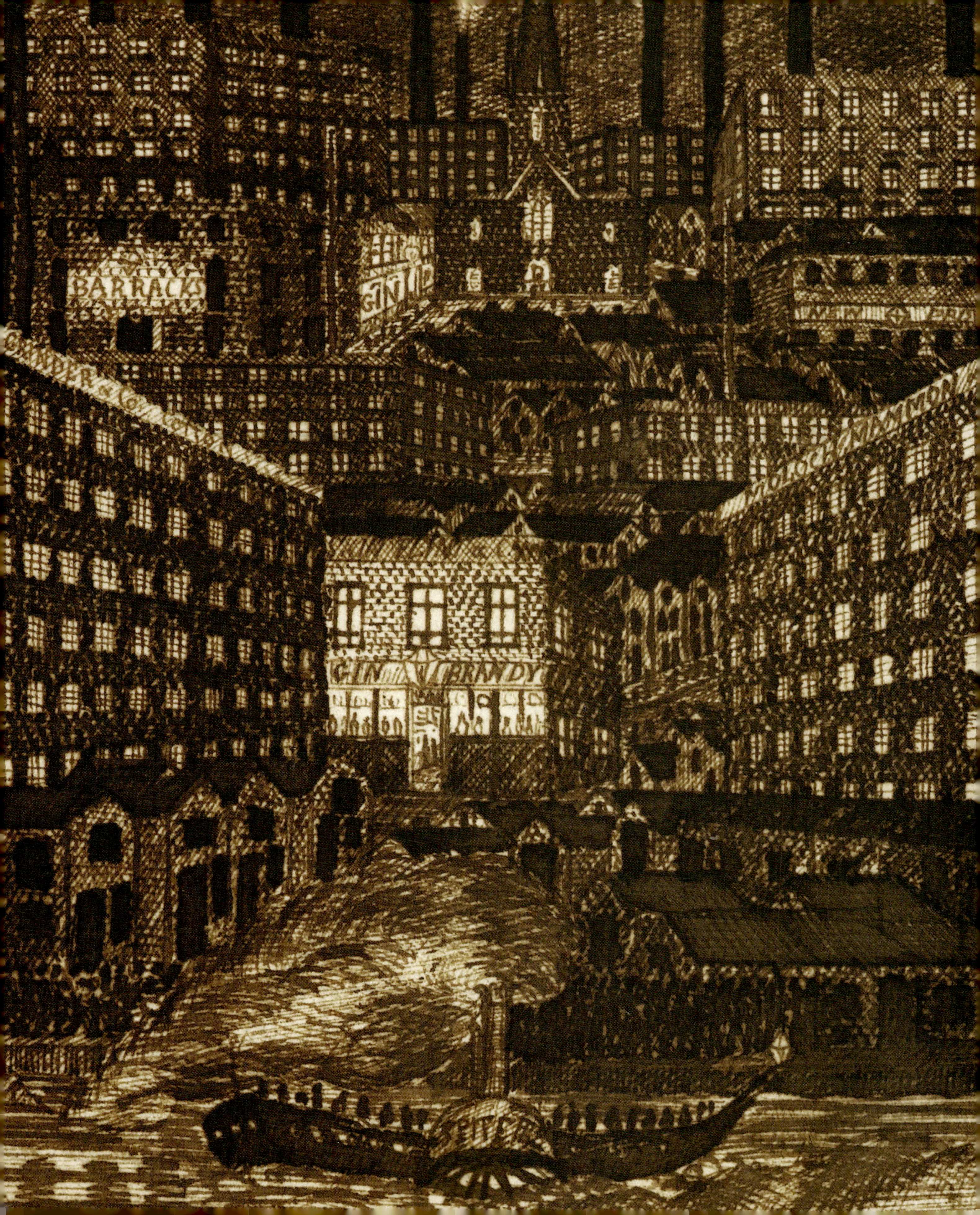
BARRACKS
GIN
BRANDY

ERNEST JONES

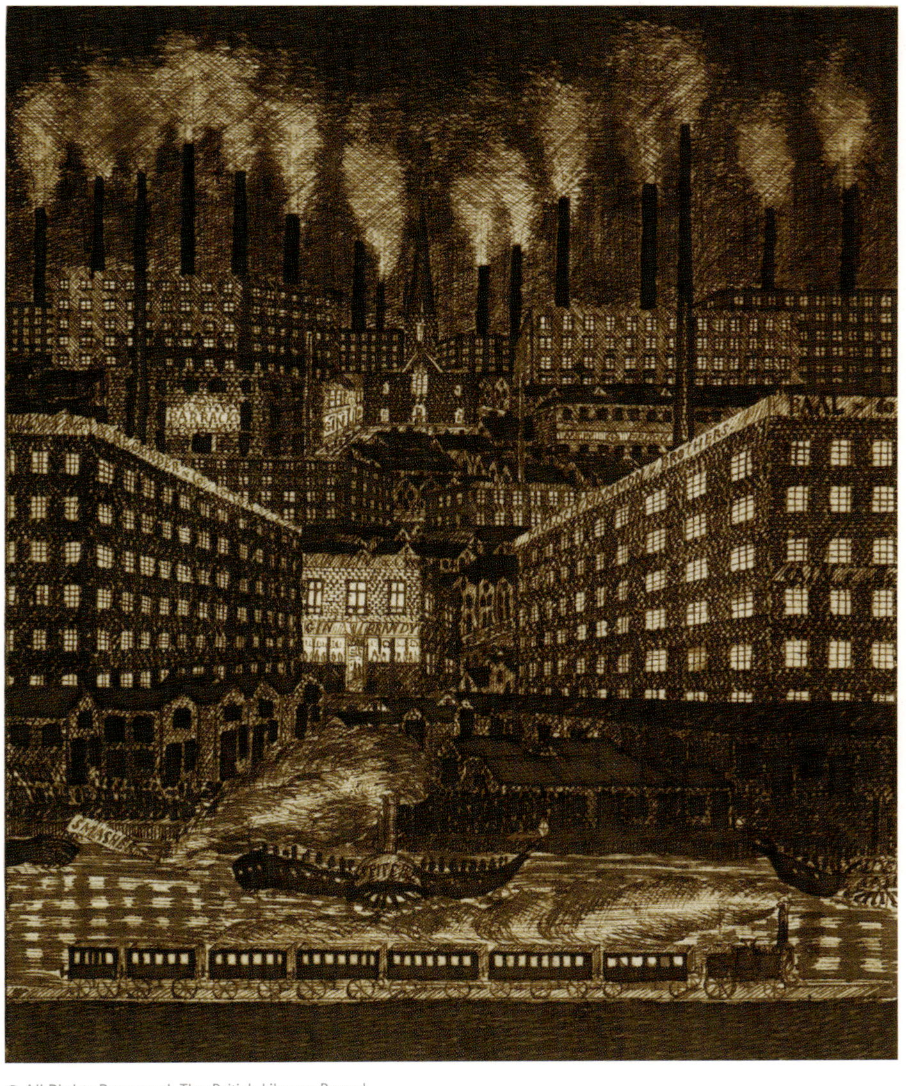

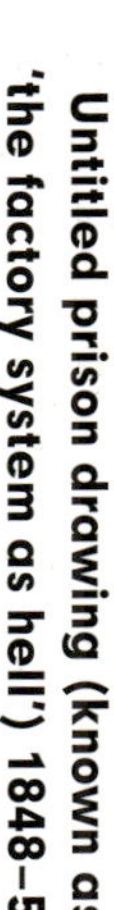

"Hell hath no limits, nor is circumscribed / In one self place: for where we are is hell."[1] **Christopher Marlowe, from 'Dr Faustus', 1604**

How far do the Victorian stereotypes of England's industrial regions continue in the popular imagination today? This little-known drawing, seemingly embodies every aspect of what William Blake called England's "dark, satanic mills", and has a tragic story. Ernest Jones was a leading Chartist, who between 1848- 50 was imprisoned for sedition. Whilst in prison, he drew this from imagination, using his paper allowance for letters. His disgust and horror at heavy industry helped forge the Chartist aim to retake control of the countryside, to help workers each have their own plot. Others agreed with the diagnosis, if not the cure. Also in 1848 Marx and Engels created a similarly apocalyptic vision of the industrial north: "in proportion, therefore, as the repulsiveness of the work increases, the wage decreases... From this foul drain the greatest stream of human industry flows out to fertilize the whole world. From this filthy sewer pure gold grows. Here humanity attains its most complete development and its most brutish."[2] Overseen by monstrous, monolithic buildings on every side, the workers in this city suffer chimneys belching smoke with only 'gin and brandy' for consolation. The buildings are owned by "Moloch, Mammon and Brothers" and "Bonegrinder & Co. Cotton."

1. Quoted in Hill, 1972, p175
2. http://www.uncp.edu/home/rwb/manchester_19c.html /

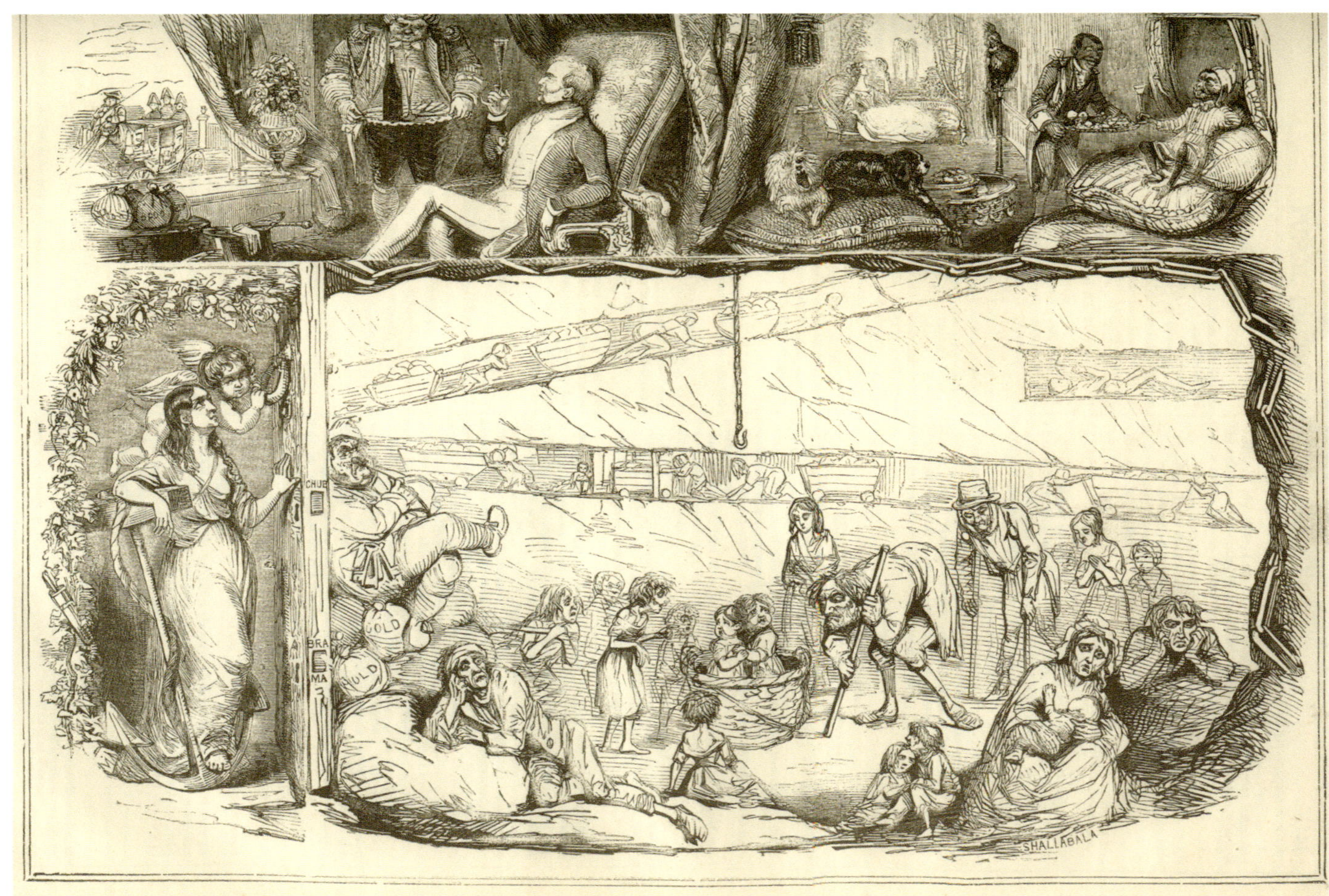

CAPITAL AND LABOUR.

Working Class Movement Library, Salford

"Our Queen reigns over the greatest nation that ever existed.' 'Which nation?' asked the younger stranger, "for she reigns over two.'... 'Yes, two nations; between whom there is no intercourse and no sympathy; who are as ignorant of each other's habits, thoughts, and feelings, as if they were dwellers in different zones, or inhabitants of different planets; who are formed by a different breeding, are fed by a different food, are ordered by different manners, and are not governed by the same laws."
'You speak of—' said Egremont, hesitatingly. 'THE RICH AND THE POOR.'[1]
Benjamin Disraeli, 'Sybil, or The Two Nations', 1845

"Manufacture centralises property in the hands of the few...Old England itself is unknown to memory and to the tales of our grandfathers... There exist here only a rich and a poor class."[2]
Friedrich Engels, 'The Condition of the Working Class in England', 1845

This image is one of the first to depict 'capital' and 'labour' in direct opposition. It was published in the same year as a Tory MP and the father of modern communism similarly observed stark contrasts between groups. Hamerton's grotesque cast are roles of absolute dominance and submission, as master and servants.

1. http://www.gutenberg.org/dirs/etext03/sybil10.txt
2. www.marxists.org/archive/marx/works/1845/condition-working-class/index.htm

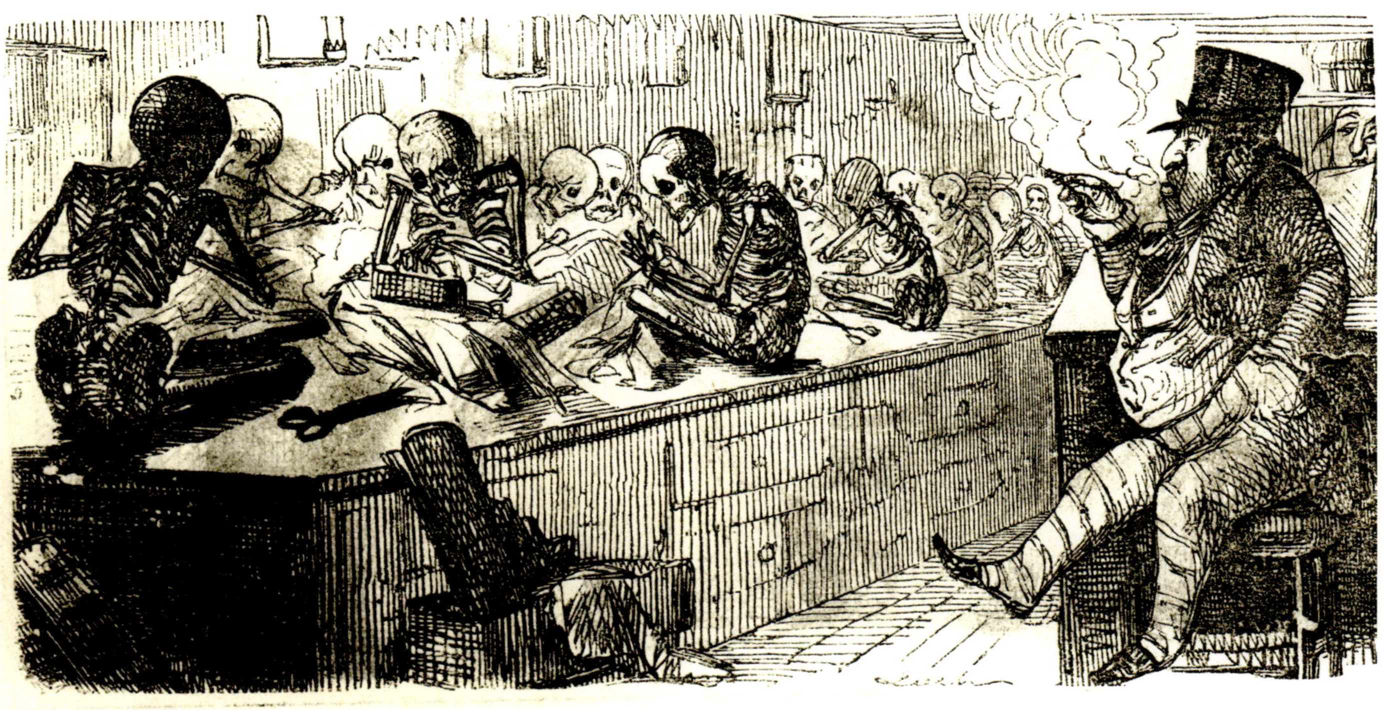

Collection Sunderland Libraries

JOHN LEECH

'Cheap Clothing' in 'Punch' 1843

"[The] restless, dynamic capitalism of the late 20th and 21st centuries, with its global scope, gross inequalities, predatory ultra-rich and powerless underclass [is] strikingly reminiscent of the capitalism of 100 years ago."[1]
David Marquand, 'Britain since 1918', 2008

The ability of the rich to consume elegant clothing has long been dependent on sweatshops. In the 1840s these were in different parts of the country; in the 21st century they are in different parts of the world. Textile workers' hours and conditions in certain 'developing' nations are not dissimilar to those of English workers of the 1840s. In its early years the magazine 'Punch' published images contrasting the living and working conditions of labourers and of Society figures. In 1843 it also published Thomas Hood's poem 'The Song of the Shirt', inspired by the case of a widow with two children who earned seven shillings a week for 50 hours work. It contained the lines: "It is not linen you're wearing out / But human creatures' lives! ...Sewing at once, with a double thread / A shroud as well as a shirt."[2] As Friedrich Engels, himself a factory owner, noted "it is a curious fact that the production of precisely those articles which serve the personal adornment of the ladies of the bourgeoisie involves the saddest consequences for the health of the workers."[3]

1. Quoted in Roy Hattersley, 'Inclement Times', Guardian Saturday Review, Sept 27 2008
2. http://www.poetry-online.org/hood_thomas_song_of_the_shirt.htm
3. www.marxists.org/archive/marx/works/1845/condition-working-class/index.htm

WALTER CRANE

'A Little Holiday, or a Day Off For All Parties' 1886

"Some animals are more equal than others."[1] **George Orwell, Animal Farm, 1945**

For Crane the labour force is a beast of burden finally shedding its shackles, having been made to 'carry' the forces of capital. Crane's drawing represents three characters as the three founding social groups identified by economists Adam Smith and David Ricardo. Ricardo saw society as based on the "three classes of the community; namely, the proprietor of the land, the owner of the stock or capital necessary for its cultivation, and the labourers by whose industry it is cultivated."[2] Ricardo uses "classes"; for Smith 40 years earlier the same groups were "constituent orders of society". Crane's print marks that the main terms of social description had shifted decisively, to see groups as competing, not complementary.

1. George Orwell, 'Animal Farm', 1945 (London: Penguin edition, 1982), p114
2. http://sticerd.lse.ac.uk/dps/darp /darp94.pdf

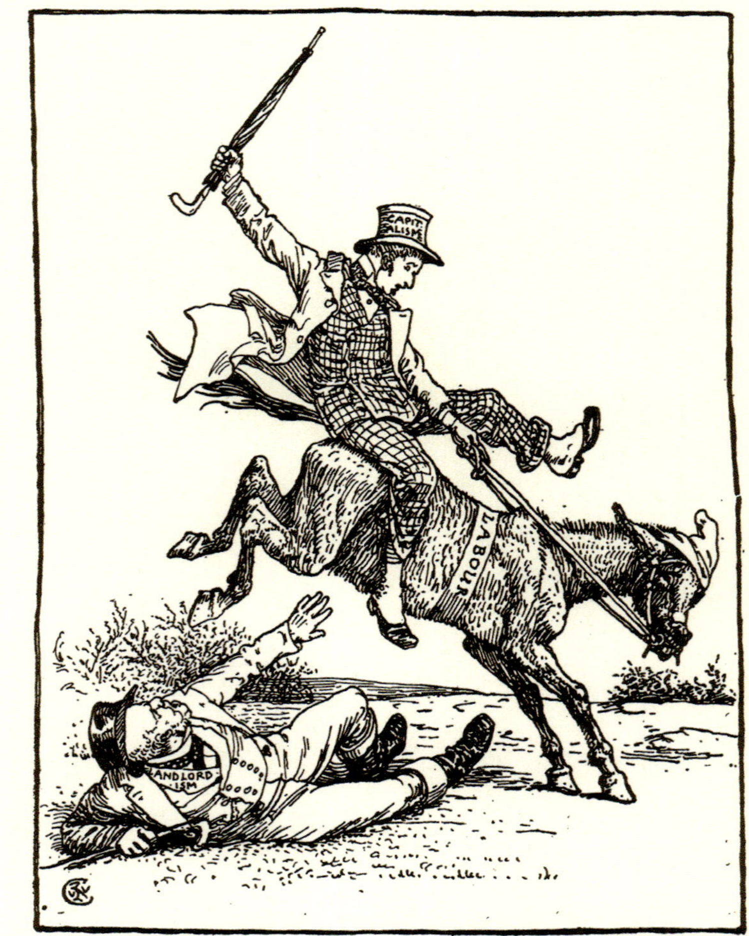

·A·LITTLE·HOLIDAY: OR·A·DAY·OFF FOR·ALL·PARTIES
[see "THE DONKEY & THE COMMON"]

Working Class Movement Library, Salford

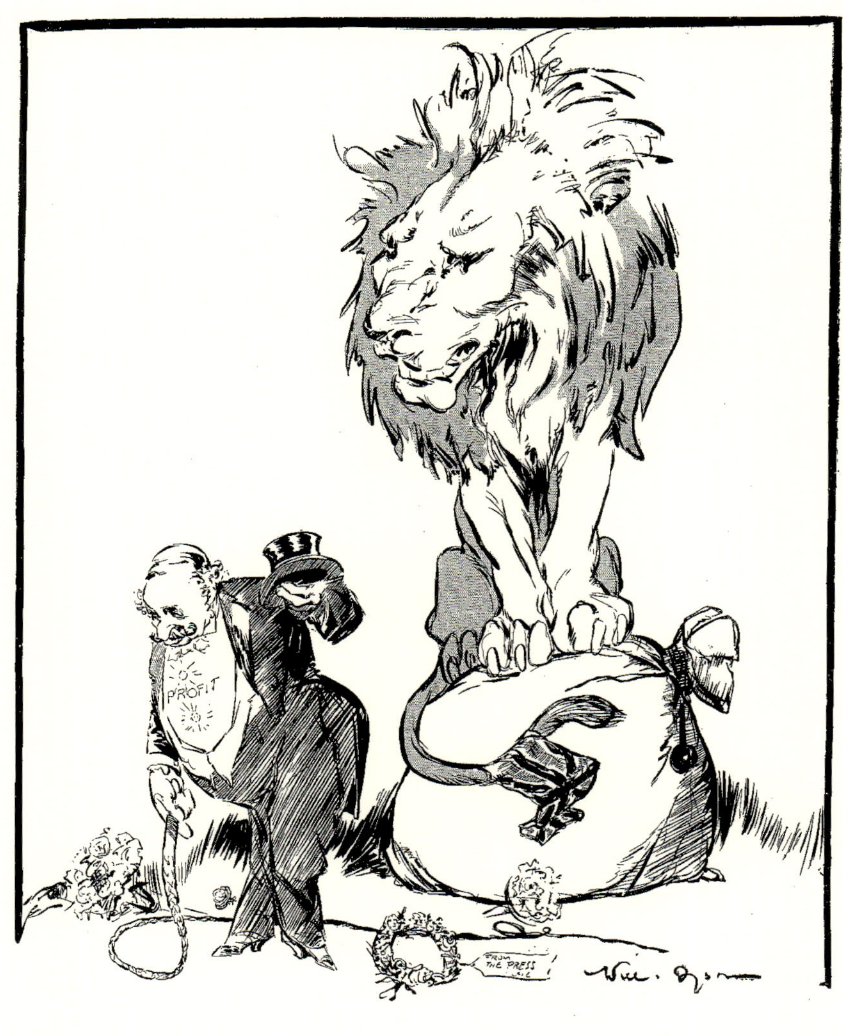

THE BRITISH LION (A Study in National Docility).

— South Africa, 1914. —

Working Class Movement Library, Salford

"Our epoch... possesses this distinctive feature: it has simplified the class antagonisms. Society as a whole is more and more splitting into two great hostile camps, into two great classes directly facing each other: bourgeoisie and proletariat."[1] **Karl Marx, 'The Communist Manifesto', 1848**

Will Dyson began his working life in Melbourne, but became well-known when working as an artist for the radical, far-left English newspaper The Daily Herald. Dyson's images make Marx's words graphic, pitting symbolic figures of each class explicitly against one another, picturing their interests as fundamentally incompatible. Dyson's polemical images promoting the interests of industrial workers echo those many created in the new Soviet Union, only a couple of years later.

1. Karl Marx, 'The Communist Manifesto', 1848, (London: Penguin 1967 edition), p80

FRED ELLIS

'Fine Lady and an Artist' 1926

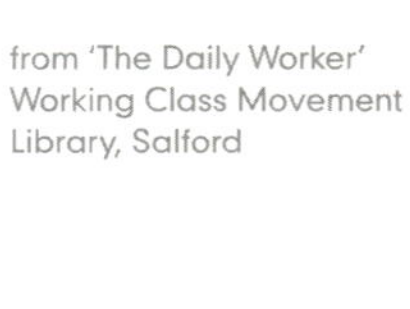

from 'The Daily Worker'
Working Class Movement Library, Salford

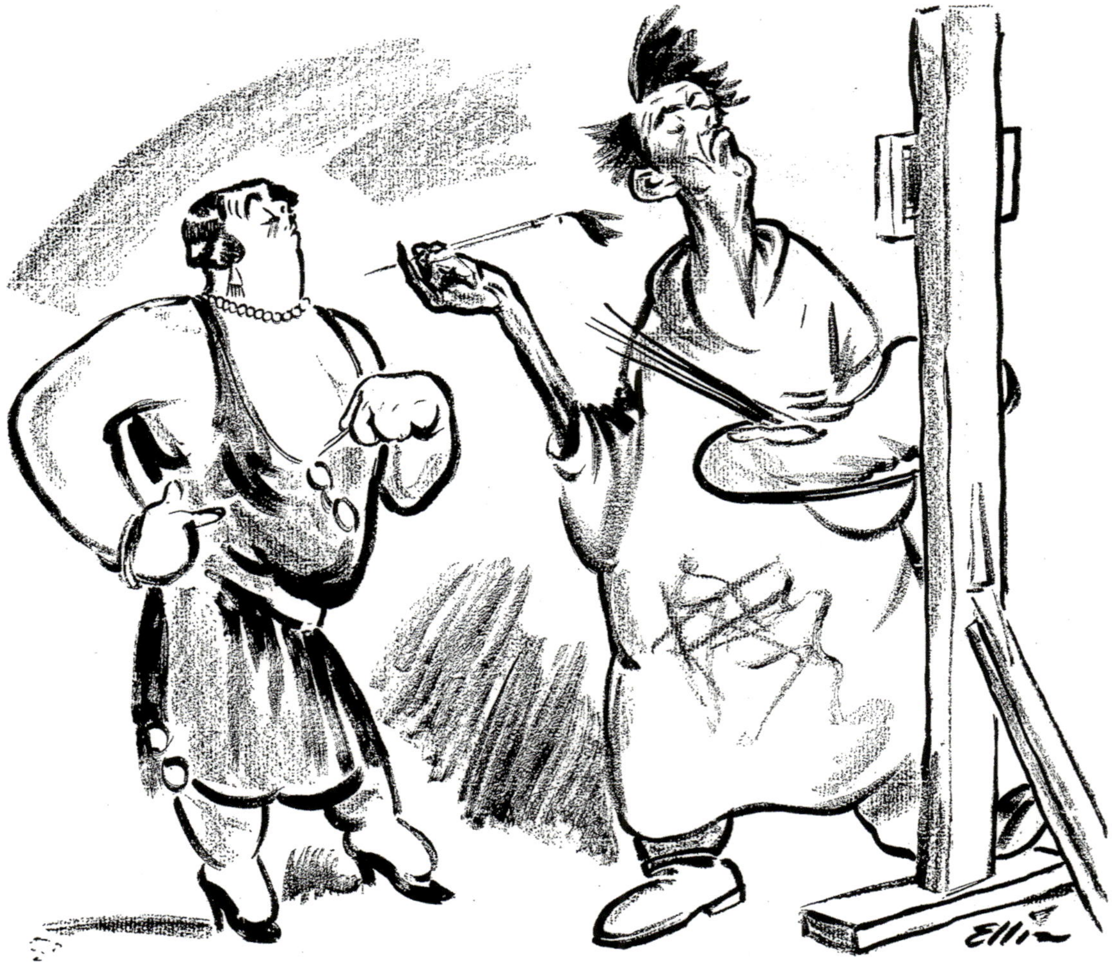

—By Fred Ellis

The DAILY WORKER
Feb. 13, 1926

FINE LADY: "Are you artists Bourgeois or Proletarian?"
ARTIST: "Well, we try to hover between the pocketbook of the Bourgeois and the soul of the Proletarian."—LE RIRE

"Making money is art and working is art and good business is the best art."
Andy Warhol

What position do artists have in the social order, and which interest group should they affiliate themselves with? Eillis's cartoon recalls the art critic Clement Greenberg's observation that – for the time being – an "umbilical cord of gold" links progressive artists to rich and conservative patrons. Barlow asks: are artists necessarily dependent on the surplus wealth of a social elite? The decisions that artists face or have faced regarding their social functions and standing, and their relationships to patronage have seldom been represented as bluntly as here. A wealthy patron of the arts enquires of an artist whether he identifies with the bourgeois class or the workers. The artist here gives an uncomfortable, hypocritical answer.
Are artists simply at the service of those in positions of economic power? Barlow's use of the graphic arts, through the newspaper The Daily Worker, and the Labour Party, argued otherwise.

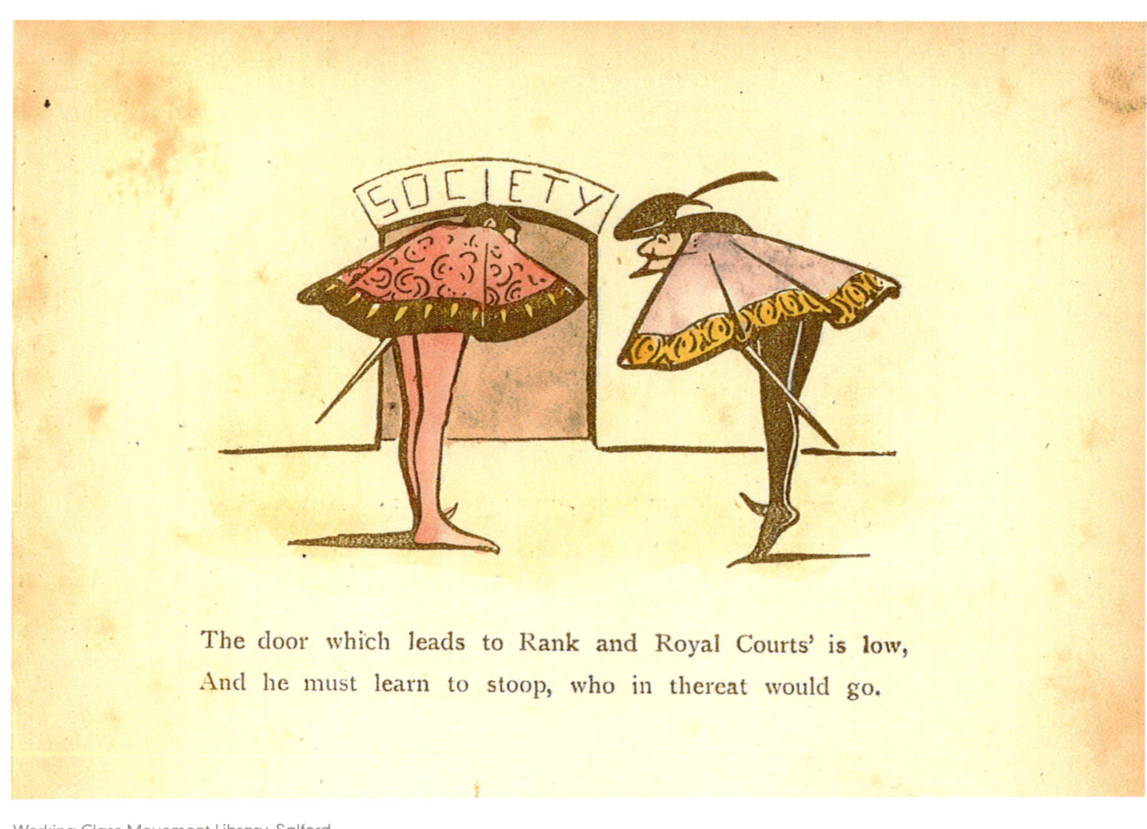

Working Class Movement Library, Salford

"Becoming class conscious.. could be compared to learning a foreign language: that is, it presents men with a new vocabulary and a new set of concepts which permit a different translation of the meaning of inequality from that encouraged by the conventional vocabulary."[1]
Frank Parkin, 'Class Inequality and Political Order', 1971

Martin Anderson produced seven volumes of self-published satires early in the 20th century under the pen-name 'Cynicus' which contain hundreds of visual parables, sometimes echoing traditional Christian principles, or forwarding anti-capitalist ideas. 'The door which leads to rank' parodies the stupidity of paying deference to imagined 'superiors' to obtain social advancement, for example. Despite forwarding a gentle humanistic socialism, with some irony Anderson became so successful that he earned enough to commission a bespoke castle for himself near Balmullo in Scotland, appropriately called 'Castle Cynicus'.

1. Frank Parkin, 'Class Inequality and Political Order', 1971 (Milton Keynes: OU), p90

"The three issues [of our time]... are: What are the facts about the distribution of wealth and incomes? Secondly, to what extent is greater equality desired in Britain today? And thirdly, has the economy been strengthened by the promotion of more equality[?]"[1]
Margaret Thatcher, speech on 15 September 1975

In the mid-1970s incomes were at their most equal levels at any point in history: the highest rates of income tax were up to 98% so that incomes were effectively capped. At the same time political ideas were increasingly polarised. Victor Burgin's seminal work of 1976 baldly exposes how incomes were distributed, using the style of advertising at the time. The original posters were billposted around Newcastle-upon-Tyne, as though the work was advertising. It asked viewers to base their identities on engagement with their society rather than on consumption choices. Since 1976, as the journalist Andrew Marr notes, "modern Britain [has been] a story of the triumph of shopping over politics."[2] The academic John Benson also notes that "the new consumerism had an anaesthetising effect: the new working-class consumer was unlikely to dwell on the inequalities that remained at the heart of British society... workers... came to regard themselves as consumers rather than producers, in fact they came to regard the new consumerism, rather than job satisfaction, religious certainty or educational advancement, as the most accessible avenue of advancement..."[3]

1. http://www.margaretthatcher.org/speeches/displaydocument.asp?docid=102769
2. Andrew Marr, 'A History of Modern Britain', 2007 (London: Macmillan) p8
3. John Benson, 'The Working Class in Britain 1850-1939', 2003 (London: IB Taurus), p147

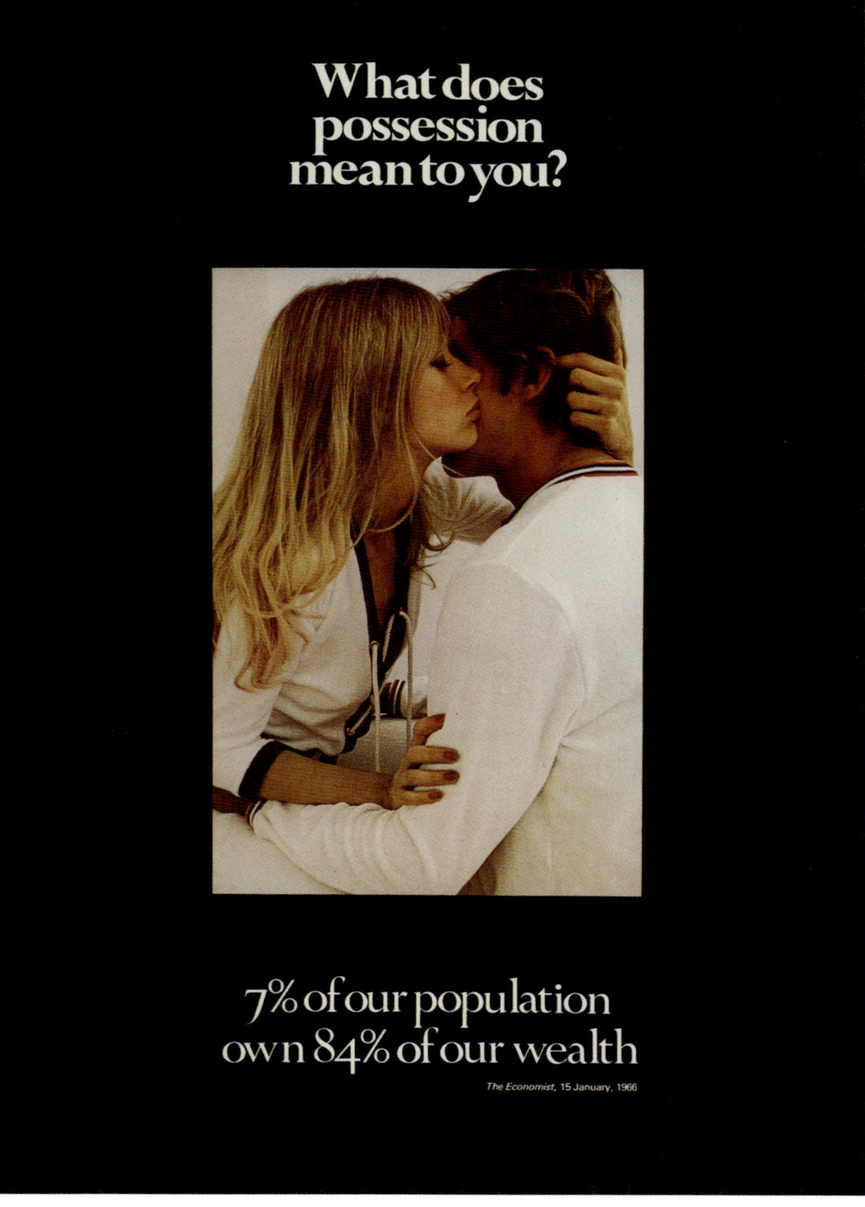

Arts Council Collection, SouthBank Centre, London

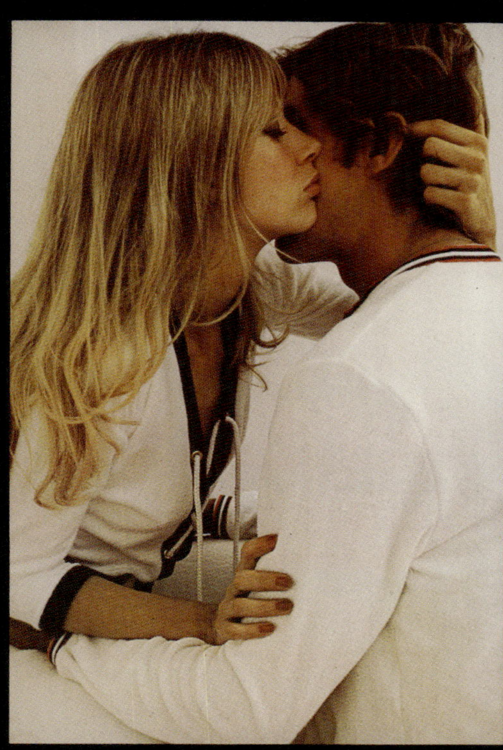

Courtesy the artist and Max Wigram Gallery, London

"From World War One to the 1970s there was slow and unsteady progress towards a more equal distribution of personal income.... Between 1976 and 1982, equalizing tendencies in the market fortunes of occupational classes came to a halt."[1] **AH Halsey, 'Change in British Society', 1986**

According to official statistics, the total pay and share options awarded to the highest paid 4,500 individuals was the same as that paid to the lowest paid 2,100,000 part-time workers in Britain.[2] As AH Halsey notes, these levels of inequality have risen since almost exactly 1976, when Victor Burgin made 'Possession' on which Hulusi's work is based. Hulusi's work is about how life feels when lived from the margins, and how inequalities are now just a fact of life rather than a matter of contention. According to the Office for National Statistics: "inequality of disposable income increased rapidly in the second half of the 1980s, reaching a peak in 1990. After 1990 the trend was downwards... [though] began to rise again, reaching a peak in 2001/02."[3] One way of thinking about how we are unequal is to calculate the difference between the 'top' and the middle. Polly Toynbee has argued that "In 1980 [company] directors were paid 10 times the average worker in their companies... In 1990 the gap had multiplied to 31.5 times. And by 2002 the top dogs were paid an enormous 75.7 times more than their average employee."[4]

1. Halsey, 1986, p39
2. From 'What Britain Earns', first broadcast BBC2 Jan 10 2008
3. Office for National Statistics study by Francis Jones. Quoted in Guardian G1 May 18 2007, p28
4. Polly Toynbee, The Guardian G1 July 7 2006, p27

'Possession' 2003/2008

OFFICE FOR NATIONAL STATISTICS

Proportions of UK wealth ownership by percentage of population, 2003

"Is Britain a peculiar capitalism, or peculiarly capitalist?"
Ellen Meiksins Wood, 'The Pristine Culture of Capitalism', 1991

How broadly is our national wealth spread? This cake shows official Inland Revenue statistics which reveal two things. First, our distribution of wealth is enormously unequal and has scarcely changed in 30 years. From 1976 to 2003 the richest 1% of the population have owned over a fifth of all assets. The entire 'bottom' half of the population still own less than one fourteenth. On the other hand, we are all much richer than ever before: the value of our collective assets has grown from £280bn to £3783bn over the last thirty years, even though inflation accounts for most of this. For those on the political left, such statistics prove that a tiny minority command a disproportionate share and we are very far from being equal. For those on the right, they prove that free enterprise has created riches (and standards of living) never seen before in history, and that we have all shared in them to some degree.

In terms of income – rather than accumulated wealth as shown here – the UK's 31m working people took home a total of £685bn in 2007. The median average salary was around £24,000, meaning the average household's disposable income had risen by a third between 1997-2007.[1] On the pessimistic side, there are clear thresholds between groups. Only 30% of workers bring home over £30,000 a year; only 10% earn over £46,000; 20% take home less than £10,000 a year.[2]

1. Michelle Harrison, Henley Centre, 'Are We Having fun Yet?',BBC4 Mar 14 2007
2. From 'What Britain Earns', BBC2 Jan 10 2008

Richest 26th – 50th%

Richest 11th – 25th%

image by Ben Branagan & Gareth Holt

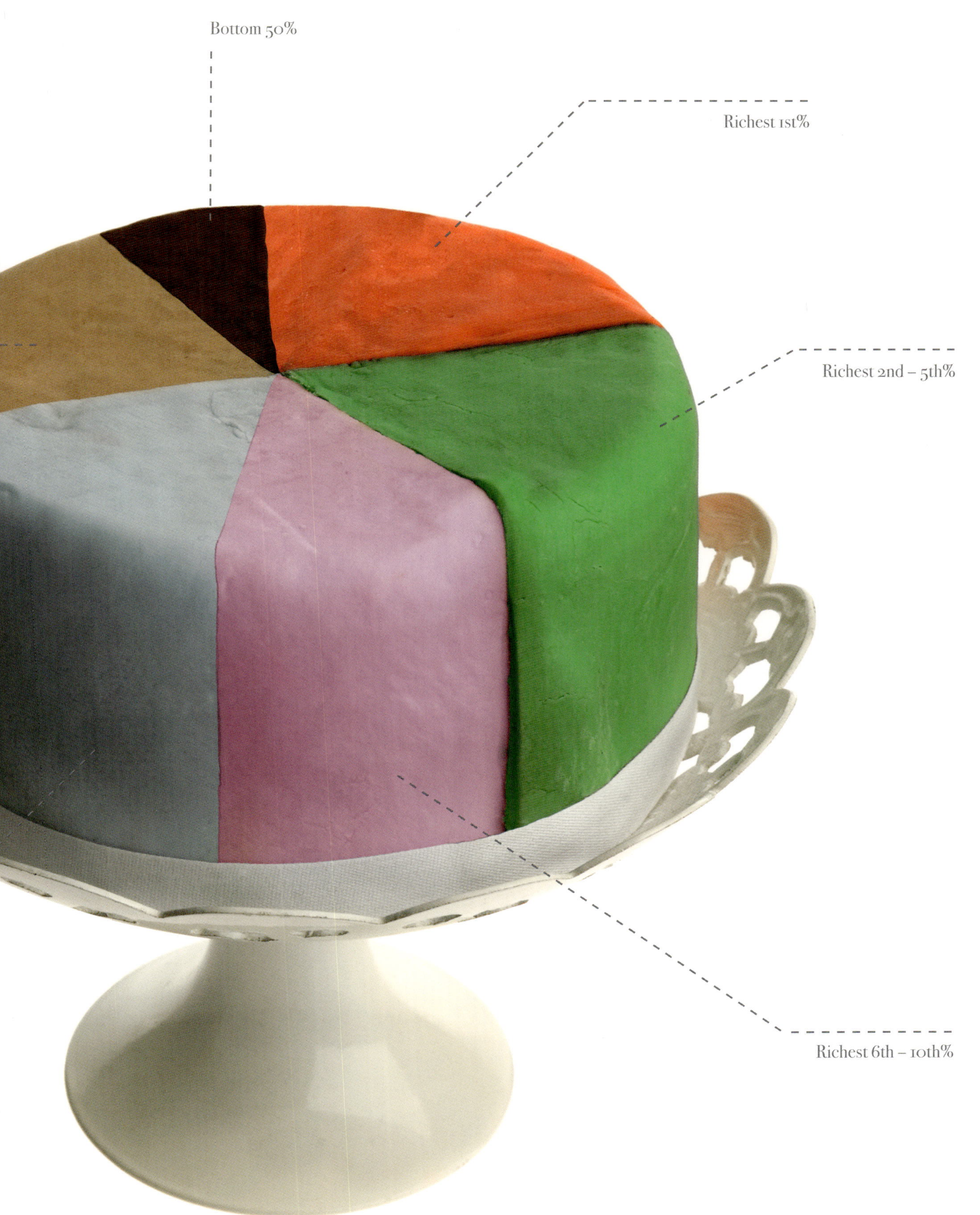
Bottom 50%
Richest 1st%
Richest 2nd – 5th%
Richest 6th – 10th%

'Untitled (The Rich Are Always With Us)' 2004

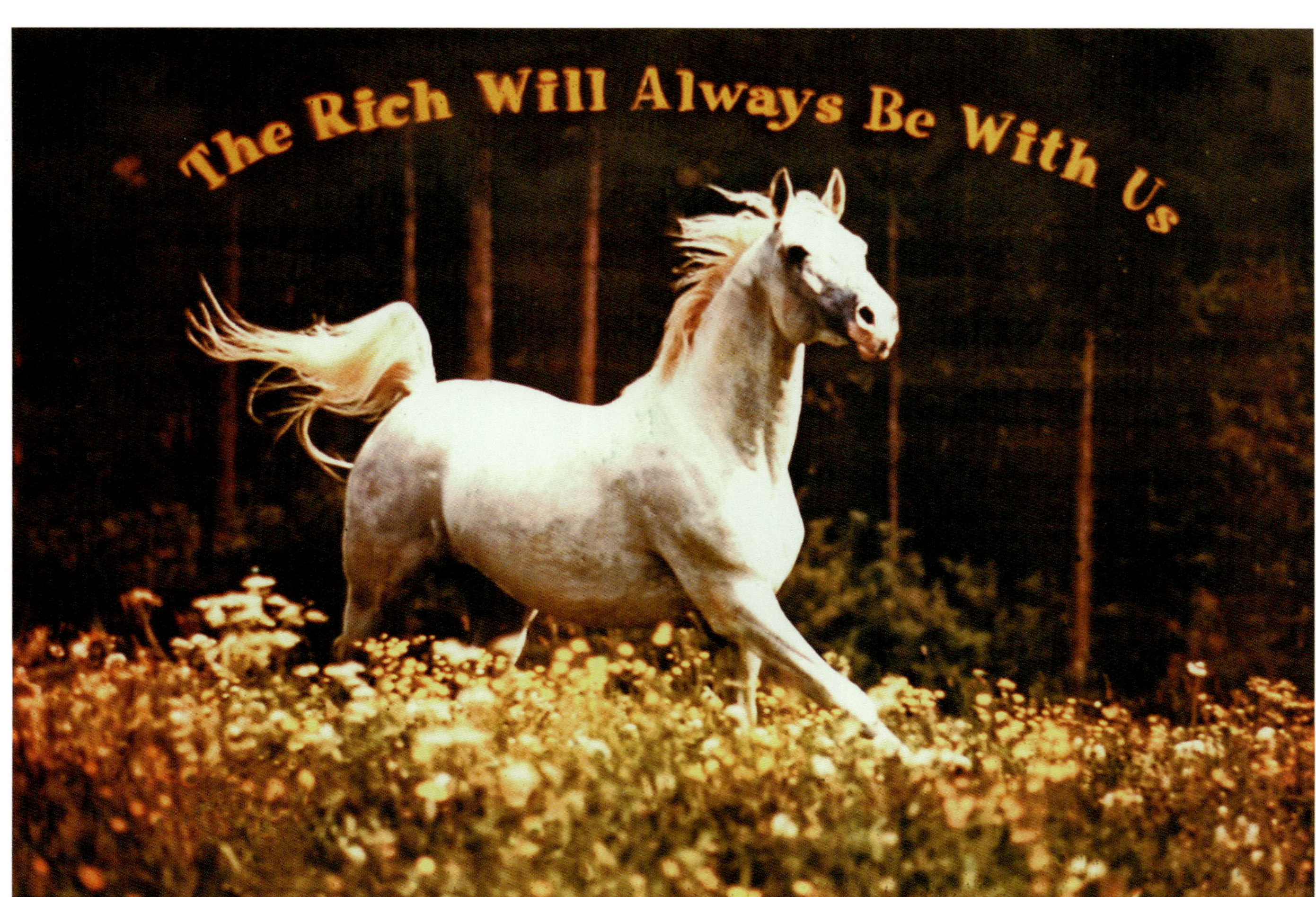

The Saatchi Gallery, London

"Inequality still remains high by historical standards – the large increase which took place in the second half of the 1980s has not been reversed."[1] **Office for National Statistics, 2007**

Simon Bedwell's works mix appropriated texts and images to create unexpected combinations. Like Victor Burgin, Bedwell works with advertising images to test how they function. Bedwell's wild horse is a clichéd image of boundless freedom – an image mostly used by corporations whose businesses carry the opposite set of connotations. Here, the phrase 'the poor will always be with you' is Biblical, indeed attributed to Jesus. Bedwell's simple inversion points out the obvious fact that if 'the poor' have always existed, then by definition 'the rich' must have as well: one term can only exist with the other. Bedwell's vision of the social order is one in which power conceals its own operations, and becomes all but invisible. Indeed it can be argued that the most notable economic development of the last decade in Britain has been the rise of what Doreen Massey has called a 'superclass', who separate themselves from the mainstream of society. The worth of the 1000 richest people tripled between 1997–2007.[2] One estimate is that there are now 425,000 millionaires in Britain.[3]

1. www.statistics.gov.uk/cci/nugget.asp?id=332
2. Daily Mail quoted by Peter Wilby, in 'Revolt of the Middle Classes', New Statesman, 21 May 2007, p14.
3. Hadfield and Skidforth, 1994,p28

THE SUNDAY TIMES

'Sunday Times Rich List' 2008

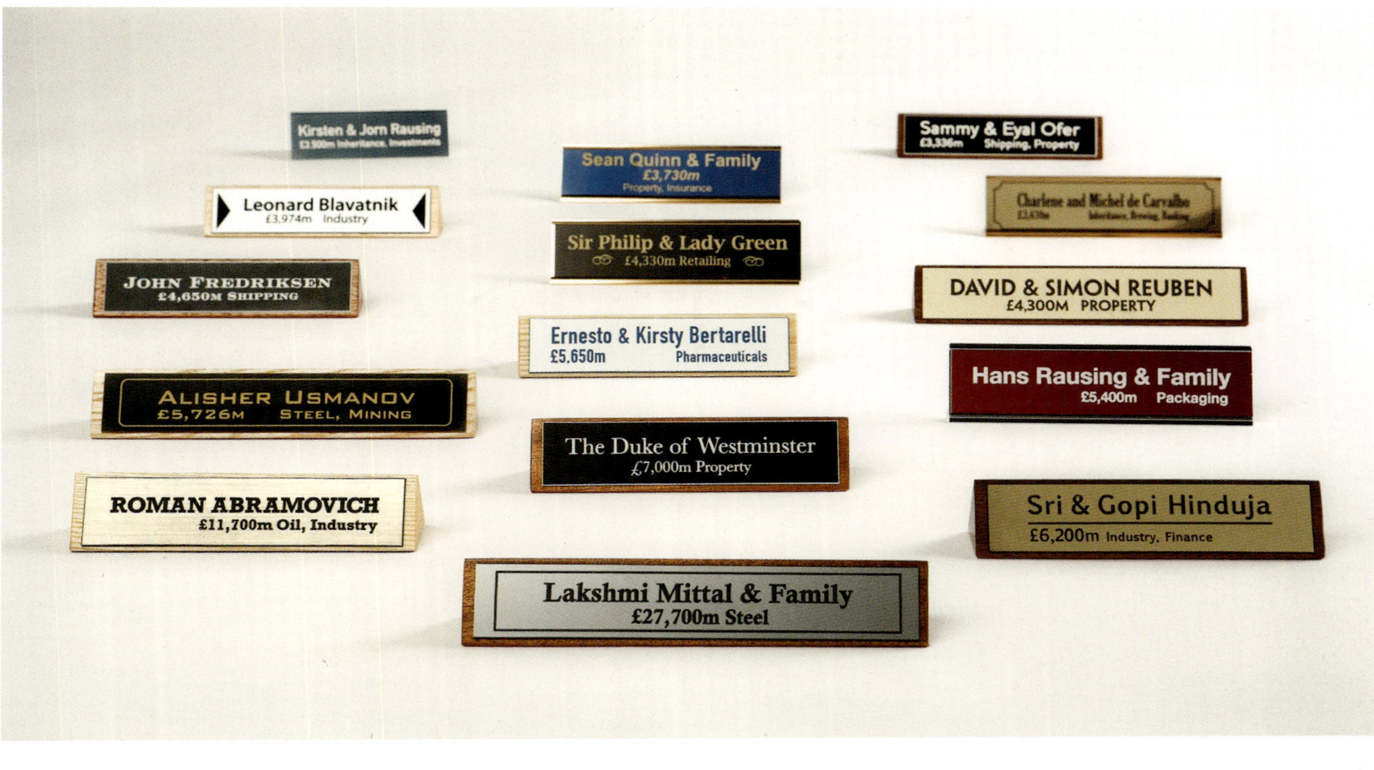

image by Ben Branagan & Gareth Holt

"Increased wage inequality is the economic fact, but the [new] social fact is the acceptance of that inequality... There is a new servant class."[1]
Richard Reeves, Director, Intelligence Agency, 2007

The Sunday Times Rich List compiles Britain's 1000 richest individuals. Nearly 750 of the richest 1000 individuals could in some sense be described as 'self-made'. Across the last three centuries, historians have debated to what extent the 'elite' stratum of society is open to others. To what extent are the very uppermost echelons of society permeable? There is contradictory evidence. Firstly, only 78 of the 1000 are women. Secondly, new wealth is concentrated in very few professions. In 2004, The Guardian newspaper's annual pay survey showed that whilst the top 190 UK company directors earned more than £1 million per year, at least 4000 City workers received over £1m in bonuses in 2007.[2] In fact they estimate that the City of London's 340,000 workers received bonuses of £64.7bn in the seven years to 2008.[3] This included some £12.8bn in 2008 and £8.8bn in 2007 – enough to distort the entire economy and large swathes of the housing market.[4]

1. Interviewed in 'Are We Having fun Yet?', first broadcast BBC4 14 Mar 2007
2. http://www.esrcsocietytoday.ac.uk/ESRCInfoCentre/about/CI/CP/seven%5Fsins/avarice
3. Jill Treanor, 'Week of fear and hope ended' The Guardian G1 Oct11 2008, p4
4. BBC4, ibid.

DARREN CULLEN

'Santa Gives More to Rich Kids than Poor Kids' 2005 / 2009

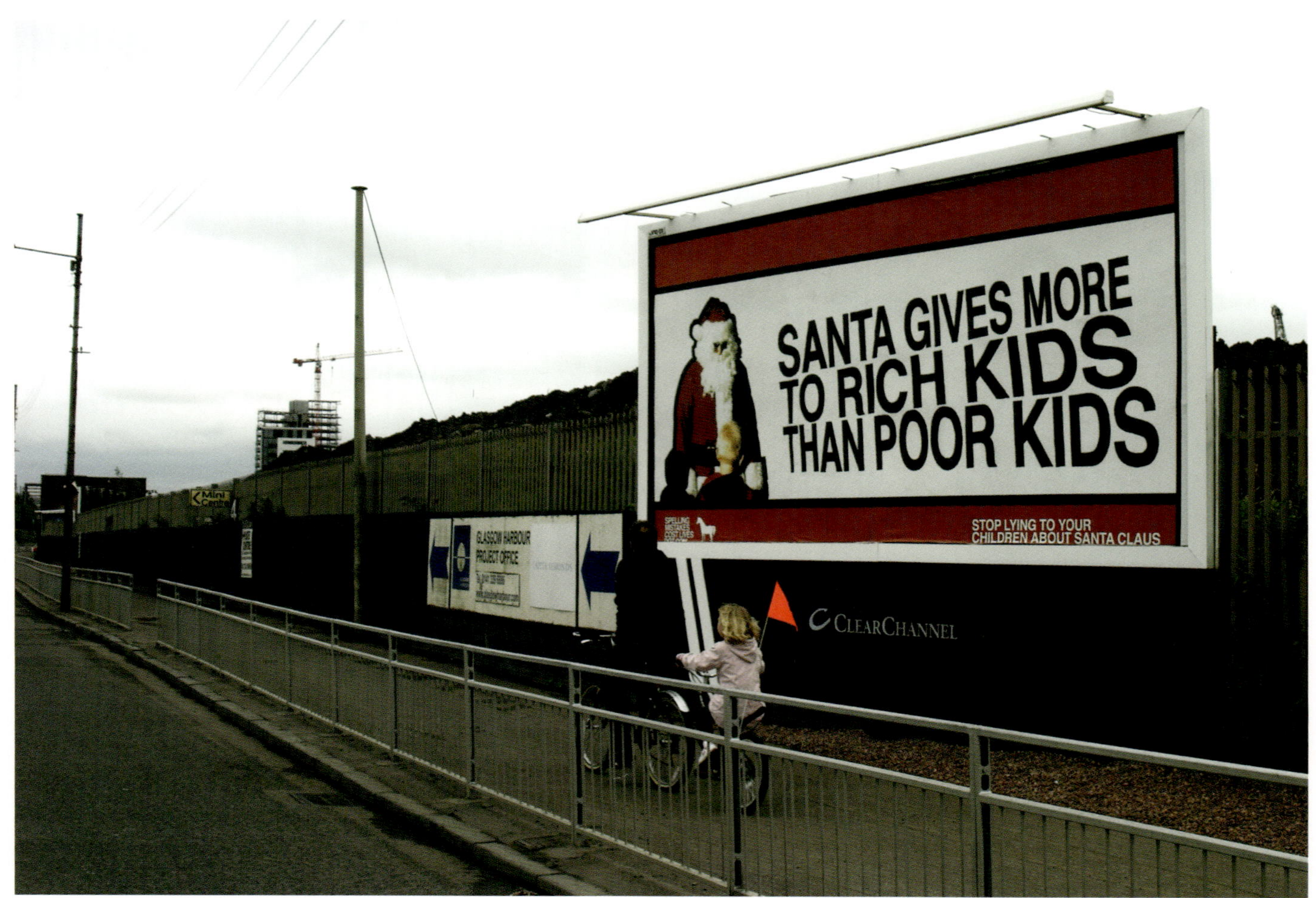

Collection the artist

"The middle classes invest in the future of their children, while the working classes spoil them in the here and now. Middle-class couples pay... to ensure that their children get the 'solid grounding' they need... The working classes, by contrast, can be seen every weekend traipsing round Toys 'R Us, their shopping trolleys stuffed"[1] **Greg Hadfield and Mark Shipworth: 'Class: Where do you stand?'1994**

Do the rituals of consumer society reinforce divisive distinctions between groups? Darren Cullen creates provocations that act as litmus tests of our prejudices. 'Santa' initially reads as a statement of the obvious. It is in fact rather more complicated. Cullen's bald statement is intended to reveal our prejudices, as it can be read in two different ways which divide people according to their assumptions about the world. Do we instinctively side with the 'underdog', and therefore imagine that the statement is true? In other words, do we agree with the academic AH Halsey that, 'what determines behaviour is not actual, but felt deprivation'?[2] Or do we agree with Greg Hadfield and Mark Shipworth? Their quotation above is based on the assumption that lower-class parents indulge rather than invest, consume rather than save, and act against their own interests. Cullen's 'Santa' was originally presented as an outdoor billboard in Glasgow in 2005. It continues Victor Burgin's strategy of using the spaces of advertising to question our worldview.

1. Hadfield and Skipworth,1994, pp 49-50
2. Halsey,1986 p39

I ♥ INEQUALITY

www.iheartcapitalism.wordpress.com

'I Love Inequality' 2008

"In more unequal societies, it is as if some people count for everything and others for nothing, making us all more concerned with how we are seen. More hierarchical societies are marked by greater social divisions and more discrimination and prejudice against those lower on the social ladder."[1] **Richard Wilkinson, 'UK Health Watch', 2005**

The group 'I Love Capitalism' use the tactics of 'guerilla marketing' to distribute their images. Their stickers are a form of 'shareware', able to be downloaded free from their website http://iheartcapitalism.wordpress.com. The group ask: if we did not love inequality, why would wealth be spread so incredibly unevenly both across the world and inside each country? There is an accepted standard for measuring a country's level of economic inequality, called the 'Gini coefficient'. This measures the size of the gap between the incomes of the richest 10% and the poorest 10% of workers. We can work out the Gini coefficient of the whole globe by comparing the incomes of the world's top 600m workers with the poorest 600m people. The difference between the two is that someone in the former group earns 103 times as much as the latter. As the Gini coefficient has a scale of 0-100 where 0 is everyone earning the same, the global Gini coefficient is 67. The gap between countries is greater than that inside any individual country, other than Namibia. Despite this, a very prosperous Brazilian earns 94 times more than a poor one.[2]

1. http://www.shef.ac.uk/geography/staff/dorling_danny/commentary.html
2. Jens Martens, 'A Compendium of Inequality: The Human Development Report 2005' http://library.fes.de/pdf-files/iez/global/04666.pdf

CHASE-DUNN / LERRO

'National GDP per capita as a ratio of world GDP per capita, 1500–2000' 2005

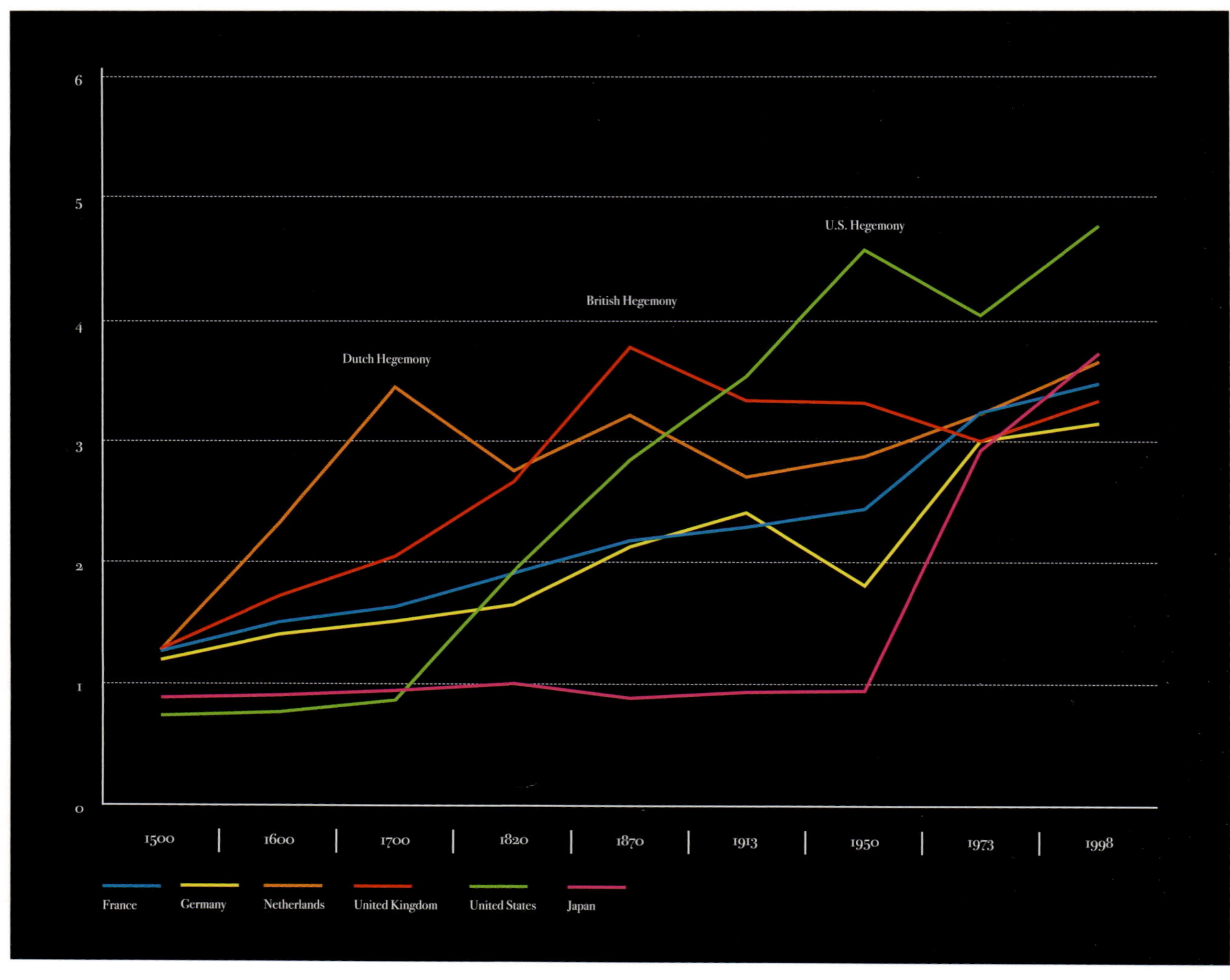

"The ways in which we image the world, our geographical imaginations, matter. The language of the 'developing' world... turns space into time... making it possible for us to deal with the horrendous facts of global inequality... [In neoliberals'] geographical imagination...the whole, variegated and unequal geography of the world is being reorganised into a historical queue... What we need is a different way of imagining geography for these times."[1] Doreen Massey, 'Is the World Really Shrinking?', 2006

The geographer Doreen Massey has asked us to think: "what is an economy for?"[2] For her, economic competitiveness is a means to other things rather than an end in itself. She has noted that the richest cities and countries are often not those with the highest standards of living in other ways. Many rich cities actually price the majority out of having high standards of living. By contrast most economists see economic output as a useful way of comparing nations. Chase-Dunn and Lerro have visualised the process by which individual nations have been economically dominant across the last 500 years.[3] Just before the graph begins, Venice and Istanbul were the world's pre-eminent trading capitals. Should we accept that the size of an economy determines a country's power internationally, or like Massey, question whether seeing countries as competitors in a race benefits us in the long run?

1. http://www.open2.net/freethinking/oulecture_2006.html
2. Ibid.
3. From 'Social Change: World Historical Social Transformations', (Los Angeles: Allyn and Bacon)

image by Ben Branagan & Gareth Holt

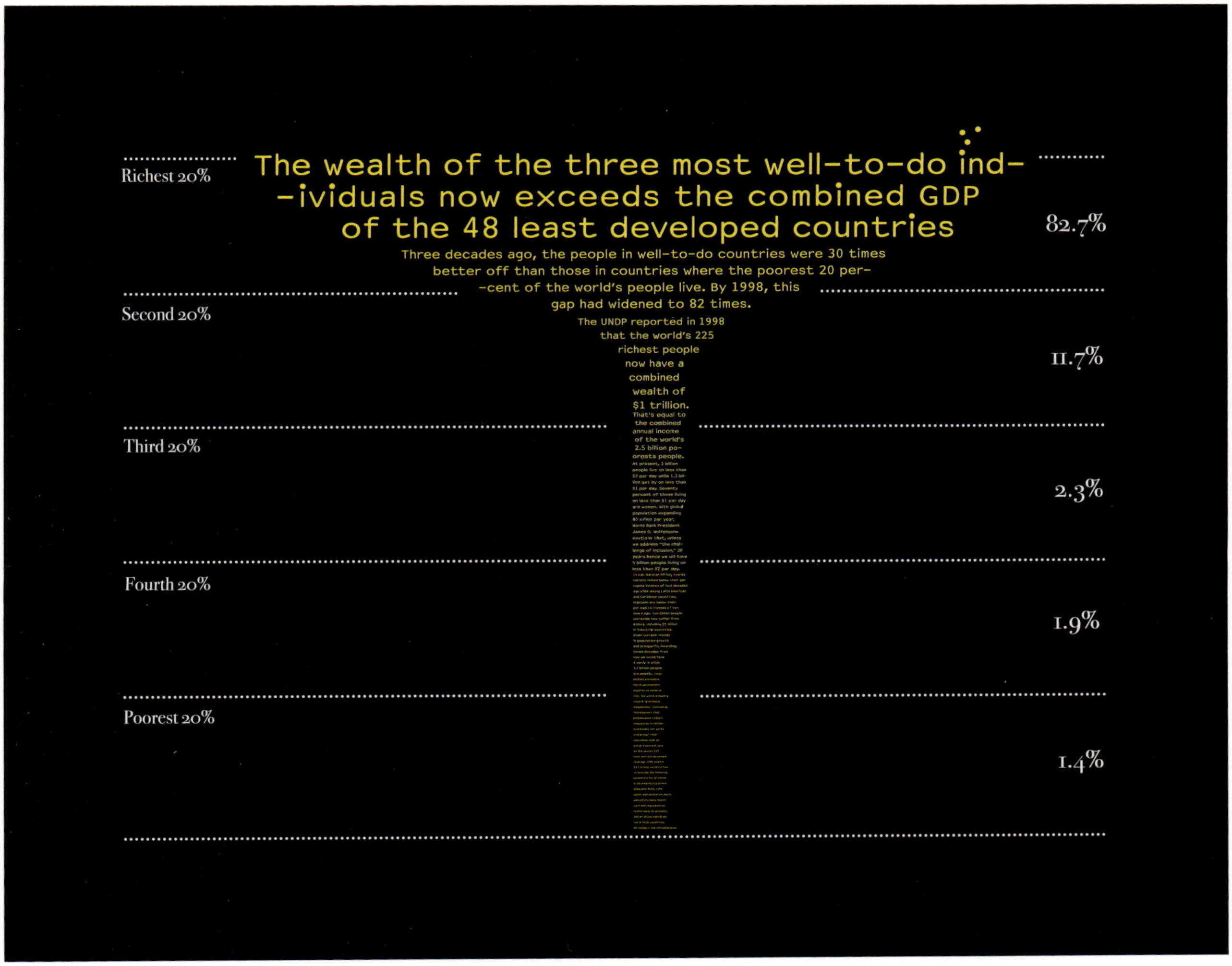

'Champagne glass' of global distribution of world wealth, 1992

Richest 20%	82.7%
Second 20%	11.7%
Third 20%	2.3%
Fourth 20%	1.9%
Poorest 20%	1.4%

The wealth of the three most well-to-do ind- -ividuals now exceeds the combined GDP of the 48 least developed countries

Three decades ago, the people in well-to-do countries were 30 times better off than those in countries where the poorest 20 per- -cent of the world's people live. By 1998, this gap had widened to 82 times.

The UNDP reported in 1998 that the world's 225 richest people now have a combined wealth of $1 trillion.

image by Ben Branagan & Gareth Holt

"In every measure that we have bearing on the standard of living, the gains of the lower classes have been far greater than those experienced by the population as a whole."[1] **Robert Fogel, 'The Escape from Hunger and Premature Death 1700-2100', 2007**

In recent years the distribution of the world's wealth has resembled a champagne glass in shape. In other words, in 1992 over 4/5 of the world's resources were commanded by 1/5 of the population. The poorest 60% provided only 6% of the world's economic output. The United Nations' image of how the world's resources are unequally shared graphically illustrates the gulf between the small number of industrialised nations and the rest. The average income of the top 20% of the world's population remains roughly 50 times that of someone in the bottom 20%. For many economists, such disparities are only to be expected; what we should pay attention to is how far poorer groups' standards of living have risen. Professor Paul Collier has argued that "since 1980 the absolute number of people in poverty globally has been falling for the first time in two centuries."[2] In wealthy countries, too, according to The Economist, "the experience of everyday consumption among the less fortunate has become in many ways more similar to that of their wealthier compatriots. The rich are [now] less different than they used to be… The increasing inequality in real consumption mirrors a dramatic narrowing of other inequalities between rich and poor, such as the inequalities in height, life expectancy, and leisure."[3] In other words, even 70% of those Americans beneath the official poverty line can afford to own a car, as 'poverty' is measured in relative terms in industrialised countries.

1. Quoted in unattributed review of Fogel, The Economist, May 14 2008
2. www.esrc.ac.uk/ESRCInfoCentre/Images/BT01_GLB_tcm6-25383.pdf
3. The Economist, ibid.

UNITED NATIONS

'Human Development Index' 2004

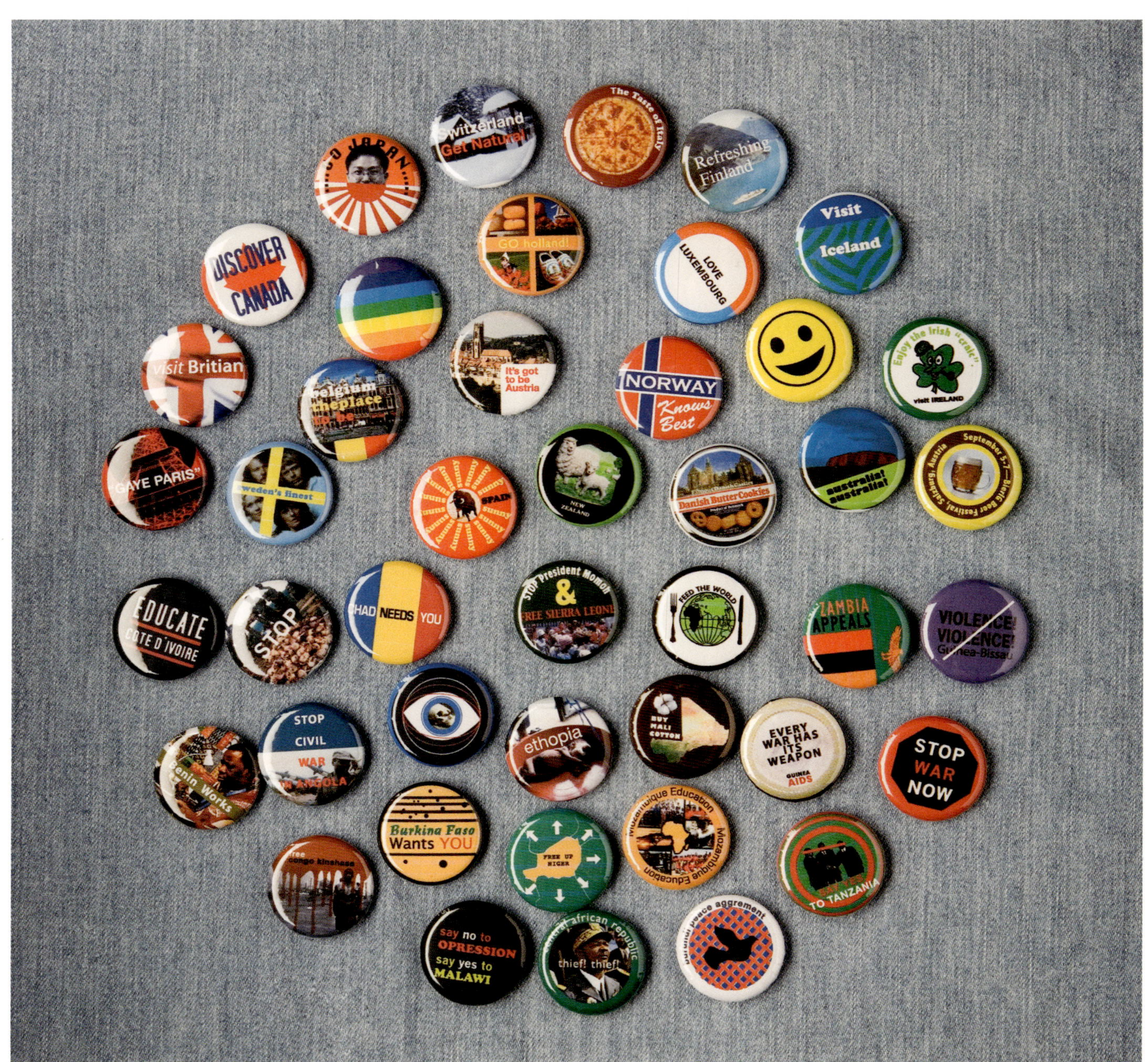

image by Ben Branagan & Gareth Holt

"Space is the dimension of the social... The cachet of [a] place uphold[s] the authority of those within it."[1]
Professor Doreen Massey, 2007

Given the choice, where in the world should we live to have the highest standard of living? 'Economic migrants' – those who move to improve their living standards – are often talked about as either threats to national stability, or sources of new skills. Yet The Economist has shown that whilst the UK has a high-performing economy, it is very far from having the highest average living standards of any country.[2]

But how can we accurately compare the standards of living experienced in different countries beyond purely economic matters? The United Nations has developed a system to incorporate life expectancy and adult literacy alongside economic welfare and wellbeing. The 'HDI' is scored from 0 to 100: over 80 is 'high'; 50-79 is 'medium' and under 50 a 'low' level of development. On this score, the residents of small countries – Norway, Iceland, Switzerland and Ireland for example – are best off by this measure. Would those born in the UK be better off by becoming economic migrants and relocating to other European states?

1. http://www.open2.net/freethinking/oulecture_2006.html
2. The Economist, 'Pocket World in Figures' 2008 (London: Profile), p28

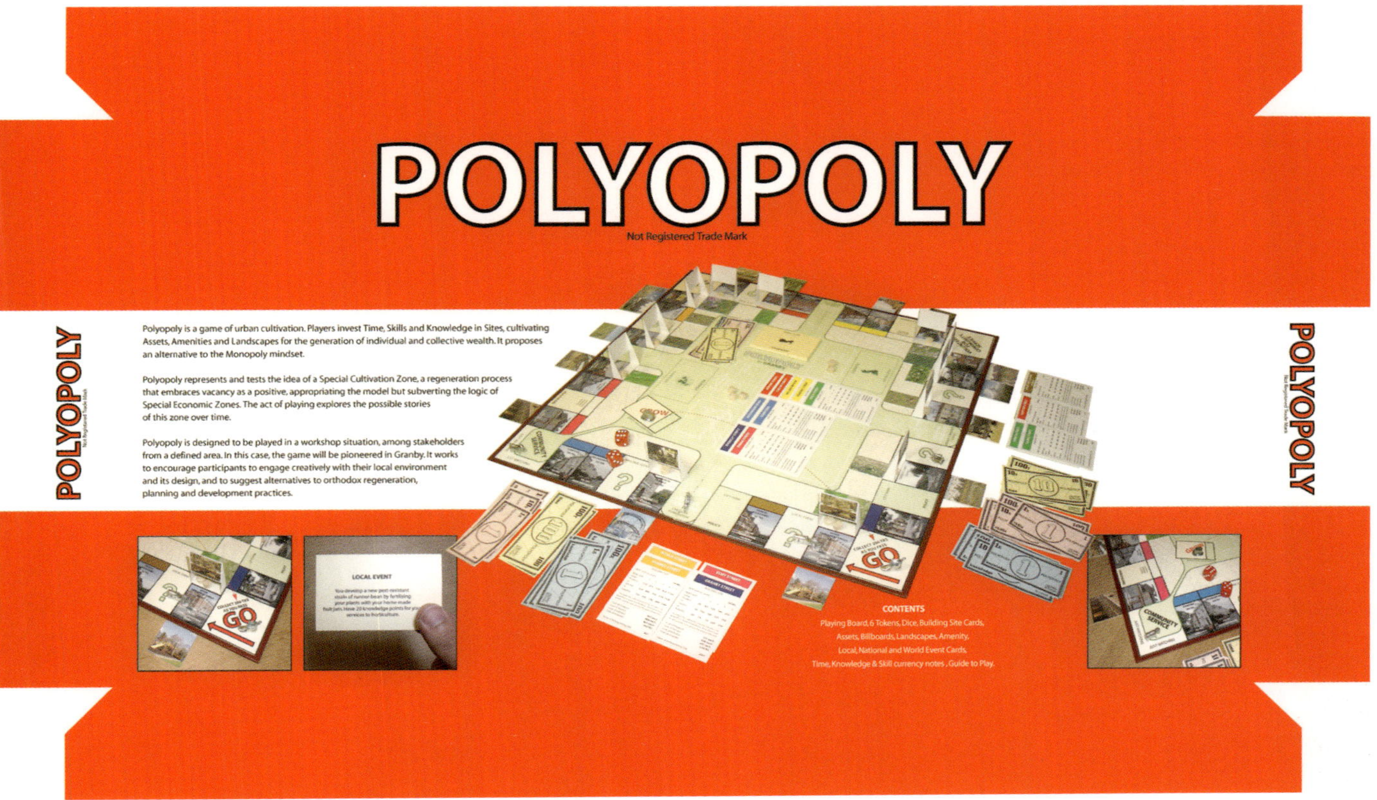

AOC Architecture (Tom Coward, Daisy Froud, Vincent Lacovara, Geoff Shearcroft)
'Polyopoly', 2008, Collection the architects

"Today's urban landscape in Britain – the undistinguished modern architecture, the neglect of public services and amenities, the general seediness... belongs to a longer pattern of capitalist development and the commodification of all social goods... Is Britain, then, a peculiar capitalism, or peculiarly capitalist?"[1]
Ellen Meiksins Wood, 'The Pristine Culture of Capitalism', 1991

"In a state of nature," Thomas Hobbes wrote in 'Leviathan', life is a game "of everyman against everyman". The game of Monopoly echoes these rules, and is a fun-sized version of life in the modern city. As the name suggests, the aim of the game is to crush your competitors. Though its exact origin is unclear, 'Monopoly' was developed at the start of the Great Depression in America. It is wholly intentional that the players' aims are punitive – each needing to bankrupt the others to win. AOC Architecture's board game 'Polyopoly' reverses the usual rules of the game. The game is a fully-fledged imaginary world where co-operation rather than competition is required to prosper; and where the most desirable locations are those with the greatest potential to be regenerated and transformed. However, the game is far from being a whimsical fantasy. It requires players to imagine ways in which they could co-operate to benefit each other, then act out alternative forms of behaviour, which can be taken into the real world. 'Polyopoly' might be seen to extend Plato's principle that "there should exist among the citizens neither extreme poverty nor again excessive wealth, for both are productive of great evil."[2]

1. Quoted Patrick Keiller, 'Robinson in Space', (London: BFI) 2006.
2. Quoted at www.constitution.org/pla/laws.htm

VICTORIA KOCHOWSKI

"Classes, like nations, are sometimes more, and sometimes less than imagined communities."[1] **David Cannadine, 'Class in Britain', 1998**

What assumptions do we carry about the relative importance of each nation in the world, about its economic power and cultural influence? Victoria Kochowski's typeface asks us to rethink what the relations between the world's 300 countries are. As she notes, economic might is tied to the spread of particular languages: English is the world's business language thanks to the US. Kochowksi has taken the symbols each country uses to represent itself on its banknotes, and transplanted them onto the alphabet, in order of their functional importance.

The 26 most traded currencies are in order of how often they are used in English, so that the US dollar becomes the letter 'E', for example. The font becomes a way to re-imagine the global economic order. For Kochowski, although we are all tied together by an increasingly globalised economy, our news and media ignore 90% of the nations in the world.

1. Cannadine,1998, p18

Letter	Rank	Country
E	1	USA
A	2	CHINA
R	3	JAPAN
I	4	INDIA
O	5	GERMANY
T	6	UK
N	7	RUSSIA
S	8	FRANCE
L	9	BRAZIL
C	10	ITALY
U	11	SPAIN
D	12	MEXICO
P	13	CANADA
M	14	SOUTH KOREA
H	15	IRAN
G	16	INDONESIA
B	17	AUSTRALIA
F	18	TAIWAN
Y	19	TURKEY
W	20	NETHERLANDS
K	21	POLAND
V	22	SAUDI ARABIA
X	23	ARGENTINA
Z	24	THAILAND
J	25	SOUTH AFRICA
Q	26	PAKISTAN

'Money Font' 2008

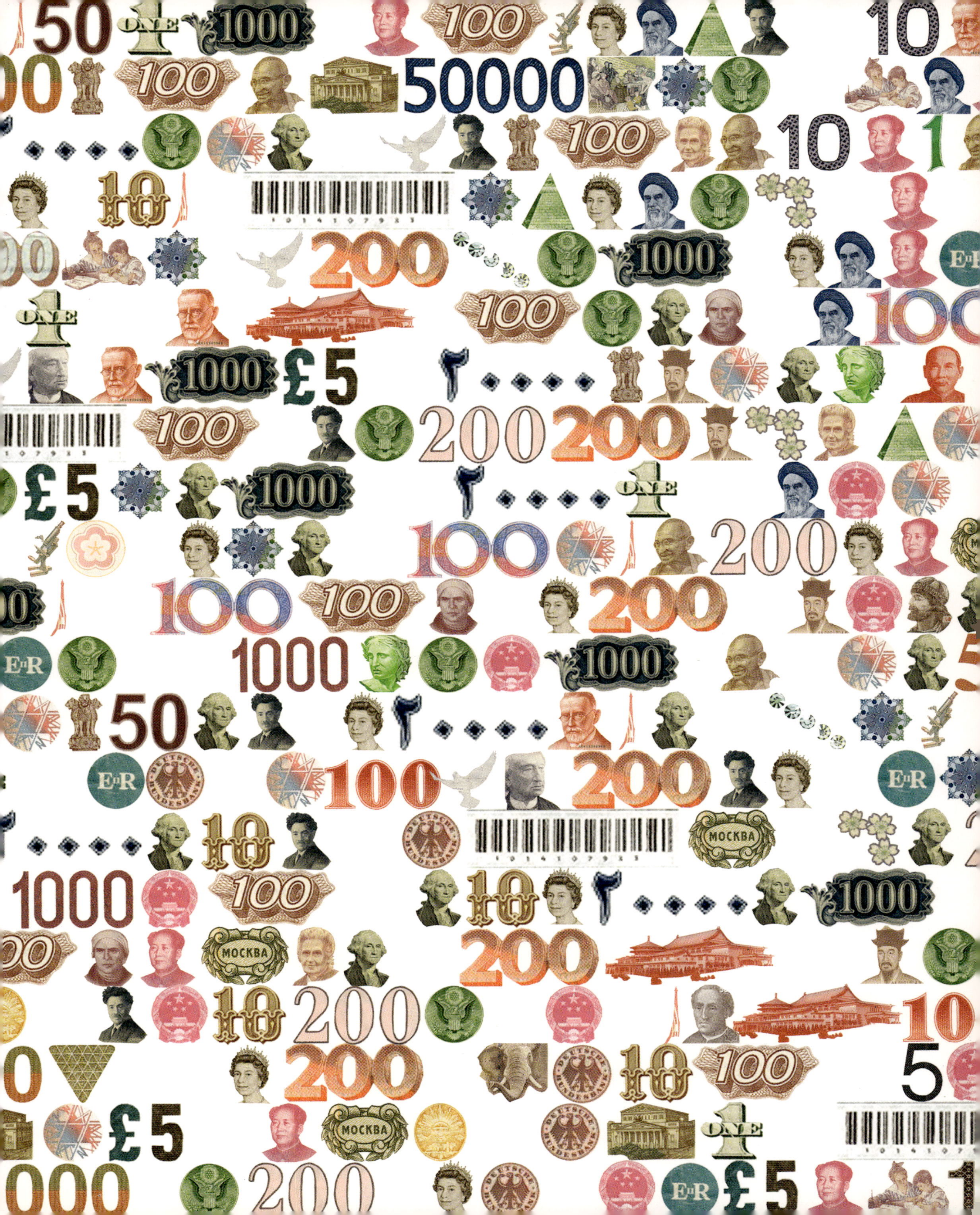

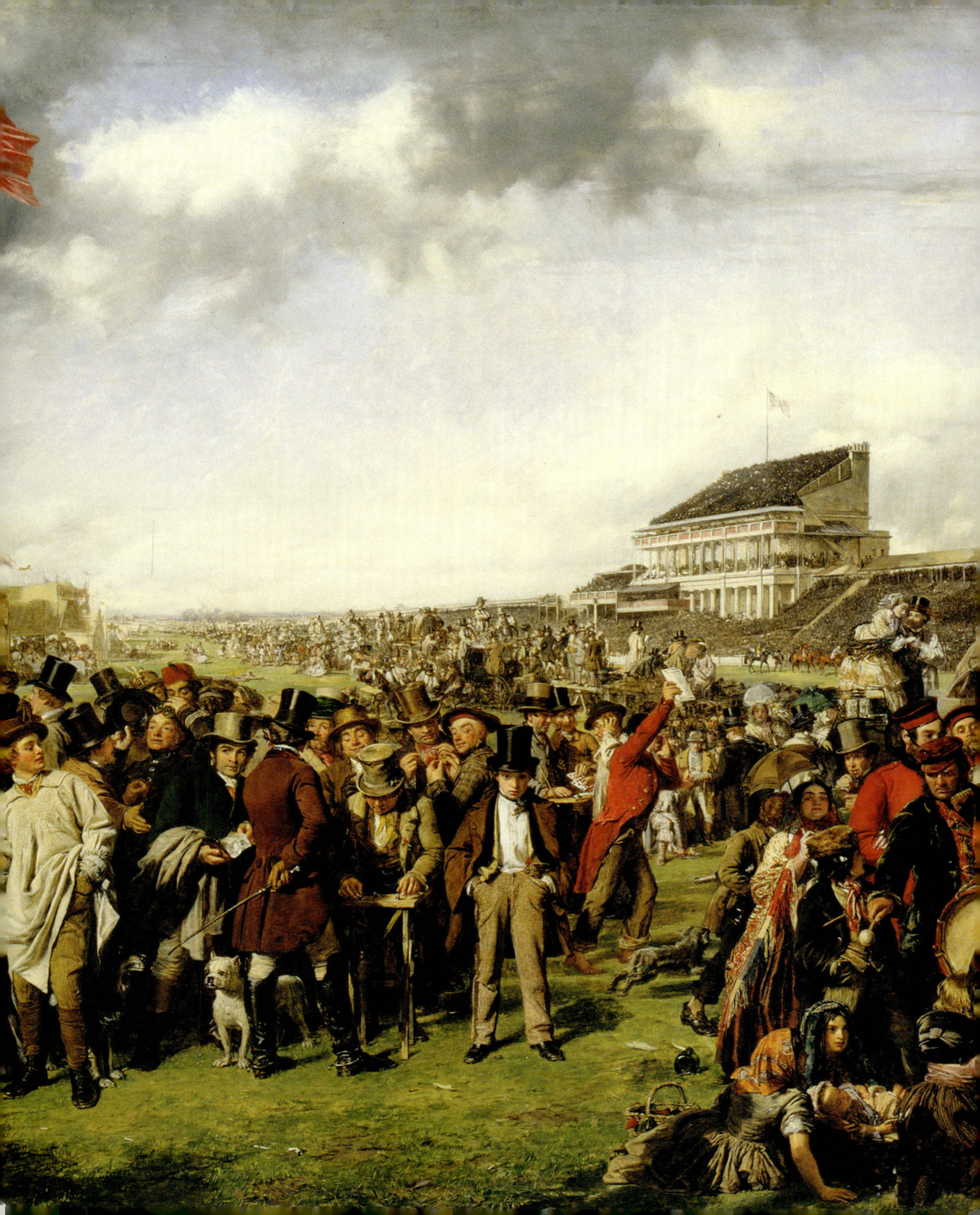